TOOLS

FOR CLASSROOM INSTRUCTION THAT WORKS

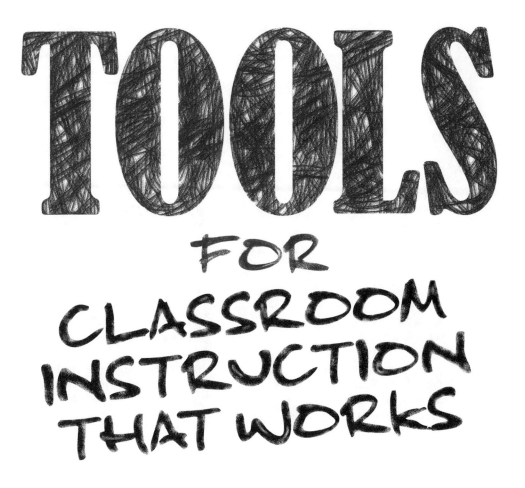

TOOLS
FOR CLASSROOM INSTRUCTION THAT WORKS

Ready-to-Use Techniques for Increasing Student Achievement

Over 50 tools for addressing key practices, including

- Setting objectives and providing feedback
- Using cues, questions, and organizers
- Summarizing and note taking
- Identifying similarities and differences
- Generating and testing hypotheses

Harvey F. Silver | Cheryl Abla | Abigail L. Boutz | Matthew J. Perini

Silver Strong & Associates
Thoughtful Education Press

McREL
INTERNATIONAL

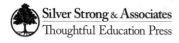
Silver Strong & Associates
Thoughtful Education Press

McREL
INTERNATIONAL

3 Tice Road, Suite 2
Franklin Lakes, NJ 07417
Phone: 800-962-4432 or 201-652-1155
Fax: 201-652-1127
Website: www.ThoughtfulClassroom.com
Email: questions@thoughtfulclassroom.com

4601 DTC Boulevard, Suite 500
Denver, CO 80237-2596
Phone: 800-858-6830 or 303-337-0990

Website: www.mcrel.org
Email: info@mcrel.org

President and Tools Series Developer: Harvey F. Silver
Director of Publishing and Tools Series Editor: Matthew J. Perini
Associate Editor / Project Manager: Justin Gilbert
Design and Production Directors: Bethann Carbone & Michael Heil
Proofreader: Lesley Bolton

CEO and President: Bryan Goodwin
Chief Innovation Officer: Ron Miletta

A number of tools featured in this book have been adapted from other titles in the Tools for Today's Educators series, including *Tools for Thoughtful Assessment* (Learning Window; Student-Friendly Learning Targets; Review/Preview; Goal Cards; PEERS; Guiding & Grading Rubrics; Effort Tracker; GOT It!; Second-Chance Test; Points Worth Praising; A Job Well Done; Vocabulary Knowledge Rating; From Topics to "Top Picks"; 4-2-1 Summarize; Graduated Difficulty), *Tools for a Successful School Year* (Rules to Live and Learn By; All for One & One for All; Community CIRCLE; Interaction in an Instant; Questioning in Style; Power Previewing; Procedural PRO; Because), and *Tools for Conquering the Common Core* (Stop, Read, Revise; AWESOME Summaries; Describe First, Compare Second).

All web links in this book are correct as of the publication date below but may have become inactive or otherwise modified since that time. If you notice a deactivated or changed link, please email questions@thoughtfulclassroom.com with the words "Link Update" in the subject line. In your message, please specify the web link, the book title, and the page number on which the link appears.

Printed in the United States of America

Quantity discounts are available. For information, call 800-962-4432.

ISBN: 978-1-58284-215-8
Library of Congress Control Number: 2017918938

25 24 23 22 21 20 19 18   1 2 3 4 5 6 7 8 9 10

Acknowledgments

First and foremost, we thank Bryan Goodwin, whose interest in combining McREL's research with Silver Strong & Associates / Thoughtful Education Press's classroom-ready teaching tools aligned perfectly with our vision and helped set this book in motion. We also thank Bryan for lending his distinctive voice to the Foreword and for providing the kind of feedback that always makes ideas—and how those ideas are expressed—better. In addition, we would like to give special thanks to our constant advisor and co-thinker, Susan Kreisman, whose insights and wisdom deeply inform this book, and to Justin Gilbert, whose "Swiss Army knife" skill set as a thinker, editor, and problem solver we continue to rely on completely.

Others who deserve thanks include Edward Thomas, whose math mind we count on to keep us out of trouble; Irena Rothaug, who stepped in when we needed her most to keep this book on schedule; and Joyce Jackson, Trisha Layden, Kristen Perini, Kimberly Nunez, Peg Whitney, and Barbara Blacher-Hecht for their assistance—and persistence—throughout the process.

We must also thank the many educators who reviewed our work, who tested and refined tools in their schools and classrooms, and who provided high-quality examples of classroom practice and student work. In particular, we would like to thank Heather Rippeteau of Manhattan/Hunter Science High School in New York, NY; Kellie Roe, Lynese Zukowski, and Beth Dome of Clear Sky Elementary School in Castle Rock, CO; Christopher Neville and Susan Bartholio of Soaring Hawk Elementary School in Castle Rock, CO; Greg Sumlin of Options High School in Littleton, CO; Kimberly Zeidler-Watters, Diane Johnson, and Stephanie Harmon of the Partnership Institute for Math and Science Education Reform (PIMSER) in Richmond, KY; Nicholas DiSanto of the Affinity Field Support Center, New York City Department of Education; Michael Scott of Langston Middle School in Oberlin, OH; David Hamilton of GST-BOCES Coopers Education Center in Painted Post, NY; Cathy Mitchell of Robert Kerr Elementary School in Durand, MI; Casey Vier and the staff at Children's Aid College Prep Charter School in Bronx, NY; the staff of Brookville Area School District (Pennsylvania); and the educators of West Babylon School District in West Babylon, NY, who were involved in contributing to and supporting the discussion of tools from the Tools for Today's Educators series on their Reflective Pathway blog, especially the blog's moderator, Lisa Granieri.

Finally, we would like to express our deepest thanks to two educators who inspired this book: Robert Wilson of Lyman Hall Elementary School in Gainesville, GA, whose passion for helping teachers and students grow led to the very first Tools for Classroom Instruction That Works institute, and Linda Ruest of Williamsville Central School District (New York), whose understanding of how tools enhance professional development always helps lead us to "the next Tools book."

For copies of the reproducibles
and other downloadable extras noted in the text,
visit **www.ThoughtfulClassroom.com/Tools**.

Contents

Foreword

What if every year, every teacher got a little bit better?

Imagine the impact on students' lives if massive numbers of teachers grew more expert at engaging students and guiding their learning. This growth could dwarf anything else we might do (or have already tried) in the name of "fixing" schools—from class-size reduction to whiz-bang technologies to value-added measures … the list goes on and on.

The partners behind this book believe that helping teachers become better every day is possible. Indeed, in school after school and district after district, we have witnessed the transformative power of improving teaching and increasing student engagement.

So, what would it look like if schools and districts everywhere were to focus not on getting better teachers, but rather, on *getting teachers better*?

We might start by asking this question: *How* do they get better? That is, how do teachers (how does anyone, for that matter) move from novice to expert? What must they learn? What skills must they develop? And what helps some people develop faster and go further with their practice than others?

Years ago, Benjamin Bloom (1985), an icon of education research, brought together a team of researchers to conduct a sweeping study of 120 immensely talented people: pianists, sculptors, tennis players, Olympic swimmers, mathematicians, and neurologists. The purpose of the study was to discover what these experts did that others did not—that is, how they developed their talents.

The results were eye opening: Although talented people differed in many ways, they followed remarkably similar phases of development. First came a "romance" period of informal training and exploration during which experts fell in love with their chosen field, followed by a period of focused "digging in." During the digging-in phase, experts sought to master the knowledge and skills of their discipline, often by mirroring and copying the works of masters.

Musicians, for example, learned to play others' songs with precision. Artists honed their talents by replicating, in fine detail, the work of the masters. Athletes dissected and modeled the techniques of top performers. Similarly, as a young man, Benjamin Franklin improved his writing skills by attempting to reconstruct, verbatim from memory, articles he admired. He then compared his own drafts with the originals. This process helped him become one of the most widely read writers of his day under the nom de plume Poor Richard (Ericsson, Prietula, & Cokely, 2007).

What mirroring does more than anything else is shorten our learning curves. Instead of spending countless hours casting about to figure out how to do something well, we learn from others' hard-earned experience and insights. What you'll find, then, in the pages of this book is a valuable "hack" for your development as a teacher: classroom techniques drawn from dynamic, expert teachers—their masterpieces, if you will—that have been curated and provided for you to apply guilt-free in your classroom. The research on expertise makes it clear that there is no shame in imitating those more masterful than us; indeed, it may be the single best way to grow professionally.

We assume you've picked up this book because you've already fallen in love with the profession of teaching—you've experienced the joy of igniting students' passions and interests and have come to see that, as a teacher, you have the power to change people's lives. Now, you're looking to hone your craft, to become even more masterful in your classroom, so you can change more students' lives even more profoundly. As you develop this mastery, you'll likely find yourself devoting mental energy to the task of learning *what* to do and *how* to do it. Musicians do the same thing as they master chords and scales and learn to read music. Athletes invest this same energy in running drills, practicing moves, and studying plays.

As professionals, we too must learn from experience and from research what works and how to do it. We've devoted this book to providing you with exactly that: research on what works and the tools for how to do it well.

When you first use these tools, you may stumble a bit. Things may not go exactly as you imagined. That's OK. Stick with the tools. Keep practicing them. The next time you use them, the results will be better—and even better the next time—until you find you can use them masterfully in your classroom.

Yet we hope your professional journey doesn't end there. These tools should not be an end but rather an important step in your professional journey—the equivalent of musicians incorporating chords, scales, and harmonies into their compositions or tennis players using slice, topspin, and blocking shots in their games.

With this in mind, here is perhaps the most important question when it comes to developing expertise: Can *you* get better?

All of us who have contributed to this book believe you can, especially if you're committed to improving your practice and are ready to dig in to your craft. With the tools in this book, you can develop greater precision and build your instructional repertoire as you learn from research and from the experience of master teachers.

So, how about it? Are you ready to dig in?

Bryan Goodwin
CEO and President
McREL International

Welcome to "Tools for Today's Educators"

The book you are holding in your hands is part of Tools for Today's Educators, a series that we began publishing more than a decade ago. We began creating tools—classroom-ready techniques for improving teaching and learning—because the teachers we worked with were asking us for simple but effective solutions for problems they faced in their classrooms. They wanted practical techniques for addressing these problems, not theoretical ones; techniques that they could implement quickly, without a lot of advance planning; and techniques that could be adapted for use in different grade levels and content areas. Most of all, they wanted techniques that would work in real classrooms with real students.

Over the years, we have kept these requests in mind as we developed the various books in our Tools line. We have also continued to ask teachers about the challenges they face in their classrooms, so that we can provide them with tools for addressing those challenges. This particular book was inspired by requests for tools that could help teachers turn key findings from education research into high-impact classroom practice. Like all our Tools books, it was designed to promote better teaching, better learning, and student engagement.

This book also represents an important milestone in the Tools for Today's Educators series, as this is the first co-published Tools title. We are truly honored to have developed and published this book in partnership with McREL International, one of the foremost education research organizations in the world. By joining McREL's renowned *Classroom Instruction That Works* framework with our years of work in developing classroom-ready tools that teachers can use tomorrow, this book will help you put the best research to work so that you and your students see real results.

Let us know how the tools are working for you and your students. We would love to hear from you!

Harvey F. Silver
Series Developer

Matthew J. Perini
Series Editor

Introduction

The Evolution of a Revolution

In 2001, *it* arrived. By identifying nine categories of instructional strategies that lead to significant and measurable gains in student achievement, it helped launch a revolution in education. It created a dramatic shift in educators' thinking, ushering in a field-wide focus on evidence-based instruction. Because it showed practitioners what really works, it inspired hundreds of thousands of educators to refine their classroom practice. It and its nine categories of instructional strategies quickly became the gold standard of effective teaching.

The *it* we are referring to is *Classroom Instruction That Works* by Robert Marzano, Debra Pickering, and Jane Pollock (2001), a book that has rightly earned its place as one of the most important and bestselling books ever published in the field of education research.

When it comes to education and research, however, 2001 is a long time ago. So, guided by a decade's worth of new studies and updated analytic techniques (see Beesley & Apthorp, 2010), the team of Ceri Dean, Elizabeth Hubbell, Howard Pitler, and Bj Stone developed the second edition of *Classroom Instruction That Works* in 2012. The second edition provided new and practical advice to help teachers ensure that the nine categories of instructional strategies remain "best bets" for raising student achievement. What are these nine "best bet" categories? They are

- Setting objectives and providing feedback

- Reinforcing effort and providing recognition

- Cooperative learning

- Cues, questions, and advance organizers

- Nonlinguistic representations

- Summarizing and note taking

- Assigning homework and providing practice

- Identifying similarities and differences

- Generating and testing hypotheses

A key goal of the second edition of *Classroom Instruction That Works* was to address common misconceptions about how to implement the research in the classroom. In some schools, for example, researchers and trainers had observed educators working their way through the list of categories— implementing them in sequence from highest to lowest effect sizes,* often without consideration of

---

*As noted in Dean et al. (2012), "An effect size expresses the increase or decrease, in standard deviation units, in the outcome (e.g., achievement) for an experimental group (e.g., the group of students who are exposed to a specific instructional technique) versus a control group. Using a statistical conversion table, we can translate effect sizes into percentile point gains" (xiii).

student needs or current practices. In other schools, teachers were using the strategies within the nine categories in a scripted or rote manner, rather than to solve problems of practice. Perhaps an even bigger concern was that many educators were using strategies in isolation. Researchers, of course, seek to isolate particular strategies to gauge their effects. When it comes to teaching and learning, however, strategies are not intended to be used in isolation; strategies work best when they are interwoven with other strategies to create a tapestry of learning experiences.

In response to these findings, the second-edition team arranged the nine categories into a framework that would help educators implement the strategies within the categories more purposefully and design instruction to address three universal goals, or components, of quality teaching: Creating the Environment for Learning, Helping Students Develop Understanding, and Helping Students Extend and Apply Knowledge. The figure below lays out these three components and shows how the nine categories of instructional strategies fit into these components.

Creating the Environment for Learning

This component helps teachers build foundations that focus learning, encourage growth, and promote a strong sense of community. It includes these three categories:

- Setting objectives and providing feedback
- Reinforcing effort and providing recognition
- Cooperative learning

Helping Students Develop Understanding

This component is about helping students process new content, organize information, and construct meaning. It includes these four categories:

- Cues, questions, and advance organizers
- Nonlinguistic representations
- Summarizing and note taking
- Assigning homework and providing practice

Helping Students Extend and Apply Knowledge

This component focuses on engaging students in complex thinking processes and challenging students to make use of their learning. It includes these two categories:

- Identifying similarities and differences
- Generating and testing hypotheses

SOURCE: Adapted from *Classroom Instruction That Works*, Second Edition (p. xvi), by C. B. Dean, E. R. Hubbell, H. Pitler, and B. Stone, 2012, Alexandria, VA: ASCD. © 2012 by McREL International. Adapted with permission.

From What to How

The first two editions of *Classroom Instruction That Works* were designed to answer important *what* questions: What strategies should I use in the classroom? What is the science behind them? What problems of professional practice do they solve?

While the first two books offered tips for implementing these strategies in the classroom, this book is designed to take that guidance to a whole new level by answering the question of *how:* How can I implement the research-based recommendations from *Classroom Instruction That Works* in a way that's meaningful and grade-appropriate—tomorrow, in my classroom, with my students? This book answers the question of how by providing practical techniques ("tools") that teachers can use to put the research to work in their classrooms.

Tools are based on the work of Harvey Silver, Richard Strong, Matthew Perini, and Abigail Boutz, who have developed and refined hundreds of instructional techniques in collaboration with educators across the country with the goal of helping teachers address specific challenges (Silver, Strong, & Perini, 2001; Boutz, Silver, Jackson, & Perini, 2012; Silver & Boutz, 2015; Silver, Perini, & Boutz, 2016).

The tools in this book are the result of a collaborative effort between McREL International, developers of the *Classroom Instruction That Works* framework, and Silver Strong & Associates / Thoughtful Education Press, creators and publishers of the Tools for Today's Educators line of books. Every tool in this book has been selected, refined, or designed for the express purpose of helping teachers implement the research-based recommendations from *Classroom Instruction That Works.*

Key Design Features of This Book

To help you understand what the book contains and how to use it effectively, we've summarized some of its key design features in the sections that follow.

Designed for users and non-users of *Classroom Instruction That Works*

Whether you're familiar with the original *Classroom Instruction That Works* text, the second edition, or neither, this book will help you improve instruction and increase student achievement. We've organized the tools into chapters that correspond to the nine categories of instruction highlighted in both editions of *Classroom Instruction That Works*, so that users of either edition can find the tools they need. We've also organized the book around the instructional planning framework found in the second edition to help users of that framework integrate tools into their instructional designs. Finally, for educators who have no experience with *Classroom Instruction That Works*, this book requires no prior knowledge of either edition or the strategies within. Each category of instruction has its own chapter introduction clarifying the relevant research, and every tool is specifically designed so that any educator can use it to improve classroom practice.

Designed for busy teachers

We know how busy teachers are, and we structured this book accordingly.

We kept things short and simple, so that tools could be put into practice quickly. A description of each tool, its benefits, and steps for implementing it can all be found on a single page. Most tools require little or no advance planning, and all have seven or fewer steps.

We formatted each tool so that critical information would be easy to find and use. Every tool contains the same four basic sections (see figure on the next page). Large, boldface headings let you jump to whichever sections you're interested in and in whatever order works best for you.

Every tool contains the same four basic sections:

1. What is it?
A brief description of
the tool and its purpose

2. What are the benefits?
A one-paragraph explanation
of how the tool enhances teaching,
learning, and/or student behavior

3. What are the basic steps?
A step-by-step description of
how to implement the tool in the
classroom; for ease of use, each
tool includes seven steps or fewer

**4. How is the tool used
in the classroom?**
A section that provides greater
clarity on how the tool can be
used and typically includes specific
examples from different grade
levels and content areas

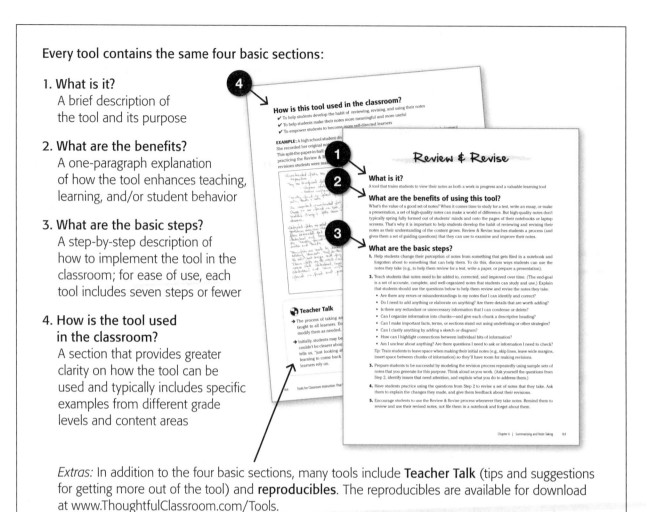

Extras: In addition to the four basic sections, many tools include **Teacher Talk** (tips and suggestions for getting more out of the tool) and **reproducibles**. The reproducibles are available for download at www.ThoughtfulClassroom.com/Tools.

We provided everything you need to get the tools going in your classroom. Besides the essentials, such as easy-to-follow steps and ready-to-go reproducibles (available both in the book and on the book's companion website, www.ThoughtfulClassroom.com/Tools), many tools include Teacher Talk, a bonus section that includes tips from practitioners, implementation suggestions, and other useful information. Skimming these Teacher Talk sections before trying a tool for the first time can help you avoid potential pitfalls and start using the tool like an expert.

We designed the book to be easily searchable, so you don't have to read it from cover to cover. Skim the one-sentence "What is it?" descriptions to find a tool that meets your needs, or use one of the book's search features:

- Use the Table of Contents (pp. vii–viii) to find tools for addressing each of the nine categories of instructional strategies from *Classroom Instruction That Works* or to find tools that align with the three components of the instructional planning framework from the second edition.

- Use the chapter introductions for Chapters 1–9 to get a quick, thumbnail description of each tool, so you can decide which tools are right for you and your students.

- Use the Index of Tools (p. 237) to search for tools by name.

Designed to work in real classrooms

The tools in this book are aligned with the updated research on raising student achievement from *Classroom Instruction That Works* (Second Edition). More than that, though, the tools are designed to work in real classrooms with real students. To get the tools working in your classroom, be sure to review them thoroughly (including classroom examples and teacher tips), modify them as needed, and use them regularly. Stop after each use to reflect on how things went and steps you might take to make the tool work even better the next time you use it.

To facilitate this kind of reflection, we've included a simple reflection form and guidelines for creating a reflection journal in the Epilogue (pp. 231–232). Whenever possible, engage in the reflective process with your colleagues, so that you can learn from each other's experiences and offer each other suggestions ("The way I simplified this tool to make it work for my English language learners was . . .").

Designed to be used across grade levels and content areas

Teachers at all grade levels are eager to do what works. But the question of how to apply the recommendations from the research is not always easy to answer. This book takes the guesswork out by including a variety of classroom examples that reflect a range of grade levels and content areas. Use the examples and Teacher Talk tips to see how tools can be adapted to meet specific content and classroom demands.

Designed to be used with colleagues

Promoting high levels of learning for all students takes commitment. The good news is that you don't have to make this commitment alone. Because this book can be used across grade levels and content areas, you and your colleagues can support each other as you learn, practice, and refine your use of individual tools. Build staff meetings and conversations around any of the nine categories of instructional strategies from *Classroom Instruction That Works* ("We really want to focus on using nonlinguistic representations this month"), as well as particular tools that will help teachers build students' skills in the targeted category. Commit to trying a new tool on a regular basis with your professional learning community (PLC). Or, do what a group of educators in West Babylon, New York, did and create a blog where teachers can share and learn from each other's experiences with specific tools (http://reflectivepathway.blogspot.com).

Why think this way? Because establishing a common language for instruction across schools and districts has been identified by researchers as a critical component of school improvement (Schooling, Toth, & Marzano, 2013). Using a research-based framework like the one laid out in *Classroom Instruction That Works*, along with classroom-ready tools that align directly to that framework, goes a long way in helping schools establish a common language for instruction.

Designed to be used by administrators as well as teachers

The tools in this book aren't just designed to help teachers; they're designed to help administrators grow their capacities as instructional leaders. Principals and other school leaders can use the tools to provide teachers with concrete suggestions for targeting particular research-based strategies and improving their classroom practice. This process is beneficial when used with individual teachers ("During my observation, I noticed that some students seemed confused about what their completed slideshows should look like. Using a tool like Guiding & Grading Rubrics would be a good way to help students develop a solid understanding of how to design a high-quality slideshow") or as part of a schoolwide initiative to target particular categories of instruction ("Many staff members are working to incorporate cooperative learning activities into their lesson designs. Over the next month, let's all commit to using at least two tools from the Cooperative Learning chapter"). Note that deciding to address particular instructional categories schoolwide is a great way to get everyone on the same page and ensure that classroom goals are aligned with school goals.

Designed to help students become better learners

The authors of *Classroom Instruction That Works* (Second Edition) remind us that the new demands of the postindustrial, information-driven world require today's teachers to "move beyond 'teaching content' to teaching students how to learn" (Dean et al., 2012, p. xix). With the tools in this book, teachers can more effectively achieve this important goal, because the tools teach students the steps in essential thinking and learning processes, including note taking and summarizing, identifying similarities and differences, and generating and testing hypotheses, among others. They also teach students the skills associated with cooperative learning and self-learning (e.g., setting goals, monitoring effort, reflecting on and improving work).

To help students learn to apply the thinking and learning skills embedded within the tools, call attention to the purpose and the process of the tools you use in the classroom ("Today we're going to be using a tool called AWESOME Summaries to help us develop summaries that are clear and concise. Here's how it works"). When relevant, model the steps to show students how you think and the learning habits you exhibit when you use particular tools. (You'll find that a number of Teacher Talk sections contain information about and tips for classroom modeling.) When students use the tools, encourage them to reflect on the process by asking them what came easy, what was challenging, what they might do differently next time, and where else—in school or beyond—they might use those tools.

. . .

Early in this introduction, we talked about the research-based revolution in education and the way in which *Classroom Instruction That Works* helped usher in and advance this revolution. This revolution led to a new promise: With clear and conclusive research behind us, we can improve learning for all our students. But a promise also requires a *how*—an approach that's manageable, that's practical, and that can work in every classroom. That's where this book comes in. With the right tools backed by the best research, we can finally fulfill the promise to help each and every student succeed.

PART I

Tools for Creating the Environment for Learning

Setting Objectives and Providing Feedback

Alice: Would you tell me, please, which way I ought to go from here?
The Cheshire Cat: That depends a good deal on where you want to get to.

—Lewis Carroll, *Alice's Adventures in Wonderland*

Setting objectives and providing feedback work in tandem. Teachers need to identify success criteria for learning objectives … [and] feedback should be provided for tasks that are related to the learning objectives; this way, students understand the purpose of the work they are asked to do, build a coherent understanding of a content domain, and develop high levels of skill in a specific domain.

—Ceri B. Dean, Elizabeth Ross Hubbell, Howard Pitler, and Bj Stone,
Classroom Instruction That Works (Second Edition)

The instructional category of setting objectives and providing feedback has a clear and positive impact on student achievement. The 2010 study (Beesley & Apthorp, 2010) that provides the research base for this category reports effect sizes of 0.31 for setting objectives and 0.76 for providing feedback, which "translate to percentile gains of 12 points and 28 points, respectively" (Dean et al., 2012, p. 4).

The logic behind these effect sizes and percentile gains should be clear enough: For students to be successful, they need to know where they are going (i.e., have clear objectives), and they need meaningful guidance about how to get there (i.e., receive feedback). It's common sense, right? Sure, but common sense is only a starting point. If we expect to see real increases in student achievement, then we need to be mindful of the *how*. Using the recommendations from *Classroom Instruction That Works* (Second Edition) as our guide, we can identify these important how questions:

When it comes to setting objectives, how can we

- Get our learning objectives just right—not too specific and not too general?
- Help students (and parents) understand the learning objectives?
- Connect learning objectives to previous learning and to upcoming learning?
- Involve students in the process of establishing their own learning objectives?

When it comes to providing feedback, how can we

- Focus students' attention on what's correct and help them see how to improve?
- Make sure that feedback is timely and will help students grow?
- Increase the power of feedback by establishing clear criteria for success?
- Invite students into the feedback process?

The tools in this chapter have been selected or developed for the express purpose of answering these questions. The first group of tools focuses on setting objectives:

1. **Learning Window** helps teachers unpack and convert their standards into four distinct types of learning objectives.

2. **Student-Friendly Learning Targets** shows teachers how to convert learning objectives into targets that are clear and easy for students to understand.

3. **Post, Discuss, Reference (PDR)** ensures that student learning objectives are fully and meaningfully integrated into the learning process.

4. **A Study In ...** invites teachers to focus learning units on rich, universal concepts that provoke student thinking.

5. **Review/Preview** helps students see where they are within an instructional sequence by highlighting what's been covered (review) and what's coming next (preview).

6. **Goal Cards** gives students a clear format for developing personal learning goals and establishing plans for achieving those goals.

The second group of tools in this chapter focuses on providing feedback:

7. **Fine-Tune Your Feedback** offers a set of guidelines for providing feedback that helps students grow—along with three techniques for delivering targeted feedback to students.

8. **PEERS** teaches students how to provide feedback to one another by spelling out five ground rules for improving the productivity of peer-feedback sessions.

9. **Guiding & Grading Rubrics** helps students understand the criteria that define high-quality work; the tool is used to promote learning and growth as well as to evaluate student performance.

Learning Window

What is it?

A framework for transforming complex standards into classroom-level learning goals—specifically, knowledge goals, understanding goals, skill-acquisition goals, and dispositional goals / habits of mind

What are the benefits of using this tool?

When learning objectives are clear, students are better able to see where their learning is headed, what's especially important, and what's giving them trouble. Clear learning objectives can also help reduce students' anxiety about achieving success (Dean et al., 2012). Unfortunately, standards are often too broad or too dense to provide the necessary degree of clarity. That's why it's so important to unpack and convert standards into smaller, more specific learning goals/targets. Learning Window facilitates this unpacking process with a window-shaped organizer that helps us determine the "core three" elements of good learning objectives: what students need to know, understand, and be able to do by the end of the lesson or unit. But Learning Window challenges us to go further by also asking us to identify the important habits of mind or dispositions we expect students to develop and the critical academic terms students will need to master.

What are the basic steps?

1. Identify the standards that you intend to address during an upcoming lesson or unit.

2. Begin to unpack the standards by scanning for useful information. Underline words or phrases that point to knowledge, understandings, skills, and habits of mind that students will need to acquire.

3. Use the questions on the reproducible Learning Window (p. 16) to help you complete the unpacking process. For help with the Habits of Mind pane, download the Habits of Mind Reference Page at www.ThoughtfulClassroom.com/Tools.

   Note: In addition to skills students will need to develop, the "be able to do" pane may also include the products/performances you expect students to complete.

4. Refer to your completed Learning Window as you map out your lesson or unit. Use it to guide the development of assessments, assignments, and activities. (If you want, you can record lesson-planning ideas directly on your window.)

5. *Optional:* Use your completed Learning Window to generate a list of student-friendly learning targets. See the Student-Friendly Learning Targets tool (pp. 17–19) for guidance.

How is this tool used in the classroom?

✔ To unpack standards, identify learning goals, and focus instruction/assessment

Teachers use Learning Window to help them unpack their standards and design their lessons and units. Two sample windows are shown here; additional samples are available for download at www.ThoughtfulClassroom.com/Tools.

EXAMPLE 1: A second-grade teacher is designing a unit on fables in which students will learn how different cultures use fables to teach life lessons. He uses a Learning Window to unpack relevant standards and clarify the knowledge, understanding, skills, and habits of mind students will develop over the course of the unit.

Common Core standards* that I intend to address

- Reading standard RL.2.2: Recount stories, including <u>fables</u> and folktales <u>from diverse cultures</u>, and determine their central <u>message, lesson, or moral</u>.

- Reading standard RL.2.3: Describe how characters in a story <u>respond to</u> major events and <u>challenges</u>.

- Reading standard RL.2.9: <u>Compare and contrast two or more versions of the same story</u> by different authors or <u>from different cultures</u>.

- Writing standard W.2.1: <u>Write opinion pieces</u> in which they introduce the topic or book they are writing about, state an opinion, supply reasons that support the opinion, use linking words to connect opinion and reasons, and provide a concluding statement or section.

- Language standard L.2.6: Use words and phrases acquired through conversations, reading and being read to, and responding to texts, including <u>using adjectives</u> and adverbs to <u>describe</u>.

LEARNING WINDOW

What will students need to KNOW?	What HABITS OF MIND will I try to foster?
• What a fable is (a story that teaches a lesson) • Critical attributes of a fable	• Appreciation for different cultures and perspectives • Persistence and cooperation (showing how persistence and cooperation help us respond to challenges)
What will students need to UNDERSTAND?	**What will students need to BE ABLE TO DO?**
• Fables are stories that teach us life lessons (in this unit, lessons about overcoming challenges). • Different cultures use fables to teach lessons.	• Describe characters using appropriate adjectives (see terms in box below) • Compare and contrast two fables from different cultures • Write an opinion essay (are the two fables more alike or different?)

What TERMS will students need to know?

Key terms: challenge, difficult, overcome, character, underdog, fable, moral, culture

Adjectives: mean, cautious, overconfident, persistent, modest, tricky, bewildered, resourceful, determined

---

*Common Core State Standards for English Language Arts & Literacy in History / Social Studies, Science, and Technical Subjects: http://www.corestandards.org/ELA-Literacy

EXAMPLE 2: After identifying the standards that she wanted to address during an upcoming exploration unit, a social studies teacher used a Learning Window to unpack those standards and design her unit. Before beginning the unit, she converted the information on her Learning Window into a list of student-friendly learning targets (not shown) and then shared those targets with students.

Standards that I intend to address

Content standards:

- Understand the <u>causes and effects</u> of <u>European overseas exploration</u> and expansion in the 15th and 16th centuries.
  - <u>Analyze</u> the <u>conditions/factors/motives</u> (political, economic, social, technological, religious) that stimulated exploration.
  - <u>Understand</u> the <u>consequences and significance</u> of European expansion (e.g., the impact on <u>Native Americans</u>).

Common Core standards:*

- <u>Write arguments</u> focused on discipline-specific content (WHST.6-8.1).
- <u>Analyze a case</u> in which <u>two or more texts provide conflicting information</u> on the same topic (RI.8.9).
- <u>Conduct research</u> to answer a question (W.8.7), and <u>gather information from multiple print and digital sources</u> (W.8.8).

LEARNING WINDOW

What will students need to KNOW?

- Conditions/factors (political, economic, etc.) that stimulated exploration
- Technological advances (navigation, map making, naval engineering) that facilitated exploration and conquest
- Consequences of expansion, including impact on Native Americans
- Names, nationalities, motivations, and accomplishments of principal explorers

What HABITS OF MIND will I try to foster?

- Seeking out reasons, explanations, and evidence
- Considering different perspectives and viewpoints
- Evaluating the quality of ideas and information

What will students need to UNDERSTAND?

- That one person's explorer can be another person's conqueror
- How technological innovations can impact the course of history
- That periods of exploration happen for a reason
  - Why did the Age of Exploration happen when it did?
  - Why was the time right for Columbus in 1492?

What will students need to BE ABLE TO DO?

- <u>Justify positions with evidence</u>
  Task: Did the times make Columbus, or did Columbus make the times? Take a position and support it in writing.

- <u>Research and report</u>
  - Gather relevant information from multiple sources.
  - Take accurate notes, summarize key points.
  - Quote or paraphrase properly; avoid plagiarism.

- <u>Investigate / Take a Position</u>
  Task: Investigate conflicting accounts of interactions between explorers and native populations. Based on your research and learning, how do you think history should remember this period? (Explorers or exploiters?)

What TERMS will students need to know?

cartography, mariner's astrolabe, caravel, New World, imperialism, Age of Exploration, Inca, Aztecs, 1492, conquistadors, colonialism, Columbus, de Soto, Cortez, de Leon, Pizarro, Prince Henry the Navigator

*Common Core State Standards for English Language Arts & Literacy in History / Social Studies, Science, and Technical Subjects: http://www.corestandards.org/ELA-Literacy

Title/topic: _____

Purpose: _____

Learning Window

What will students need to KNOW?	**What HABITS OF MIND will I try to foster?**
(terms,* facts, formulas, events, procedures, etc.)	
*Record key terms in the "windowsill" portion of the organizer.	
What will students need to UNDERSTAND?	**What will students need to BE ABLE TO DO?**
(big ideas, concepts, principles, "hows & whys")	(thinking and learning skills like summarizing, researching, and data analysis, as well as products and performances that students will need to create)

What TERMS will students need to know?

Student-Friendly Learning Targets

What is it?

A tool for developing learning targets that are clear, specific, and easy for students to understand

What are the benefits of using this tool?

Setting clear learning objectives "reassures students that there is a reason for learning and provides teachers with a focal point for planning instruction" (Dean et al., 2012, p. 2). By encouraging students to think of objectives as targets, and by presenting those targets in student-friendly language, this tool helps make objectives more understandable and assessable by our students. It also reminds us that learning objectives can't be posted and then forgotten; rather, they need to be revisited, reinforced, and assessed throughout the course of instruction.

What are the basic steps?

1. Generate a list of learning objectives for an upcoming lesson or unit. To do this, ask yourself what you want students to know, understand, and be able to do by the end of the lesson or unit.

   Tip: Be sure to list *objectives* (what you want students to know, understand, and be able to do) rather than *activities* (the things students will be doing in class).

2. Turn your list of objectives into student-friendly targets. To do this,

   * Write the objectives in "I will" or "I can" format. ("I will know / understand / be able to _____.")
   * Frame the objectives in simple, age-appropriate language that students will understand.
   * Be specific. A well-written target should tell students what they're trying to achieve and let them assess their ability to achieve it.

   Note: Because *understanding* can be hard to define and assess, you may want to replace the word *understand* with something more specific when framing your targets (e.g., "I will be able to *explain* _____" instead of "I will *understand* _____").

3. Post the list of targets in a prominent location and leave it there throughout the lesson or unit. Discuss the targets with students so that they're clear about what they're aiming for and why it's worthwhile (e.g., "We'll be learning how to use a book's index. This is important because …").

   Note: Alternative methods of sharing learning targets are discussed in Teacher Talk.

4. Refer to the list regularly to show students how the things they're doing in class (tasks, activities, assignments) relate to the things they're supposed to be learning (targets).

   For example: Today, you'll be examining *yes* and *no* examples of prime numbers (activity). The goal of this activity is for you to understand and be able to define what a prime number is (target).

5. Remind students to revisit the list of targets throughout the lesson or unit to gauge their progress.

How is this tool used in the classroom?

✔ To make learning objectives easy for students to understand

✔ To enable students to assess and monitor their learning

EXAMPLE 1: Here's how an elementary teacher transformed a specific math standard into a set of student-friendly learning targets:

Standard that I intend to address:

4.NF.A.2 Compare two fractions with different numerators and different denominators, e.g., by creating common denominators or numerators, or by comparing to a benchmark fraction such as 1/2. Recognize that comparisons are valid only when the two fractions refer to the same whole. Record the results of comparisons with symbols >, =, or <, and justify the conclusions, e.g., by using a visual fraction model.*

Student-friendly learning targets:

- I will be able to define these terms in my own words and give an example of each: *fraction, equivalent fraction, numerator, denominator,* and *value.* I will also be able to explain what it means to *compare* two things.

- I will know what these three symbols mean and how and when to use them: >, =, <.

- I will be able to compare fractions with different numerators and denominators.

- I will be able to tell when fractions are equivalent.

- I will be able to show and explain how fractions can be equivalent even though they may look different.

- I will be able to express fractions using visual models (like pictures or number lines) as well as numbers.

---

*Common Core State Standards for Mathematics: http://www.corestandards.org/Math/Content/4/NF

EXAMPLE 2: A high school history teacher has developed a mini-unit in which students explore the meaning of the American Dream using two famous speeches as lenses. The student-friendly learning targets for the unit appear below.

- I will be able to explain the historical significance of two great American speeches: Ronald Reagan's "Address at Moscow State University" and Dr. Martin Luther King, Jr.'s "I Have a Dream" speech.

- I will be able to conduct a close reading of both speeches.

- I will be able to identify key elements that make each speech particularly persuasive.

- I will be able to compare and contrast the speeches and explain how each provides a different perspective on the American Dream.

- I will be able to explain what the American Dream means to me and support my explanation with evidence from both speeches.

EXAMPLE 3: In order to make learning targets clearer for young learners, a teacher makes two moves: She limits the learning targets that students will be focusing on at any one time to three or fewer, and she incorporates simple visuals to make each learning target more memorable.

I will be able to explain why sleep is important.

I will know what I need to do before I go to bed.

🔘 Teacher Talk

→ The simple, everyday language of learning targets makes it easier to communicate your objectives to parents, which helps them "understand and become engaged in what their children are learning" (Dean et al., 2012, p. 7).

→ Learning targets are often introduced at the start of a lesson or unit to guide the learning process, but they *can* be shared at other points in an instructional sequence as well—and in a number of different ways. Instead of telling students the targets, you could invite them to uncover the targets for themselves by having them analyze a culminating assessment task ("What will you need to know and be able to do in order to complete this task successfully?") or complete an activity ("What did we learn by creating a plot of temperature versus elevation?"). And instead of simply posting targets on the board, you could use an engaging hook or activity to concretize and give context to the targets. ("What's the difference between the subtraction problems we learned to solve yesterday and the new ones on the board? Today, we're going to learn how to use a technique called 'borrowing' to tackle these new problems.")

Ultimately, the time and method that you use to share your targets should be determined by the content and purpose of your lesson. Regardless of how and when you share your targets, students should be able to explain what they're supposed to be learning long before that learning is assessed. Check their ability to do this by posing questions like these: "Why are we doing this?" and "What's our goal?"

Post, Discuss, Reference (PDR)

What is it?

A tool that tells us how to use classroom learning objectives once we've developed them

What are the benefits of using this tool?

Setting clear learning objectives is essential to teaching and learning. But what do we do with those objectives once we've set them? This tool provides the answer in the form of an acronym that reminds us to **P**ost our learning objectives, **D**iscuss them with students, and **R**eference them throughout the instructional process. Collectively, these three steps remind us that setting objectives isn't good enough; in order to make learning objectives true catalysts for student learning, we must share those objectives with students in a way they can understand—and help students see the connection between what they're doing in class and what they're supposed to be learning.

What are the basic steps?

1. POST the learning objectives at the start of a lesson or unit. Present the objectives using simple, age-appropriate language. See the Student-Friendly Learning Targets tool (pp. 17–19) for guidance.

Note: Remember to use the posted objectives to focus and drive your instructional plans. Ensure that the activities you plan are designed to help students achieve the posted objectives.

2. DISCUSS the learning objectives as a class, both before instruction begins and regularly after that.

- Clarify what students are trying to achieve and why it's important. ("The goal is for you to be able to craft a well-supported argument. Being able to do this is important because …")
- Highlight connections to previous lessons/units, future lessons/units, real-world applications, and/or central course themes. ("Last week, we learned what a *claim* is. Today, we'll see how …")
- Encourage student participation by inviting students to explain objectives in their own words, ask questions, and share personal reactions.

3. REFERENCE the learning objectives throughout the lesson or unit.

- Point out connections between the objectives students are working to achieve and the things they're doing in class. (How does each lesson/activity relate to the posted learning objectives?)
- Assess, and encourage students to assess, their progress toward achieving each objective. Develop, and encourage students to develop, concrete plans for advancing their achievement.

4. *Optional:* Invite students to generate personal learning goals within the context of your lesson or unit by asking them what else they want to know, understand, or be able to do.

How is this tool used in the classroom?

✔ To move from posting objectives to helping students understand and achieve those objectives

A Study In...

What is it?

A simple technique for framing instructional units around core concepts that focus student learning and provoke student thinking

What are the benefits of using this tool?

In addition to having clear learning objectives, a good instructional unit should also be what Art Costa (2008) calls "a home for the mind"—a place where students explore content, make connections, and develop new insights. One way to build this "thinking-centric" quality of our units is to frame them around core concepts or universal themes. This tool encourages teachers to search their units for the biggest of the big ideas—that conceptual powerhouse that puts all the other concepts into line—and to use it as an organizing principle for student learning.

What are the basic steps?

1. Identify the key understandings that you expect students to develop over the course of a unit. For help with this step, see the Learning Window tool (pp. 13–16).

2. Ask yourself, "What core concept or universal theme unites these key understandings and can serve as a lens for investigating the content of this unit?" For a list of universal concepts that provoke deep thinking, see Teacher Talk.

3. Turn your concept into a unit title using this format: "(Unit Topic): A Study in (Core Concept)."

   Note: You are not simply restating the topic of your unit, so think conceptually rather than literally. A conceptual title such as "The Water Cycle: A Study in Renewal" will provoke student thinking about the importance of water far more than "The Water Cycle: A Study in Precipitation."

4. Use the core concept to guide student learning throughout the unit. Some ways to do this include

   - *Using the concept as a hook for the unit.* Introduce the title of the unit, and invite students to think about what they know about the topic and the core concept.

   - *Designing essential questions around the concept.* Have students explore the concept deeply using essential questions. See Teacher Talk for more on the relationship between core concepts and essential questions.

   - *Developing a culminating assessment around the concept.* For example, a unit titled "The Water Cycle: A Study in Renewal" might culminate with a task that asks students, "What can the water cycle teach us about nature's power to renew itself?"

   - *Encouraging regular reflection.* Come back to the concept throughout the unit. Ask students to think about how their understanding of the concept is growing.

   - *Building interdisciplinary thinking.* Teachers can work together to build units that highlight common concepts. For example, how might a concept like *design* play out in three different units, one focused on literature, one focused on art, and one focused on STEM?

How is this tool used in the classroom?

✔ To use rich, universal concepts as lenses that focus student learning

✔ To develop students' ability to think conceptually

✔ To increase students' interest in academic topics

Teachers at all grade levels use this tool to frame their units around thought-provoking concepts. Below are some examples of unit titles developed with this tool.

Frog and Toad: A Study in Friendship

The Four Seasons: A Study in Change

The Energy Crisis: A Study in Responsibility

Equations: A Study in Balance

The Civil Rights Movement: A Study in Courage

The Grapes of Wrath: A Study in the American Dream (or Nightmare?)

Four Films by Hitchcock: A Study in Obsession

 **Teacher Talk**

➔ Are you looking for some universal concepts that dependably lead to robust thinking? Try these:

Adaptation	Creativity	Patterns
Balance	Design	Perception
Caring	Discovery	Perspective
Cause and effect	Ethics	Prejudice
Change	Friendship	Relationships
Community	Inequality	Renewal
Competition	Interdependence	Representation
Composition	Interpretation	Revolution
Conflict	Needs and wants	Structure and function
Convergence	Order	Supply and demand
Courage	Organization	Survival
Craftsmanship	Parts and wholes	Systems

➔ Use the power of collaborative professional learning to build conceptually driven units. For example, a team of middle school ELA teachers wanted to help all students develop the skill of argument. In developing an argument unit as a team, these teachers brainstormed a variety of core concepts that might serve as the unit theme, including *perspective*, *balance*, and *persuasion*. The group settled on "Argument: A Study in Craftsmanship," because the concept of *craftsmanship* drew the greatest attention to the idea that arguments need to be crafted with care and to the larger goal of teaching students how to build (craft) strong arguments.

➔ The core concept that you derive using this tool can be an ideal basis for developing essential questions for your unit. For example, the ELA team discussed above that designed the unit titled "Argument: A Study in Craftsmanship" asked students to explore the following essential question during the unit: What does it mean to craft a convincing argument?

Review/Preview

What is it?

A tool that helps students understand where they are within an instructional sequence by pointing out what they've already covered (review) and what's coming up next (preview)

What are the benefits of using this tool?

When we begin an instructional unit, *we* know exactly what we plan to cover and in what order. Our students, on the other hand, don't have the benefit of this big-picture vision—and without it, they can easily get lost. This tool keeps them oriented by giving them a road map for instruction and helping them track their progress. (What topics and learning targets have we already addressed? Where are we going next?)

What are the basic steps?

1. Create a road map for an upcoming unit by listing the topics and learning objectives/targets you plan to address. If you'll be covering these topics/targets in a specific order, your map should reflect that.

   Note: Your map can be as simple or creative as you want—anything from a list of learning targets to a drawing that looks like an actual road map. Here are a few examples:

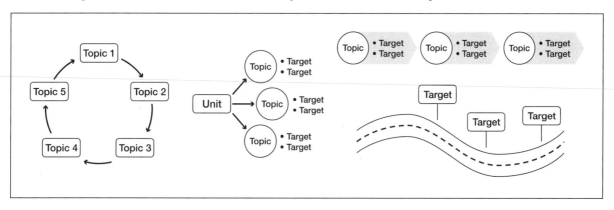

2. Share the map with students before instruction begins. Keep a copy on display throughout the entire unit so you can refer to it.

3. Stop at various times throughout the course of instruction to point out where you are on the map. ("At this point, we've already covered ____ and ____ . Next, we're going to be learning ____ .")

4. Help students improve their big-picture understanding of the material by pointing out how the topics, targets, and lessons within your unit connect to one another. A web or flowchart-style map can make these connections easier for students to see.

How is this tool used in the classroom?

   ✔ To give students a road map of the learning to come
   ✔ To help students keep track of where they are within an instructional sequence

Goal Cards

What is it?

A tool that prepares students to become more self-directed and successful learners by giving them a framework (a Goal Card) that they can use to record personal learning goals, establish plans for achieving those goals, and reflect on their progress

What are the benefits of using this tool?

The most successful learners are self-regulating; they set their own goals for learning and monitor their progress along the way. Goal Cards gives teachers a powerful way to develop this kind of self-direction in all students, so they can become lifelong learners. The tool invites students to identify personal learning goals, establish plans for achieving them, and reflect on their accomplishments. It also calls students' attention to the way that their actions (planning, effort, strategy use) can impact their success.

What are the basic steps?

1. Invite students to establish personal learning goals. Examples 1–7 highlight some of the different kinds of goals students might choose to pursue.

2. Have students record their goals and plans for achieving them on a Goal Card. Choose one of the three Goal Card formats on pages 27–28, create your own format, or use blank index cards.

3. Meet with students one-on-one to review and discuss their plans. Once an acceptable plan has been agreed upon, sign—and have students sign—their Goal Cards.

4. Remind students to follow through with their plans, monitor / gather feedback about their progress, and adjust their plans as needed. If you want, have them check off each step in their plan as it's accomplished, as shown in Example 7.

5. Acknowledge students who worked hard and achieved their goals. Call their attention to the ways that their actions (e.g., effort, strategy use) influenced their success. For example, "This draft is much smoother than your last one. The strategy of reading your work aloud really helped you improve."

6. Use questions like these to help students reflect on the impact that effort, persistence, and use of strategies can have on their success:
   - What strategies did you use to tackle your goal? What impact did they have?
   - How did it feel to achieve (or make progress toward achieving) your goal?
   - Can effort level, strategy use, and persistence influence achievement? How?
   - Do you have the power to influence your academic success?
   - Did you learn anything that could help you be more successful in the future?

How is this tool used in the classroom?

✔ To have students set goals, establish plans for achieving them, and monitor their progress

✔ To help students see that planning, effort, and strategy use can facilitate achievement

Students can establish personal learning goals at any point in the instructional process. (They can create these goals from scratch or select teacher-generated goals that they'd like to pursue with greater intensity.) The examples that follow highlight some of the many different kinds of goals that students might choose to pursue—personal-interest goals, process goals, task-related goals, etc.

EXAMPLE 1: Learn about something that interests me

After introducing an upcoming unit about ancient Egypt, a sixth-grade teacher invited his students to generate some goals of their own. ("What are you interested in learning about this topic?") One student's Goal Card is shown below.

This Goal Card belongs to *Anthony Coleman*

Goal: *To learn how structures as amazing as the pyramids were built using the tools available at the time*

Date goal established: *January 12th*　　　　　　**Date goal achieved:** *January 26th*

Action plan: *I will ask the librarian if she knows of any good books about this topic. I will also look on Wikipedia and other websites to see what I can find. Maybe my shop teacher would be interested in helping me with this project since it relates to tools. I will have to check about that. Once I find my information, I will make a poster to show what I learned.*

Student signature: *Anthony Coleman*　　　　　　**Teacher signature:** *Mr. R Engel*

EXAMPLE 2: Try out a specific strategy

A fourth-grade teacher encourages students to try different strategies to improve their writing.

Goal: *To use more figurative language in my descriptive writing this week.*
Strategy: *I will use two similes when I am describing Sarah's character from my book during book club time.*
How did I do? *I used three similes in my writing, so I surpassed my goal. It was much easier than I thought. The similes helped paint a picture of what type of character Sarah is.*

EXAMPLE 3: Develop a specific attitude, behavior, or habit of mind

A high school homeroom teacher helps his students grow as learners by encouraging them to identify attitudes, behaviors, and habits of mind that could help them be more successful in school. Students record their thoughts on paper and show their commitment to developing the attitudes, behaviors, and habits they've identified by signing their names to their plans.

My goal is to develop the courage to participate more and ask questions when I am lost in calculus class. For starters, I am going to commit to raising my hand at least once per class. I will try a self-talk strategy ("Why do you care what other people think?" "What's the worst that could happen?" "Other people are probably lost too") to see if it helps me.

— Jennifer

EXAMPLE 4: Focus on one of the learning goals/targets from a lesson or unit

Midway through a unit on magnetic forces and fields, a physics teacher asked his students to assess their progress toward the various learning targets they had been working on in class. (Students made this assessment after reviewing completed assignments, quizzes, and teacher feedback.) He challenged them to identify the target that was proving hardest to hit, record it on a Goal Card, and map out a plan for achieving it. He offered specific suggestions for each of the targets in question (readings, activities, study strategies, etc.) but left it to students to develop a course of action.

EXAMPLE 5: Revisit a learning goal/target that was missed the first time around

At the end of a unit on graphic design principles, a teacher had students review their culminating assessment tests, identify learning goals they hadn't yet achieved, and develop plans for achieving them.

EXAMPLE 6: Complete a task or assignment

A second-grade teacher uses Goal Cards to help his students focus their attention and effort on specific tasks. He has students choose a goal to work on at the start of each week and reflect on their accomplishments at the end of that week. In the interim, he encourages students to share their Goal Cards with their parents to keep them abreast of the things that they're working on.

GOAL OF THE WEEK by *Christine*

What is my goal for the week? *My goal for this week is to read the two books we have to read for our animal project.*

How did I do? What did I learn? *I ran out of time and only got to read one book. I maybe should have started reading on Monday.*

EXAMPLE 7: Tackle one specific part of a larger goal or task

Fifth-grade students were training for increased fitness in gym class. After three weeks of assessing and monitoring their progress in different fitness exercises, students identified the exercise that was hardest for them, established a goal for improvement, and developed a plan for achieving that goal. One student's Goal Card is shown here:

This goal card belongs to *Arturo*   **Date:** *April 6th*   **Subject:** *Gym*

Ultimate goal: *Satisfy the requirements for all five exercises.*

Intermediate goal: *By the end of the month, I will be able to run a mile in under 8 minutes. Current time is 8 minutes, 6 seconds.*

Action plan (✓off each step that you accomplish)	Completion Date:
☑ 1 *I will ask my teacher for tips on improving my form.*	*April 7*
☑ 2 *I will run with my dad every weekend this month.*	*April 9, April 16*
☑ 3 *I will try to take 5 seconds off my time by next week.*	*April 15*
☐ 4 *I will try to cut 5 more seconds off by the end of the month.*	
☐ 5 *I will stretch after every run so that I don't pull a muscle.*	*Ongoing*

Basic Goal Card

This Goal Card belongs to _____

Start date: _____ Achievement date: _____

My goal is to

Here is what I will do to try and achieve my goal:

Goal Card with Action Plan

This Goal Card belongs to _____ Date: _____

Goal:

Action plan (✔ off each step that you accomplish and record the completion date)	Completion date
☐ 1	
☐ 2	
☐ 3	
☐ 4	
☐ 5	
☐ 6	

Student signature: _____ Teacher signature: _____

Expanded Goal Card

This Goal Card belongs to _____

Start date: _____ Achievement date: _____

The goal that I will be working to achieve is …

What do I already know that can help me achieve this goal?

What will I need to know in order to achieve this goal?

What will I need to be able to do in order to achieve this goal?

People, materials, and resources that might help me achieve this goal include …

Steps that I will take to try and achieve this goal include …

Student signature: Teacher signature:

Fine-Tune Your Feedback

What is it?

A tool that outlines general principles and a set of specific techniques for providing effective feedback

What are the benefits of using this tool?

Education researcher John Hattie (2012) explains that "while feedback is among the most powerful moderators of learning, its effects are among the most variable" (p. 129). In other words, not all feedback is equally effective. Fine-Tune Your Feedback lays out a clear set of principles for providing the kind of feedback that encourages students to analyze and improve their work. The tool also includes three practical feedback techniques that teachers can use to put these principles into action.

What are the basic steps?

1. Familiarize yourself with the principles of effective feedback as summarized in the STAIRS acronym (see The STAIRS to Effective Feedback box on p. 30 for more on each principle):

    Specific

    Task focused, not student focused

    Age appropriate

    Improvement oriented

    Regular

    Selective

2. Discuss with students the importance of feedback to the learning process.

    Tip: To help students better understand the value of feedback, ask them to think about something that they learned with help and the role that feedback played in their improvement.

3. Review an assignment or task that students have completed. Ask yourself, "What does this work tell me about the student's progress toward relevant learning targets / criteria for success?"

    Note: Remember to share the criteria for success with students before they begin working.

4. Decide how you'll give students feedback about their work. (See Three Techniques for Thoughtful Feedback, pp. 31–32, for options. Notice how these techniques incorporate the principles of effective feedback from Step 1.)

5. Give students an opportunity to use the feedback you have provided, either by allowing them to revise their work or by encouraging them to apply the feedback to a future assignment.

How is this tool used in the classroom?

✔ To help students understand how they are progressing toward learning targets

✔ To teach students how to review, reflect on, and improve their work

There are several ways to provide feedback, and on pages 31–32, we present three feedback techniques that have the power to enhance student achievement. All feedback, however, should be guided by a general understanding of what makes feedback particularly effective. The STAIRS to Effective Feedback box below outlines a simple set of principles to help ensure that the feedback you provide to students will promote growth. For more on the principles of effective feedback, see Brookhart (2008), Chappuis (2009), Hattie and Timperley (2007), and Shute (2008).

The STAIRS to Effective Feedback

Effective feedback is **S**pecific.

Replace vague comments like "good job" or "needs work" with specific comments that identify

• What is right or was done well ("Your explanation lays out three important factors that led to McCarthyism")

• What is incorrect or needs attention ("Your lab report needs a Materials and Methods section")

• What is needed to improve ("Remember to follow the order of operations")

Effective feedback is **T**ask focused, not student focused.

Avoid comments that focus on the student ("You're so smart!"). Comment instead on the work that students have done—products they've created, strategies / thinking processes they've used, assessment criteria they have or haven't yet satisfied, learning targets they have or haven't yet met, the impact of their efforts, or the progress they've made ("The extra effort you put into analyzing the significance of your results paid off. This is much improved!").

Effective feedback is **A**ge appropriate.

If students can't understand your feedback, they won't be able to act on it. Use student-friendly language and avoid technical jargon like "shows partial command of writing conventions."

Effective feedback is **I**mprovement oriented.

Corrective feedback should teach students what they can do to improve their work and encourage them to do it. Instead of correcting students' work for them, give students suggestions and strategies that they can use to take their work to the next level. ("Refer to the rubric to see how you can make this conclusion stronger" or "One of your homework problems is incorrect. Can you figure out which one and fix the error?") Adjust the amount of guidance that you provide according to students' individual needs and abilities.

Effective feedback is **R**egular.

Good feedback should be regular and paced to match instructional goals. Research suggests that when students are acquiring procedural skills, developing reading fluency, or focused on learning that requires accurate recall, feedback should be immediate so that students don't practice incorrectly; however, students may benefit from delayed feedback when learning concepts (Franzke, Kintsch, Caccamise, Johnson, & Dooley, 2005; Mathan & Koedinger, 2002; Shute, 2008).

Effective feedback is **S**elective.

Prevent corrective feedback from becoming overwhelming by forcing yourself to be selective. Instead of pointing out *everything* that needs fixing, identify a few important things for students to work on and leave the rest for another time.

Three Techniques for Thoughtful Feedback

Glow & Grow

Teachers use Glow & Grow (Boutz, Silver, Jackson, & Perini, 2012) to boost students' confidence and help students understand the attributes of quality work by identifying what they have done well (what glows in their work). The tool also empowers students to take a direct role in improving their work by pinpointing specific areas for improvement (where the work can grow). What's more, the tool's simple, student-friendly format helps ensure that the feedback won't overwhelm students.

An important element of Glow & Grow is that the *grow* feedback often includes enough *how* language to help the student think through how the improvement can be achieved, without simply telling the student what to do. Below are two examples of the Glow & Grow technique in action.

EXAMPLE 1: A first-grade teacher asked students to identify their favorite toy and give three reasons why it is their favorite. She discussed her Glow & Grow feedback with students during one-on-one conferences and had them use it to revise and improve their work.

Three ways your work GLOWS:
☀ Your sentences start with capital letters and end with periods.
☀ You remembered to give three reasons why you like your toy.
☀ You stuck to the topic. Everything is about your favorite toy.

Two ways your work can GROW:
🍸 Four of your sentences start with the word "my." Can you start some of them with a different word?
🍸 Your letter "z" is backwards. Can you find and fix your mistakes?

EXAMPLE 2: A high school computer science teacher is working with a business teacher to help students develop functional websites for their model businesses. The teachers use Glow & Grow to give students feedback on their home pages and site maps before students move on to building their websites.

Where your website GLOWS	Where your website can GROW
1. Your home page is welcoming and bright, which works well for a business that focuses on outdoor activities.	1. You have identified a lot of pages on your site map. Is there a way you can organize them around three or four core services/products?
2. Your home page offers a lot of information to visitors and uses different forms of media.	2. Can you shorten your domain name so customers can find and remember it more easily?

What & Why Feedback

What & Why Feedback (Boutz et al., 2012) puts a premium on explaining to students why particular elements of their work are of high quality and why others need attention. To use the tool as a feedback technique, indicate *what* was done well and *what* needs to be improved when you review students' work. Then, provide a *why* for each *what* you identify.

What: Your paragraph isn't as descriptive as it could be.
Why: You use the words *good* and *fun* a lot. Can you find some words on our word wall that might do a better job of describing your vacation?

What: Your current batch of marinara tastes better than your last batch.
Why: You took the time to slowly sweat your onions and garlic, which gave the sauce a milder taste.

What: Your lab report lacks a proper conclusion.
Why: You've reported your results, but you haven't explained what the results tell you.

The "Ps" to Better Work

With The "Ps" to Better Work (Boutz et al., 2012), teachers challenge and encourage students to analyze their work through multiple lenses, leading students to think more deeply about how they can make improvements. To use the tool, review students' work against the learning targets / criteria for success and look for opportunities to

PRAISE specific things that were done well. For example:

- Your story has a clear beginning, middle, and end.
- I can see that you checked your work, found all of the errors, and corrected them.
- Beginning your report with an essential question and coming back to the essential question multiple times created strong cohesion throughout your report.

Use **P**ROMPTS to remind students of things they've been taught but have forgotten to do. For example:

- Remember to double-check your measurements before mixing any substances.
- Don't forget to simplify all fractions in your answers.
- Remember to bend your knees before you take your foul shot.

Use **P**ROBING QUESTIONS to encourage students to explain or expand on their work. For example:

- Does your answer make sense? Could an acid have a pH of 10?
- Can you clarify how this paragraph relates to your overall thesis about Hamilton and Federalism?
- I am intrigued by your choice of a minor key for your composition. Why a minor key?

PROPOSE specific ways for students to improve their work. For example:

- What if you rewrite your story in the first person? How might that increase the immediacy of the incident for the reader? Try it and see!
- A few well-chosen visuals will help make the ideas in your presentation more concrete.
- Your birdhouse is still rough to the touch. Try using sandpaper with a finer grain.

PEERS

What is it?

A tool that improves the productivity of peer-review sessions by outlining steps for students to follow (adapted from Brookhart, 2008); each step is spelled out by a different letter in the PEERS acronym

What are the benefits of using this tool?

Allowing students to reflect on their performance and exchange feedback with their fellow learners can be a powerful way to develop lifelong learning skills. If not done strategically, however, peer feedback can amount to a waste of precious classroom time. This tool makes peer-review sessions more focused and productive by reinforcing that the purpose of feedback is to help students improve and by teaching students five simple steps for giving and responding to feedback. Because these steps are spelled out by the letters in the PEERS acronym, they're easy for students to remember and follow.

What are the basic steps?

1. Pair students up. Explain that they'll be assessing each other's work on an assigned task using a process called PEERS.

2. Explain and model each step in the PEERS process:

   Preview the assessment criteria or rubric before reviewing each other's work.

   Examine each other's work, keeping the assessment criteria in mind.

   Explain what was done well and what could be improved. Be as specific as possible.

   Review the feedback you received. *Think:* How can you use it to improve your work?

   Share your thoughts with your partner and discuss plans for revision.

3. Give students a list of assessment criteria or a rubric for the assigned task. Review and discuss the criteria as a class.

   Optional: Convert the list of criteria into a feedback form like the ones on page 34.

4. Have students review each other's work on the assigned task using the PEERS process (post the PEERS acronym in a prominent location so that they can easily refer to it). Tell students whether to speak their feedback to their partners or record their comments on paper.

   Note: Before having students use the PEERS process on their own, you might want to have them practice as a class (i.e., go through the process step-by-step using one or more samples of work).

5. Listen in as students work to confirm that they're staying on task and using the PEERS process properly. Remind them that their feedback should address the criteria for successful work: Which criteria have their partners satisfied? Which criteria have yet to be met?

6. Give students an opportunity to use the feedback they receive by allowing them to revise their work.

   Optional: Have students submit a copy of the feedback and a note explaining how they used it (or why they didn't) along with their completed work.

How is this tool used in the classroom?

✔ To teach students how to give each other focused feedback

✔ To have students revise and improve their work with guidance from their peers

Many teachers convert their lists of assessment criteria into feedback forms that students can use to review each other's work (see below for two examples).

EXAMPLE 1: A first-grade teacher uses simple forms in conjunction with the PEERS process to help his students provide feedback on each other's work. Two feedback forms are shown below.

WRITING A SENTENCE	😐	🙂
The sentence begins with a capital letter.		
The sentence ends with a punctuation mark.		
The sentence makes sense.		

MATH PROBLEM CHECKLIST	😐	🙂
The key words in the problem are underlined.		
The problem is drawn out using pictures.		
The correct number model is shown.		
The answer is boxed.		
The answer is correct.		

EXAMPLE 2: A middle school teacher used his state's writing standards to help him develop a list of assessment criteria for persuasive essays. He then converted this list into a feedback form that students could use to review each other's drafts throughout the year. (The feedback that one student received from a classmate is shown below.) This teacher also used the form himself to give students detailed feedback about their work. (He stapled a completed form to each student's paper.)

Assessment Criteria	Keep Working	Almost There	Excellent	Comments/Suggestions
POSITION: Position or claim is clearly stated.			✓	Position is clear and easy to find.
EVIDENCE: Position is supported with relevant evidence or reasons. Conflicting evidence/claims are addressed where appropriate.	✓			I am not clear how your third piece of evidence supports your position. Also, you didn't address any alternative positions.
CONCLUSION: Conclusion follows from and summarizes the argument/evidence.		✓		Don't think new evidence should be presented in a conclusion.
ORGANIZATION: Paper is structured as follows—position, evidence, conclusion. Evidence is linked together in a clear and logical sequence.		✓		Overall organization is great, but would your first two pieces of evidence make more sense if you reversed their order?
WRITING: Style is formal, yet easy to understand. Ideas flow smoothly, and paper is free of errors.		✓		Your writing is clear, but there are a lot of spelling mistakes. Did you forget to spell-check?

Guiding & Grading Rubrics

What is it?

A tool that describes what work looks like at different levels of quality; it is used to both assess students' performance on an assigned task and guide students' thinking as they work

What are the benefits of using this tool?

We often use rubrics to look at students' work, figure out where it lies on a scale, and give students a grade. But when fully integrated into the instructional process, rubrics can shift the focus from evaluation to learning. Presenting a rubric at the beginning of a unit helps students understand what high-quality work looks like and how to produce it. Students refer to the rubric throughout the process, measuring their work against the descriptions and seeking ways to move it up the levels. Finally, the rubric greatly enhances the feedback process by giving us and our students an objective scale for assessing their work and discussing ways to make it better.

What are the basic steps?

1. Create a rubric that can be used to guide and grade students' work on an upcoming task. Follow the steps below, use the examples on pages 36–37 as models, and see page 39 for a list of tips.

   - Decide what criteria to focus on when assessing students' work (e.g., depth of understanding, organization of ideas, creativity).

   - Describe three or four levels of performance for each criterion (e.g., explain what *creativity* looks like at the expert, proficient, and novice levels). Use simple but specific language.

   - Decide whether to weight some criteria more than others when evaluating students' work (e.g., "I'll count *depth of understanding* twice as much as *creativity*").

2. Review the rubric with students before they begin working. Explain that its purpose is to clarify expectations, give them concrete targets to aim for, and help them assess their work along the way.

3. Remind students to refer to the rubric on a regular basis to see how their work stacks up and how they can improve it. (What does expert-level work look like? What does *my* work look like? What can I do to close the gap?)

4. Use the rubric to grade students' completed assignments, provide students with feedback about their work, and explore strategies for improvement (e.g., "Let's look at the word-choice section of the rubric to see if it tells us how you could convey the events in your narrative more precisely").

How is this tool used in the classroom?

✔ To teach students what high-quality work looks like

✔ To help students assess and improve their performance on assigned tasks

✔ To evaluate and give students specific feedback about their work

EXAMPLE 1: A high school biology teacher challenged her students to develop an extended simile that answers this question: "How is the human nervous system like a computer?" In their writing, students had to incorporate at least ten vocabulary terms and identify and explain three connections between the human nervous system and a computer. The criteria and rubric this teacher used to guide and assess student writing appears below.

	Excellent	Almost There	Keep Working
Development of Simile	You provided three strong connections between the human nervous system and a computer, and you elaborated on each one.	You identified three connections between the human nervous system and a computer, but could have elaborated more on the connections.	Make sure you have identified three connections. Try to make your connections stronger by elaborating on each one.
Use of Critical Vocabulary	You incorporated ten or more critical vocabulary terms meaningfully in your response to show you have a deep understanding of the human nervous system.	You incorporated ten terms in your response, and most of them were used meaningfully or in context.	Try to use vocabulary terms in context to show that you know what they mean.
Clarity of Writing	Your ideas are presented clearly and are easy to follow. Your use of transitions creates a strong sense of flow from one idea to the next.	Your ideas are presented clearly. You can use stronger transitions to guide the reader from one idea to the next.	Make sure that each paragraph is about one big idea. Use transitions to help the reader follow your thinking.
Use of Appropriate Conventions	Your writing follows all of the conventions of written English and is free from any significant errors.	Your writing follows most of the conventions of written English with only a few errors.	You can eliminate significant errors by going back over your work carefully.

EXAMPLE 2: To develop the kinds of thinking skills that today's standards and tests call for, a math teacher assigns complex problem-solving tasks on a regular basis. He gives his students the same exact rubric for every assignment, both to save himself some time and to help them internalize the attributes of high-quality work. (The rubric appears on the next page.) He also requires his students to revise and resubmit novice-level work.

DIMENSIONS TO BE ASSESSED

		Problem-solving strategy	Problem-solving process	Solution quality
LEVELS OF PERFORMANCE	**MASTER** 5 points	You selected an appropriate strategy for tackling the problem.	Your strategy, steps, and reasoning process are clearly explained.	Your solution is correct!
	APPRENTICE 4 points	You chose an appropriate overall strategy, but got off track due to a conceptual error, misunderstanding, or incorrect assumption.	You showed your work, but your explanation is unclear and/or incomplete.	Your solution is incorrect due to a careless or simple calculation error.
	NOVICE Revise and resubmit.	See me to discuss strategies for tackling this problem. Then give the problem another try and resubmit your work.	You need to show your work / explain what you did. Try again and resubmit your work.	Your solution needs to be completed or corrected. Try again and resubmit your work.

Variation 1: Single-Dimension Rubrics

Not all work that students undertake calls for the development of a multidimensional rubric. Indeed, in many cases, a rubric designed around a single dimension may be all that is needed. In *Classroom Instruction That Works* (Second Edition), the authors identify two types of single-dimension rubrics: rubrics that focus on knowledge/understanding of content and rubrics that focus on the mastery of processes or skills. In the case of content-focused rubrics, you can design the levels to assess students' understanding of particular concepts or topics. For process/skill rubrics, you can design the levels to assess mastery in terms of accuracy, proficiency, or speed.

Below and on the next page are examples of single-dimension rubrics. The first was designed by a teacher who assigned students a timeline task on the lead-up to the American Revolution and developed the corresponding rubric to assess how well students' timelines demonstrated understanding of key events. The second rubric focuses on a skill. It assesses students' speed and accuracy in solving two-digit multiplication problems. Note that both rubrics can be customized to fit whatever content or skill you are teaching.

CONTENT-KNOWLEDGE RUBRIC ("Road to the American Revolution")

Performance Level	Performance Description
4	Thorough understanding of the events leading up to the American Revolution with detailed explanation of the big events
3	Clear understanding of events, showing key details leading up to the war
2	Partial understanding of events with limited detail
1	Limited understanding of key events with minimal detail
0	No timeline presented at this time

SKILL / PROCESS RUBRIC (Two-Digit Multiplication)

Performance Level	Performance Description
4	The student was able to complete all of the multiplication problems with complete accuracy within the required timeframe.
3	The student was able to complete at least three-quarters of the multiplication problems with complete accuracy within the required timeframe.
2	The student was able to complete at least one-half of the multiplication problems with complete accuracy within the required timeframe.
1	The student was able to complete less than one-half of the multiplication problems with complete accuracy within the required timeframe.
0	The student was unable to complete any problems correctly within the required timeframe.

Variation 2: Student-Created Rubrics

Involving students in the process of developing rubrics for the work they will be doing is a great way to teach them about quality—what it is, what separates quality work from average work, and what's involved in producing high-quality work. Students who have had a stake in developing their own rubrics approach a task with a deep understanding of what's expected of them. The process of collaborative rubric development also ensures that the language of the rubric is understood by all students.

For example, a fifth-grade class was learning about how to take good notes. After reviewing what students know about notes and rubrics, the teacher broke students into groups of four and challenged each group to create a four-level rubric for taking notes. As groups shared their rubrics, the teacher worked with the class to synthesize the best ideas into a single rubric for the whole class (see below).

Note-Taking Rubric

	1	2	3	4
Understanding	I need to show my understanding in my notes.	My notes show I understand parts of the topic.	My notes show I understand almost all of the topic.	My notes show I understand the topic thoroughly.
Ideas	I need to do more than copy information.	I include a few of my own ideas.	I include several of my own ideas.	My notes are really my own.
Neatness & Organization	I need to make my notes neater so someone else can read them.	My notes have some neat parts and some sloppy parts.	My notes are neat and somewhat organized.	My notes are neat and well organized.

Tips for Developing Good RUBRICS

Remember your audience.

A rubric isn't for academics or content-specialists. It's for students! Make sure yours is student friendly by asking yourself questions like these: Is it too much to process? Can I simplify it? Have I described the levels using simple language that will make sense to students? Confirm that students understand the information on your rubric by discussing it with them, giving them concrete examples, and/or challenging them to restate the characteristics of quality in their own words (younger students can use pictures).

Underscore what's important; unload extraneous criteria.

When deciding what to include on your rubric, focus on the criteria that are essential for a quality performance. In the case of a slide-show presentation, this might include *accuracy of content knowledge*, *readability of text/images*, and *logical organization of slides*. (Something like *use of multiple fonts*, on the other hand, shouldn't appear on your rubric since using multiple fonts isn't essential to giving a good presentation.) The goal is to include all the elements that define quality work while avoiding arbitrary or irrelevant criteria.

Borrow ideas from others.

Developing rubrics doesn't need to be a solo endeavor. Talk to colleagues about the tasks they assign and the rubrics they use. Trade notes, borrow ideas, and adapt each other's rubrics to suit your purposes.

Another option: Invite students to help you define the attributes of quality work. When done well, involving students in the process of generating assessment criteria can help them "internalize the criteria and bring them to bear on their own work" (Stiggins, Arter, Chappuis, & Chappuis, 2006, p. 209).

Reuse if possible.

To save time and help students internalize the qualities of top-notch work, design rubrics for recurring types of tasks (e.g., writing an argument essay, preparing a lab report, solving a word problem) and reuse them throughout the year. (The "repeat rubric" concept is illustrated in Example 2 on pages 36–37.)

Inspire growth.

Rubrics should be used to help students become better thinkers, learners, and problem solvers. To inspire growth, replace descriptions that emphasize what's wrong (e.g., *contains numerous grammar, punctuation, and spelling errors*) with ones that map out a path for improvement (e.g., *proofread more carefully to root out avoidable grammar, punctuation, and spelling errors*); use the "Keep Working" column in Example 1 (p. 36) as a model.

Another option: Encourage students to revise and resubmit novice-level work (or anything less than expert-level work) as shown in Example 2.

Clarify expectations.

Replace "fluffy" descriptions that are too vague to be helpful with descriptions that are specific and clear. (It's one thing to ask for a *meaningful* conclusion; it's quite another to ask for one that *follows from and summarizes the information in the preceding paragraphs*.) Whenever possible, help students understand what each level of performance entails by providing examples for them to look at (e.g., Level 1, 2, and 3 concluding statements from a previous year's class).

Stop and review.

Whenever possible, test-drive your rubric using samples of student work (e.g., samples from a previous year's class, a different class period, a colleague's students, or a previous assignment of the same type) and make sure you feel good about the scores that you come up with. If your rubric is causing you to give low scores to samples of work that you feel are strong—or high scores to samples of work that aren't that great—take time to revise it. Change your criteria, your level descriptions, or your weighting system / point values.

🔵 Teacher Talk

➔ Since the notion of levels of performance can be abstract and hard to grasp, especially for younger students, look for ways to make the rubric concept more concrete. A first-grade teacher we know introduced the concept of differing levels of quality by laying out four spoons: a flimsy plastic spoon, a durable plastic spoon, an everyday flatware spoon from her kitchen, and a sterling silver spoon from her fine china cabinet. After having students discuss the qualities that distinguished one spoon from the next, she used this four-spoons activity to introduce the rubric concept. For the remainder of the year, she included pictures of the four spoons on every rubric to remind her students of the difference between "flimsy plastic work" and "sterling silver work."

➔ Teach students what quality work looks like and help them better understand the criteria on a rubric by showing them samples of work that represent the different levels (e.g., essays with excellent, average, and below-average concluding sentences). Choose representative samples from a previous year's class or different class period (remove identifying information to protect students' privacy)—or create your own samples from scratch as shown in the example below.

Samples of work at five different levels of quality:

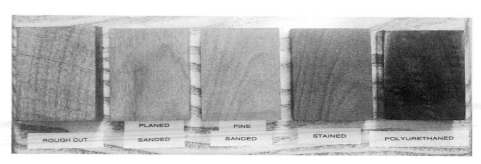

SOURCE: David Hamilton, Career and Technical Education Program, GST-BOCES Coopers Education Center, Painted Post, NY.

A career and technical education teacher initially made this series of five blocks to illustrate the different levels of quality in a finished woodworking product, but we often use the blocks ourselves (he made us our own set) to illustrate the levels-of-quality concept in a more general way. Because each block in the series is smoother and more polished than the one before it, the set as a whole helps students see that creating a "finished" final product involves a series of steps—and that they can move their work from rough to polished one step at a time.

➔ To save time, you may want to take advantage of the many rubrics and rubric-designing tools that are available online. Some of the most commonly used rubric-design templates can be found at sites such as edutopia.org, rcampus.com, rubistar.4teachers.org, and teach-nology.com. But be selective! Since the quality of available rubrics can vary significantly, it's important to assess and improve them as needed before using them with your students (use the tips on p. 39 to help you).

Another option: Borrow scoring rubrics from state assessment tests (rewrite them in student-friendly language before giving them to students). Besides saving time, using these rubrics in your classroom can help students develop the kinds of skills they'll need to succeed on these tests.

Reinforcing Effort and Providing Recognition

Continuous effort—not strength or intelligence—is the key to unlocking our potential.

—Winston Churchill

Reinforcing effort is a process that involves explicitly teaching students about the relationship between effort and achievement and acknowledging students' efforts when they work hard to achieve. When teachers emphasize this connection, they help students develop a sense of control over their academic learning.

—Ceri B. Dean, Elizabeth Ross Hubbell, Howard Pitler, and Bj Stone,
Classroom Instruction That Works (Second Edition)

As a category of instruction, reinforcing effort and providing recognition has the power to reshape students' beliefs about their own competence, deepen their sense of control over the learning process, and establish greater purpose for working toward academic goals. Perhaps most important, reinforcing students' effort and recognizing the hard work students put forth increases their intrinsic motivation, or their inner drive to engage in learning and see their undertakings through to completion. Indeed, when teachers emphasize the relationship between effort and achievement and make sure to acknowledge students' effort, their students "often become more tenacious and resilient; they will persevere when a task is difficult and success doesn't come immediately" (Dean et al., 2012, p. 21).

This chapter is about developing that inner drive in students—that deep and abiding commitment to learning that is a hallmark of successful students and successful people in general. To meet this important teaching goal of increasing students' willingness to pursue even difficult learning challenges, the authors of *Classroom Instruction That Works* (Second Edition) recommend six research-based practices. The tools in this chapter are designed to help teachers bring these six practices to life in the classroom.

1. **I Can & I Will** helps teachers address the practice of *teaching students about the relationship between effort and achievement*. The tool fosters a growth mindset in students, teaching them that they can achieve goals through hard work and committed effort.

2. **Rules to Live and Learn By** helps teachers address the practice of *providing students with explicit guidance about what it means to expend effort*. It empowers teachers to work collaboratively with students to identify actions and behaviors that promote success in the classroom.

3. **Stop, Read, Revise** gives teachers a second tool for addressing the practice of *providing students with explicit guidance about what it means to expend effort*. This tool applies specifically to the writing process, and it teaches students how to review, analyze, and make improvements to their written work.

4. **Effort Tracker** helps teachers address the practice of *asking students to keep track of their effort and achievement* by encouraging students to rate their effort, reflect on their performance, and identify strategies that lead to success.

   Because of its strong focus on the importance of effort, this tool is also a powerful technique for addressing the practice of *teaching students about the relationship between effort and achievement*.

5. **GOT It!** helps teachers address the practice of *promoting a mastery-goal orientation* that prioritizes learning and progress over performance. The tool trains students to assess their starting level of achievement and chart their **G**rowth **O**ver **T**ime (the "GOT" in GOT It!).

   This tool's emphasis on monitoring progress also makes it an ideal way to address the practice of *asking students to keep track of their effort and achievement*.

6. **Second-Chance Test** is another tool for addressing the practice of *promoting a mastery-goal orientation*. It treats every test as an opportunity for improvement by asking students to analyze their errors and see what they can learn from their mistakes. Students then take another test, giving them a second chance to demonstrate their learning.

7. **Points Worth Praising** helps teachers address the practice of *providing praise that is specific and aligned with expected performance and behaviors*. The tool shows teachers how to identify evidence of student learning and reinforce that learning with effective praise.

8. **A Job Well Done** helps teachers address the practice of *using concrete symbols of recognition*. This tool outlines a set of easy-to-use techniques for celebrating student effort and achievement.

I Can & I Will

What is it?

A tool that empowers students to achieve at higher levels by facilitating an "I can & I will" attitude

What are the benefits of using this tool?

Carol Dweck's (2016) work shows that students with a "growth mindset" (i.e., students who believe that hard work and effort matter) are far more likely to succeed than students who believe that achievement is determined by innate ability. I Can & I Will provides insight into students' existing beliefs about and attitudes toward learning. More important, it helps students develop a growth mindset by highlighting the relationship between effort, attitude, and achievement.

What are the basic steps?

1. Use the Agree/Disagree form on page 44 to uncover—and help students uncover—their existing beliefs about factors that impact success and achievement. Have students decide whether they agree or disagree with each statement and explain why. Discuss students' responses as a class.

2. Teach students that they have the power to control their own success—that ability isn't a fixed trait but rather something that can be improved via effort and a can-do attitude.

3. Help students internalize the lesson that effort level and attitude make a difference by having them identify examples from their own lives where their attitude, actions, or level of commitment helped them get better at something. Invite them to share their examples with the class.

4. Ask students to make an "I can & I will pledge" before tackling a specific learning target or task. ("I believe that I CAN improve my performance through effort, and I WILL give 100% to this task.")

   Optional: Ask students to formalize their pledge by completing a contract like the one on page 45.

5. Clarify that having an "I can & I will" attitude is only the first step—that students need to know how to channel their efforts productively in order to be successful. Prepare them to do this by

   - Helping them identify attitudes and behaviors from their past successes (see Step 3) that can help them (e.g., a can-do attitude or a willingness to persevere through challenges).
   - Defining what "giving 100%" means in the context of the assigned task. Before having students read a challenging passage, for example, you might clarify that giving 100% means reading slowly, checking for understanding after each paragraph, and asking for help if needed.

6. Teach students to talk themselves through rough patches by repeating the phrase "I can & I will."

How is this tool used in the classroom?

✔ To uncover students' existing attitudes about the factors that impact success

✔ To help students develop a growth mindset

Agree/Disagree

Anyone can get better at anything.

Agree or disagree?

Explain:

When it comes to doing well in school, all that matters is how smart you are.

Agree or disagree?

Explain:

Hard work pays off.

Agree or disagree?

Explain:

When things get difficult, it's OK to give up.

Agree or disagree?

Explain:

Name: _____   Date: _____

I Can & I Will Contract

Here is what I am trying to learn or do …

Attitudes or actions that might help me include …

☐ I believe that I CAN learn more and do a better job if I work hard.
☐ I promise that I WILL work as hard as I can.

Write or sign your name here: _____

Rules to Live and Learn By

What is it?

A technique for establishing behavioral guidelines that promote a positive learning environment

What are the benefits of using this tool?

The authors of *Classroom Instruction That Works* (Second Edition) emphasize the importance of helping "students develop an operational definition for what it means to work hard by being explicit about the actions and behaviors associated with effort" (Dean et al., 2012, p. 25). Rules to Live and Learn By invites students directly into this process of identifying those "actions and behaviors" that lead to academic—and social—success. By using this tool to develop classroom guidelines that promote learning rather than compel students to behave, teachers can change the culture of the classroom from one focused on discipline and consequences to one focused on learning and responsibility.

What are the basic steps?

1. Pose the following question at the start of the year: "What is the primary purpose of coming to school?" (The response you want to hear is, "To learn.") Ask students what learning means to them, and record their ideas on the board.

2. Tell students that you'll work hard to help them learn and that you expect them to do the same. Explain that there are two rules you'd like them to follow and that the purpose of the rules is to help them learn. Have students meet in small groups to discuss what each rule means to them.

   RULE 1: Be the best student you can be, and learn as much as possible.

   RULE 2: Make the classroom a good place for everyone to live and learn in.

3. Explain that while you created the rules, it's up to students to figure out how to follow the rules. Have students brainstorm a list of things they could do to support each rule (e.g., ask questions in class, listen when others talk, treat classmates with respect), and record their ideas on the board.

4. Fine-tune this list of rule-supporting behaviors (behavioral guidelines) as a class. Help students eliminate or combine similar ideas, express ideas clearly, and replace negative language with positive (guidelines should state what students *should* do rather than what they shouldn't do).

5. Generate and post a final list of behavioral guidelines. Explain and model each guideline.

6. Make classroom rules and guidelines "a way of life" rather than "a first week of school thing."

   - Target specific guidelines for review throughout the year. (Before a problem-solving lesson, you might review guidelines such as *ask questions if you're confused* or *learn from your mistakes*.)

   - Enforce compliance with posted guidelines throughout the year. Invite students to monitor and assess compliance as well. ("How well have *you* been following our guidelines? How has the class as a whole been following our guidelines?") Discuss strategies for improvement if needed.

7. Acknowledge students' efforts to make the classroom a great place in which to live and learn by praising individual students (or the class as a whole) for following agreed-upon guidelines. Be specific so that students are clear about what they've done well.

How is this tool used in the classroom?

✔ To establish rules and guidelines that promote student learning and inspire effort

✔ To involve students in the process of establishing classroom rules and guidelines

EXAMPLE: The ideas that a class of elementary students generated during the initial brainstorming session (Step 3) are shown in the box below.

What can we do to be the best students we can be and learn as much as possible? (Rule 1)

- Participate in class and ask questions.
- Learn from our mistakes.
- Ask for help if we need it.
- Keep trying. Don't give up if we're stuck.
- Check our work to make sure it's complete and done well.

- Practice the things that we learn.
- Make notes in class and study our notes.
- Write down our assignments.
- Find a quiet place to do our homework.
- Listen to and learn from our classmates.

What can we do to make the classroom a good place for everyone to live and learn in? (Rule 2)

- Listen quietly when the teacher or someone else is talking.
- Take good care of books and other classroom supplies.
- Be polite. Say "please," "thank you," and "you're welcome."
- Find something quiet and productive to do when we finish our work.
- Treat other people the way that we want to be treated.

- Don't use "put downs," only "put ups."
- Clean up any messes that we make.
- Help and support our classmates.
- Be friendly to everyone.
- Use people's names when we speak to them.

With their teacher's help, these students refined, cut, and combined the ideas from their original brainstorming session to create the list of official classroom rules and guidelines shown below.

CLASSROOM RULES AND GUIDELINES

RULE 1: Be the best students we can be, and learn as much as possible.

- Pay attention, ask questions, and participate in classroom activities.
- Practice the things that we learn, and keep up with our assignments.
- Carefully check our work before turning it in. Only turn in work that we are proud of.
- Learn from our classmates and our own mistakes, not just from the teacher.
- Ask for help if we are confused.

RULE 2: Make the classroom a good place for everyone to live and learn in.

- Be quiet when other people are talking or working.
- Treat people and things the way we would want others to treat us and our things.
- Be friendly, respectful, and polite.
- Help our classmates learn.
- Instead of putting people down, put them up! Offer encouragement instead of criticism.

🎯 Teacher Talk

→ While sharing the responsibility for establishing classroom rules and guidelines with students might seem counterintuitive, it can actually be extremely beneficial. Why? Because students are more committed to guidelines that they have a stake in creating, and they are more likely to comply with guidelines whose purpose they understand.

→ Don't assume that behavioral guidelines are self-explanatory. Explain and illustrate these guidelines for students at the start of the year using modeling, role-playing, and concrete examples. (Teaching guidelines directly is particularly important at the primary and elementary levels.) Try using charades for reinforcement: Ask a student to act out one of the guidelines, let whichever student guesses the guideline correctly act out the next one, and continue on in this manner until all the guidelines have been modeled. Remember that the time you invest in establishing rules and guidelines at the start of the year will pay off later in the form of increased time on task and enhanced student achievement.

→ Don't skip Step 6! Developing effective guidelines is the key to *establishing* a productive learning environment, but reviewing, revising, and enforcing these guidelines throughout the year is the key to *maintaining* that environment.

→ Use friendly and age-appropriate language when discussing concepts like rules and guidelines. When asking students to generate rule-supporting behaviors in Step 3, for example, you might avoid an unfriendly term like *behavioral guidelines* and ask students to generate a list of "here's hows" instead. ("Here's how we can support each rule …")

→ Turn your list of rules and guidelines into a "classroom compact" by having students sign their names to the final document (see example below). By signing their names, students indicate their commitment to following the guidelines that they developed as a class.

Rule #1: Be the best scholar you can be, and learn as much as possible

*Use your active listening skills and follow all directions

*Be honest. Tell the truth

Rule #2: Make the classroom a good place for everyone to live and learn in

*Respect your classmates, teachers, and life coaches

*Raise a quiet hand before speaking or leaving your seat

*Stop and think. Keep your hands and objects to yourself

*Use walking feet

Stop, Read, Revise

What is it?

A tool that teaches students what "working hard at writing" means by outlining a clear process and concrete criteria for improving written work

What are the benefits of using this tool?

When students take the time to review their writing, they often find that important words are missing or that their ideas aren't as clear as they thought. Stop, Read, Revise gets students in the habit of reading their own writing so they can root out mistakes and communicate their ideas with greater power and precision. It also provides students with explicit guidance (in the form of "Seven Cs") about how to make their work better.

What are the basic steps?

1. Talk to students about the importance of reading what they write. Help them generate a list of reasons why the reading-after-writing habit is so good to develop.

2. Give students a writing task. Tell them to skip lines so they'll have room to revise their work.

3. Ask students to read their completed pieces to themselves. Tell them to check their work for the "Seven Cs" (explain the Cs beforehand; adjust them as needed for specific kinds of writing tasks):

   Completeness: Did I leave out any words, details, or big ideas?

   Coherence: Are my ideas presented in a logical and orderly way? Do they make sense?

   Clarity: Are my ideas clear and easy to understand? Is my writing clear and easy to read?

   Correctness: Are there any spelling, grammar, and/or factual errors that I need to correct?

   Composition: Do I have a topic sentence / thesis, supporting information, and conclusion?

   Congruence: Does my response address the specific question or task I was given?

   Communication skills: Would someone who's unfamiliar with this topic understand what I wrote?

4. Instruct students to revise their work as needed.

5. Invite students to reflect on and share what they learned by reading their own writing.

6. Teach students that the Stop, Read, Revise process is one that they can and should use on their own. Help them make it habitual by having them use it as often as possible.

How is this tool used in the classroom?

✔ To help students evaluate and improve the quality of their written work through reflection

EXAMPLE: A middle school teacher who wanted students to learn to write powerful personal narratives revised the Seven Cs to fit narrative writing as follows:

Completeness: Did I leave out any words, details, or events?

Coherence: Does my narrative make sense? Do my ideas fit together in a logical way?

Clarity: Is my narrative clear and easy to understand? Is my writing clear and easy to read?

Correctness: Are there any spelling, grammar, or factual errors that I need to correct?

Composition: Does my narrative have a clear beginning, middle, and end?

Congruence: Does my narrative address the assigned writing task?

Catchiness: Will my narrative engage an outside reader? Can I make it more interesting?

A student used these Seven Cs to guide her revision of a personal narrative about overcoming a challenge (learning how to hit a softball). She then shared what she learned from the process in her reflection journal (as called for in Step 5).

When I reread my personal narrative carefully, it helped me to hear my own voice the way a reader would hear it. Using the Seven Cs helped me figure out what I could do to make my narrative better and more engaging. The two Cs that jumped out at me during my reading were clarity and composition.

For clarity, I noticed that my narrative was a little unclear because some of the events just happened one after the other. To make my narrative clearer, I added some transitional words, and I separated my first paragraph about always striking out from my second paragraph about learning how to relax and wait on the ball.

For composition, I noticed that I didn't really take the time to set up my challenge, which means that I didn't really have a strong beginning. So I added two sentences to my original opening that showed the reader how frustrated I was because I was striking out so much.

🌑 Teacher Talk

→ The Seven Cs reinforce many standards-based writing and language skills—skills like adjusting writing to fit task, purpose, and audience; presenting ideas in a clear and logical way; using the conventions of Standard Written English; and improving writing via editing and revision.

Effort Tracker

What is it?

A tool that helps students see the link between effort and achievement by having them rate the amount of effort they put into their assignments and reflect on the way it influences their success

What are the benefits of using this tool?

One of the most important ways to help more students succeed is to help them understand that "success comes because of effort and that they control the amount of effort they put forth" (Dean et al., 2012, p. 24). Effort Tracker builds this success-oriented mindset by inviting students to explore the way that effort affects performance and by using concrete examples to show that effort really *does* matter. Teaching students that they have the power to improve their academic performance is an extremely valuable lesson—one that can increase their motivation, encourage them to persevere in the face of challenges, and enable them to achieve at higher levels (Alderman, 2008; Dweck, 1975, 2007).

What are the basic steps?

1. Initiate a conversation about the relationship between effort and achievement. Specifically,

   - Use personal, fictional, or real-world examples to illustrate and reinforce the effort-achievement relationship; see Teacher Talk for ideas. Then encourage students to share their own examples.

   - Ask students what effort looks like in a classroom setting. (Is it always giving 100%? Asking for help if you're stuck? Proofreading work before turning it in?) Record their ideas on the board.

2. Help students understand that effort involves more than spending time working. Teach them to consider these five criteria (adapted from Moss & Brookhart, 2009) when assessing their performance on an assigned task:

   - *Degree of effort:* How hard did you concentrate or try?

   - *Time spent:* How much time did you spend on this task?

   - *Level of care:* How carefully did you check and correct your work?

   - *Willingness to seek help:* Did you ask questions or seek help if you were stuck or confused?

   - *Use of strategies:* What (if any) strategies did you use while working on this task?

3. Give students a task to work on (e.g., review for a test or make three consecutive free throws).

4. Prepare students to work productively by introducing or reviewing specific strategies that can help them (strategies for writing a focused paragraph, what-to-do-when-stuck strategies, etc.).

5. Have students rate their effort using an Effort Tracker Form (p. 54, Questions 1–5) *before submitting their work*. Have them reflect on the effort-outcome link *after seeing their graded work*.

6. Talk to students whose achievement level doesn't reflect their effort level. Help them identify possible reasons for the discrepancy by posing probing questions like these: What do you mean when you say that you worked hard? Did you use any of the strategies that we discussed?

How is this tool used in the classroom?

✔ To have students reflect on and learn from their classroom experiences

✔ To help students recognize the relationship between effort and achievement

✔ To increase students' intrinsic motivation and willingness to put forth effort

EXAMPLE: The form below was completed by a sixth grader.

EFFORT TRACKER FORM

Name: Alana

Assignment: Writing a basic lab report

1) How hard did I concentrate or try?

0 (not at all) — 5 (somewhat) — ☆ — 10 (as hard as I could)

Explanation:

Being able to write a lab report is important in science, and I want to be a scientist, so I gave this task my full effort.

2) How much time did I spend studying, practicing, or working on this assignment?

0 (none) — 5 (a fair amount) — ☆ — 10 (a lot)

Explanation:

This was our first lab report. It took me a while to really understand what every section needed to include. I worked longest and hardest on the conclusions section because that was the most challenging.

3) How carefully did I check and correct my work?

0 (not at all) — 5 (somewhat) — ☆ — 10 (extremely)

Explanation:

It wasn't easy to go through and review my whole report carefully. I went through it once to make sure I had all the sections completed properly. If I had more time, I would have reread it one more time.

4) Did I ask questions or request help if I was confused?   Yes ☒   No ☐   I didn't need help ☐

5) Which (if any) strategies did I use? Ms. Redding gave us a model lab report and a checklist to help us through our own reports. I used both of them to help me make my report better.

REFLECTION: Did my actions (strategies used + amount of effort) affect my success?   Yes ☒   No ☐

Working hard and using the model report and checklist helped me make sure my report was complete. Sticking with it when the conclusion section was giving me trouble was satisfying because Ms. Redding said my conclusion was very well done. Overall, I am happy with my effort and the final result!

⬤ Teacher Talk

→ Seeing concrete examples helps students recognize that their actions and attitudes can actually influence their level of success. The examples that you present in Step 1 can be personal, real world, or fictional:

- *Personal:* Share stories from your own life. (What have you been able to accomplish by working hard? What disappointments or failures do you owe to a lack of effort rather than a lack of ability?)

- *Real world:* Discuss famous individuals (athletes, politicians, scientists, artists, actors) whose work ethic, determination, and perseverance in the face of setbacks enabled them to succeed. Alternatively, identify individuals whose lack of effort prevented them from achieving their full potential.

- *Fictional:* Use familiar stories to illustrate the idea that effort can be more valuable than innate ability (try "The Tortoise and the Hare") or that working hard and believing in yourself can impact your success (try *The Little Engine That Could*).

→ To use this tool with younger students, simplify the reproducible form as needed. Among other things, you can replace the number lines with smiley faces and frown faces as shown here:

→ Head off disappointment by having a discussion about realistic expectations *before* returning graded work. Remind students that hard work won't guarantee them a perfect score and that success takes time and sustained effort. Use the examples from Step 1 or a tool like GOT It! (pp. 55–58), which has students examine the impact of effort on achievement over time, to reinforce this point.

→ To encourage regular self-assessment, you can have students complete Effort Tracker Forms on a daily basis (all but the reflection section) rather than just at the end.

Name: _____   Date: _____

Assignment: _____

Effort Tracker Form

1) How hard did I concentrate or try?

├─────────────────────────┼─────────────────────────┤
0 (not at all)   5 (somewhat)   10 (as hard as I could)

Explanation:

2) How much time did I spend studying, practicing, or working on this assignment?

├─────────────────────────┼─────────────────────────┤
0 (none)   5 (a fair amount)   10 (a lot)

Explanation:

3) How carefully did I check and correct my work?

├─────────────────────────┼─────────────────────────┤
0 (not at all)   5 (somewhat)   10 (extremely)

Explanation:

4) Did I ask questions or request help if I was confused?   Yes ☐   No ☐   I didn't need help ☐

5) Which (if any) strategies did I use?

REFLECTION: Did my actions (strategies used + amount of effort) affect my success?   Yes ☐   No ☐

Explain your answer on the back of this worksheet and/or share your ideas with the class.

GOT It!

What is it?

A tool that has students assess and chart their progress as they work to achieve specific learning goals or targets; the "GOT" in GOT It! stands for **G**rowth **O**ver **T**ime

What are the benefits of using this tool?

Classrooms that build intrinsic motivation and promote self-confidence in students tend to have what researchers call a "mastery-goal orientation" (Dean et al., 2012, p. 29). In other words, students do better when the classroom focuses on personal progress and the achievement of goals rather than on comparing student performances. Few tools do more to help teachers promote a mastery-goal orientation than GOT It!, which teaches students to assess their starting level of achievement, develop strategies for improvement, and chart their progress over time. By enabling students to visualize their growth and by celebrating improvement, this tool also serves as a powerful reminder to students that their effort and commitment pay off over the long term.

What are the basic steps?

1. Identify a learning goal or target that students will be working to achieve.

   Note: A well-crafted goal/target describes what students will need to know, understand, be able to do, or be like—and is framed in clear and student-friendly language.

2. Ask students to assess and record their starting (pre-instruction) level of achievement on a GOT It! form. Customize the reproducible form on page 58 (fill in the blanks to create an appropriate rating scale), or create your own form using the ones in Examples 1 and 2 as models.

   Tip: Try using graphing software such as the Create A Graph tool (found at nces.ed.gov/nceskids) to help students build their proficiency with relevant technology, as shown in Example 2.

3. Make it clear that improvement is what matters, not starting knowledge or ability.

4. Help students create a visual record of their progress over time by stopping at various points (after a quiz, lecture, assignment, etc.) to have them reassess and record their level of achievement.

5. Facilitate forward progress between each checkpoint:
   - Review students' GOT It! forms to gauge their progress and overall level of achievement. Identify steps that you can take to help all students (or specific students) improve.
   - Encourage students to take responsibility for their own success. Ask them what *they* could do to improve before the next checkpoint, and help them implement their plans.

6. Help students process and learn from the overall experience by having them respond to the reflection questions/prompts at the bottom of their GOT It! forms.

How is this tool used in the classroom?

✔ To help students assess and track their progress

✔ To help promote a mastery-goal orientation

As shown in Examples 1 and 2, teachers often adjust the format and wording of their GOT It! forms to match the age, needs, and interests of their students—or the goals that their students are working on.

EXAMPLE 1: A first-grade teacher used the race-themed GOT It! form shown below to inspire her students to master their addition facts. Students charted their progress by pasting stickers on their forms.

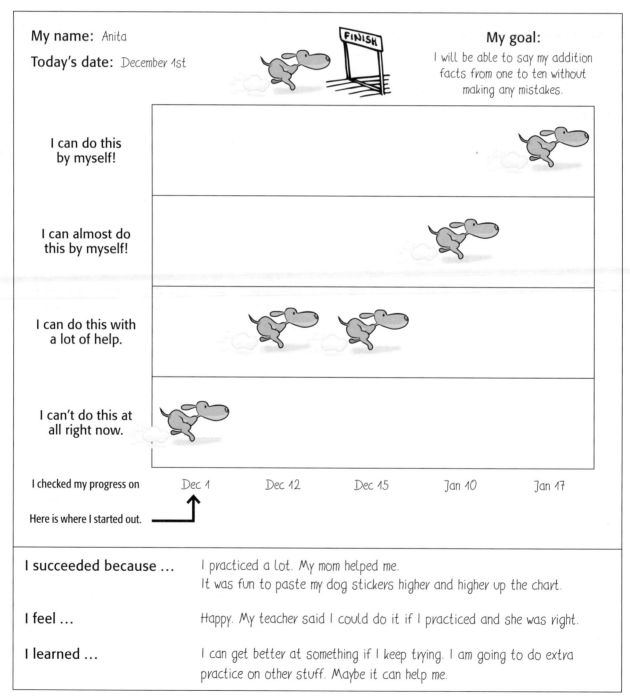

EXAMPLE 2: A high school teacher teaches students how to track their growth over time using an online graph-making tool. To better help her students see how effort pays off over the long term, she asks students to chart their level of achievement at each stopping point. One student's work is shown below.

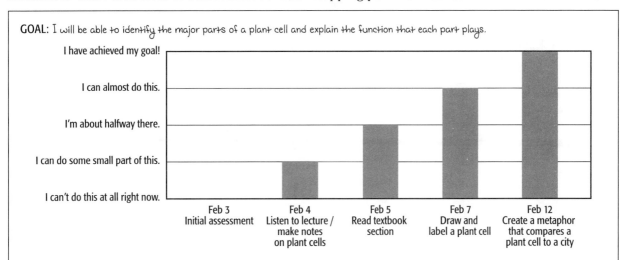

GOAL: I will be able to identify the major parts of a plant cell and explain the function that each part plays.

(Bar graph with vertical axis labels, top to bottom:)
- I have achieved my goal!
- I can almost do this.
- I'm about halfway there.
- I can do some small part of this.
- I can't do this at all right now.

(Horizontal axis labels:)
- Feb 3 — Initial assessment
- Feb 4 — Listen to lecture / make notes on plant cells
- Feb 5 — Read textbook section
- Feb 7 — Draw and label a plant cell
- Feb 12 — Create a metaphor that compares a plant cell to a city

REFLECTION QUESTIONS:

What helped you improve?

Learning about the plant cell in different ways helped my understanding grow. We took notes, read, did a diagram, and created a metaphor.

How do you feel about what you've accomplished?

I am proud of myself. There are a lot of parts and functions to learn about, and I feel like I really know this material well.

Did you learn anything else from this experience that you could use in the future?

Metaphors are fun, but they also really help you understand the content.

What effect did your effort level have on your achievement?

I kept my effort level high the whole time. I told myself I would give this my all, and it really worked!

🌀 Teacher Talk

→ For more on crafting student-friendly learning objectives/targets (Step 1), see the Student-Friendly Learning Targets tool (pp. 17–19).

→ Emphasizing the idea that improvement is what matters (not existing knowledge or ability) will help students who know very little at the start of the process feel comfortable. It will also discourage students from comparing their performance with that of their peers, thus eliminating the pressure and negative feelings that such comparisons often produce.

→ This tool is commonly used to have students track their progress with regard to teacher-established learning goals/targets, but it can also be used to have students track their progress toward goals or targets that they've established for themselves. What's more, it can be used to help students track progress toward social/behavioral goals (e.g., staying focused and ignoring distractions during silent reading time) as well as academic goals.

Name: _____   Date: _____

Learning goal/target: _____

GOT IT!

INITIAL ASSESSMENT: Check off your starting level of achievement on the scale below.

☐ Level 5: _____

☐ Level 4: _____

☐ Level 3: _____

☐ Level 2: _____

☐ Level 1: _____

TRACKING MY PROGRESS:

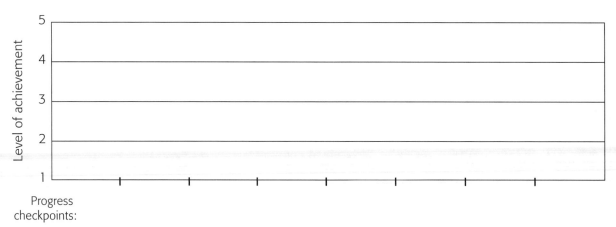

Progress
checkpoints:

REFLECTION QUESTIONS:

What helped me improve (people, resources, strategies, attitudes)?

How do I feel about my accomplishments?

Did I learn anything from this experience that might help me in the future?

Second-Chance Test

What is it?

A tool that transforms classroom tests into learning opportunities by having students analyze their errors, learn from their mistakes, and take second-chance tests on the same material

What are the benefits of using this tool?

The learning process does not stop with the test. Indeed, assessment expert Susan Brookhart (2008) reminds us that "an analysis of test results can be a gold mine of information, but only if students know that they will get a chance to use the information" (p. 66). This tool, which draws on Brookhart's work, encourages students to reflect on their performance, learn from their mistakes, and take another test on the same material. Developing students' self-assessment skills in this way can boost motivation, learning, and confidence. What's more, the process of taking multiple tests can actually promote retention of the tested material (Pashler et al., 2007).

What are the basic steps?

1. Return a graded test to students. Explain that they'll be given the opportunity to take another test on the same learning goals / material at a later time.

2. Help students analyze and learn from their mistakes:
   - Explain why it's important to analyze the types of errors they made: "Once you know what kinds of errors you made, you can figure out how to fix them and avoid making them again."
   - Discuss the different types of errors listed on the bottom of the Error Analysis Form (p. 61).
   - Have students use the form to indicate which types of errors they made on which questions.

3. Teach students strategies for addressing different kinds of errors—time-management strategies, strategies for writing coherent and well-organized paragraphs, study strategies, etc.

4. Help students generate and record specific plans for improvement on the Error Analysis Form.

5. Remind students that their fix-it plans should reflect the types of errors they made. For example, it wouldn't make sense for a student who forgot to answer part of a question to restudy the material. Instead, that student should plan to read the test questions more carefully the next time around.

6. Give students time to implement their plans. Then administer a second test. (Test questions should be different than the ones on the original test but target the same material.)

7. Have students reflect on what they've learned about the content, the kinds of errors they tend to make and how to address them, and/or their study habits and how to improve them.

How is this tool used in the classroom?

✔ To help students learn from their mistakes and achieve at higher levels

✔ To boost motivation by giving students multiple chances to succeed

✔ To help students reflect on and improve their test performances

EXAMPLE: A middle school student used the Error Analysis Form below to identify and develop strategies for avoiding future mistakes after a test on time-distance-rate problems. Later in the week, the student took a second-chance test.

· Error Analysis Form ·

WHICH question did I get wrong?	WHY did I get this question wrong?	HOW can I avoid making this same type of error the next time around?
#2	Careless division error	—check my work before turning my test in
#11	didn't read the question carefully and missed some key information	- read questions more slowly and carefully - underline important bits of information
#14	didn't notice that time was given in minutes, not hours so didn't convert min→hours	- pay attention to units - convert one unit type to another if needed before performing calculations
#25-30	ran out of time	- practice these kinds of problems A LOT so I get better at doing them faster

TYPES OF ERRORS: Use the suggestions below to help you complete column two.

☑ I didn't check my work (careless error).

☐ I didn't know/understand this material.

☐ I didn't study this material/didn't think it would be on the test.

☐ I didn't answer the question that was asked.

☐ I didn't understand the question or directions.

☑ I ran out of time.

☐ I knew the material; my writing skills were the problem.

☐ I knew this material, but forgot it on the test.

☐ I forgot to answer part(s) of the question.

☑ Other didn't read question carefully didn't pay attention to units

Name: _____   Date: _____

Test topic: _____

· Error Analysis Form ·

WHICH question did I get wrong?	WHY did I get this question wrong?	HOW can I avoid making this same type of error the next time around?

TYPES OF ERRORS: Use the suggestions below to help you complete column two.

☐ I didn't check my work (careless error).

☐ I didn't know/understand this material.

☐ I didn't study this material / didn't think it would be on the test.

☐ I didn't answer the question that was asked.

☐ I didn't understand the question or directions.

☐ I ran out of time.

☐ I knew the material; my writing skills were the problem.

☐ I knew this material but forgot it on the test.

☐ I forgot to answer part(s) of the question.

☐ Other: _____

Points Worth Praising

What is it?

A tool that helps us provide praise that's specific and that addresses established learning goals

What are the benefits of using this tool?

How many students associate the word *feedback* with "all the things I did wrong"? By shifting our focus from "points that need fixing" to "points worth praising," we not only prevent students from becoming discouraged, we also teach them what they've done well so they can continue doing it on future tasks and assignments.

What are the basic steps?

1. Review an assignment that students have completed.

2. Identify "points worth praising" by looking for the following:

- Evidence that a specific learning goal or target has been met
- Evidence that the piece fulfills specific criteria for success (e.g., criteria on a rubric or checklist)
- Evidence that all the required elements are present or that the appropriate steps were followed
- Evidence of progress (Is there an aspect of this piece that shows improvement?)
- Evidence that the student has mastered critical vocabulary terms, content, or procedures
- Evidence the student has responded to prior feedback
- Evidence that the student has put forth significant effort
- Evidence that the student has used appropriate strategies / thinking processes to complete the task (e.g., outlining thoughts before writing, using a rubric to self-assess work)

3. Share these positive points with students, either verbally or in writing. Be as specific as possible so students are clear about what they've done well.

4. Encourage students to take note of things they did well and make a conscious effort to continue doing them (e.g., "I'll continue to repeat my experiments multiple times to validate my results").

How is this tool used in the classroom?

✔ To acknowledge quality work and reinforce student effort

🌐 Teacher Talk

➜ Praise should address specific aspects of students' work, not the students themselves.

➜ The Points Worth Praising framework can be used to help students assess the strengths in their own work as well. To use the tool in this way, give students the list of points worth praising from Step 2 (shorten or simplify it as needed), explain the list in terms they can understand, and instruct them to "mark and describe the positives" in their assignments before submitting them.

A Job Well Done

What is it?

A set of quick and easy-to-use techniques for recognizing and celebrating students' achievements

What are the benefits of using this tool?

We all want our classrooms to be joyful places, where students feel recognized for their accomplishments and where students support one another through the learning process. This tool helps us create such an environment by using classroom celebration and concrete symbols of recognition to honor each student's efforts and achievements. The recognition techniques it presents are easy to incorporate into any lesson, and they encourage students to take note of—and actively participate in recognizing—one another's successes.

What are the basic steps?

1. Familiarize yourself and your students with the recognition techniques described on page 64.

Optional: Invite students to generate some techniques of their own. Add them to the list.

2. Identify an action, attitude, accomplishment, or attribute of a student's work that deserves to be acknowledged (e.g., Did a student use an appropriate strategy to tackle a task? Exhibit a high degree of effort or persistence? Satisfy specific assessment criteria? Improve on prior performance?).

3. Acknowledge this "job well done" using the recognition technique of your choice.

4. Accompany the acknowledgment with a specific description of what was done well. ("You did a great job of finding textual evidence to support your position" instead of "Great job.")

How is this tool used in the classroom?

✔ To provide recognition and help students learn from their achievements

Recognition Techniques

Oohs and Aahs

Have students acknowledge behaviors or qualities of work that deserve recognition by making "ooh and aah" sounds. Oohs and aahs can be initiated by you (identify something specific that a student has done well, and ask the class to ooh and aah in appreciation) or by your students (ask students to ooh and aah when they see or hear something they think is worth praising). In either case, the action, attribute, or attitude that's being acknowledged should be clearly explained as illustrated in the examples below.

Teacher initiated: "Ellen spent a lot of time practicing her waltz, and the improvement in her rise and fall is evident. Let's acknowledge her hard work and progress. Ooh … aah …"

Student initiated: "I oohed and aahed when I heard Franklin's story because it had a lot of strong verbs and adjectives like a good story is supposed to have."

Variations on Oohs and Aahs

There are many variations on Oohs and Aahs. Some of our favorites include

Round of Applause: Students clap their hands in a circular motion to create a "round" of applause. ("Let's give a round of applause to all the students who had the courage to speak up and say 'I'm lost' during today's lecture.")

Na Na Na Cheer: Students swing their arms back and forth over their head while singing, "Na na na na! Na na na na! Hey, hey, hey! Good job!"

Coaster Cheer: Students lean their heads back and say, "Click, click, click," as if they are going up a roller coaster. Then, they throw their arms up and say, "WHEEEEE!"

Big OK: Students make an "OK" sign with their hands instead of making sounds of appreciation. For truly exceptional work, students can make a "big OK" (touch the fingertips/thumb on their left hands to the corresponding fingertips/thumb on their right hands to create a larger O shape with both hands) instead of a normal OK sign.

Shout-Out

Identify actions or accomplishments you want to acknowledge, and ask the class to give the appropriate student(s) a "shout-out" for those accomplishments. Be specific about what the shout-outs are for so that everyone can learn from the experience. For example, "Let's give Ivy a shout-out for using our explanatory-writing rubric to review and revise her work."

Paper Plate Awards

Create awards out of paper plates to acknowledge students' efforts and/or achievements. (If you prefer, you can have students create plates for each other.) In either case, awards should state the recipients' names and explain exactly what behaviors or quality characteristics are being recognized.

This award goes to
JAIME
for his never-give-up attitude on the daily problem set.

HappyGrams

If you want to acknowledge a student's actions or achievements in a more private way, you can send that student a HappyGram. To do this, create a form that looks like a telegram, address the outside with the student's name and a happy face, and write a message to the student on the inside explaining what you're happy about. ("Dear Jack: It made me very happy when you offered to help Bobby practice his number facts without being asked. That was very thoughtful of you!") Encourage students to share their HappyGrams with their parents.

Cooperative Learning

The fun for me in collaboration is … that working with other people just makes you smarter; that's proven.

—*Hamilton* creator, Lin-Manuel Miranda

In the layers of a complex world, the students of today need to possess not only intellectual capabilities but also the ability to function effectively in an environment that requires working with others to accomplish a variety of tasks.

—Ceri B. Dean, Elizabeth Ross Hubbell, Howard Pitler, and Bj Stone
Classroom Instruction That Works (Second Edition)

Cooperative learning is one of the most well-known, commonly used, and theoretically grounded instructional strategies. It is also a demonstrably high-yield strategy, as the authors of *Classroom Instruction That Works* (Second Edition) note an effect size of 0.44, or a gain of 17 percentile points, in student achievement across twenty different studies on cooperative learning (Dean et al., 2012). Yet, studies on teachers' perceptions and use of cooperative learning indicate that it is one of the most misunderstood of all instructional strategies (Antil, Jenkins, Wayne, & Vadasy, 1998; Koutselini, 2009). Perhaps the most common misconception is that any kind of group work counts as cooperative learning. In reality, cooperative learning activities—the kind that lead to deep learning, ensure positive contributions from all group members, and promote the gains suggested by the research—are built around key principles that differentiate them from other kinds of group work.

The authors of *Classroom Instruction That Works* (Second Edition) present three recommendations that should guide teachers' use of cooperative learning in the classroom:

- Design cooperative learning activities so that they promote both positive interdependence ("We're all in this together") and individual accountability ("I need to be responsible and contribute my fair share").
- Keep group size to five or fewer students.
- Use cooperative learning consistently and systematically in the classroom.

In this chapter, we present four tools designed to help teachers put these recommendations into practice and, more broadly, to engage students in learning with and from each other:

1. **All for One & One for All** provides cooperative learning structures that ensure positive interdependence and individual accountability.

2. **Community CIRCLE** empowers students to explore content collaboratively and helps teachers create a classroom environment that fosters respect and active listening among all students.

3. **Interaction in an Instant** gives teachers quick and easy ways to get students talking to and learning from their classmates.

4. **Jigsaw** uses a well-designed cooperative learning structure to build students' research and communication skills.

All for One & One for All

What is it?

A tool that helps students get more out of cooperative learning experiences by teaching them how to work together, support each other, and take personal responsibility for group success

What are the benefits of using this tool?

In reviewing the work of cooperative learning pioneers Johnson and Johnson (1999), the authors of *Classroom Instruction That Works* (Second Edition) conclude that the two most critical elements of effective cooperative learning activities are positive interdependence and individual accountability (Dean et al., 2012). In other words, when students work cooperatively, they must recognize that they are a team that works together (positive interdependence) and that they have a personal responsibility to do their fair share (individual accountability). All for One & One for All provides teachers with six ready-to-use structures that ensure both positive interdependence and individual accountability, so that students are engaged in truly cooperative work.

What are the basic steps?

1. Identify a learning goal or task that is suited to cooperative work. Decide which of the cooperative learning structures on pages 68–69 is the best fit for your chosen goal or task.

2. Organize students into mixed-ability-level teams of three to five students each. Describe the goal or task you want them to work on and the cooperative structure that you selected. Confirm that students understand their roles and responsibilities within the selected structure.

3. Introduce the principles of individual accountability and positive interdependence (adapted from Johnson & Johnson, 1999) using simple and student-friendly language:

   - *Individual accountability* means that everyone is responsible for doing his or her fair share and for learning and being able to explain all the relevant material.

   - *Positive interdependence* means that teammates are in it together—that all members need to work together and/or help each other learn in order to be successful.

4. Clarify that effective group work involves both of these principles. Discuss the way that these principles work to promote learning, productivity, and positive relationships among teammates.

5. Observe students as they begin working. Use questions like these to help them assess and improve their performance (their own as well as their team's):

   - How did you decide who would do what? Is this a fair distribution of labor? Why or why not?

   - How are you personally contributing to the success of your team? How are you helping others?

   - Do you understand this material well enough to explain it to someone else?

   - How is your team as a whole ensuring that everyone understands the relevant material?

6. Help students assess and learn from the overall experience by posing reflection questions (e.g., What are some benefits of working collaboratively? How did your team function? What could you do better next time?) or distributing Team-O-Graph forms (see pp. 70–71 for options).

How is this tool used in the classroom?

✔ To make cooperative learning experiences more positive and productive

✔ To establish clear behavioral expectations for cooperative learning experiences

✔ To help students develop collaborative and supportive relationships with their peers

Teachers use the cooperative learning structures that follow to engage students in a range of activities, including reviewing content, researching topics/issues, and solving complex problems.

Cooperative Learning Structures

United We Stand

With this technique, team members demonstrate their learning by producing and submitting a single product (e.g., essay, diorama, skit, lab report) that everyone has contributed to in some way. Students are responsible for deciding who will do what and for dividing tasks fairly. (A brief note explaining the division of labor should be included with the final product.) Students understand that they will receive a shared grade for their work and are responsible for all the relevant material.

To Each His Own

With To Each His Own, team members work together to research, discuss, or practice the assigned material but ultimately produce their own products. Students understand that their final grades will be a reflection of everyone's work, either an average of all team members' scores *or* the sum of the team average plus their own individual scores (your decision, but tell students in advance).

Note: You can tell students what type of product to create or let them show what they know using any format that appeals to them ("Research the causes/effects of climate change as a team. Then create products—one per person, any type of product you want—that show what you learned").

Divide and Conquer

Here, the materials students need to complete an assigned task, project, or problem are distributed to different team members so that students must work together and share resources in order to be successful. For a map-based measuring task, one student might be given the map, another might be given a centimeter ruler, a third might be given the instructions, and so on. For a document-based essay task, different students might be given different primary documents. For a solve-the-mystery task, one student might be given background information, while the rest receive relevant clues.

Sign Off

With this technique, which is designed to prevent students from sitting back and letting others do the work, every member of the team has to sign off on completed work before submitting it. The trick is that students can only sign off if they agree that every member of the team (1) has contributed to the final product, (2) has encouraged his or her team members to contribute/participate, and (3) grasps the relevant content well enough to present or explain it if called on. Students understand that their work won't be accepted by the teacher until it receives everyone's signature.

Note: Sign Off can be used in combination with other cooperative learning techniques that require team members to produce a single final product or response.

Pick 'Em at Random

Here, students begin by working together to solve a problem, answer a question, or learn about a specific topic/concept. One student from each group is then randomly selected to share the group's response. Students understand that their grade will be determined by the quality of this person's response. Note that numbering group members in advance and calling on numbers rather than names ("Can all the twos stand up and share?") can help keep the selection process random.

Meet, Then Compete

With this technique, students review and practice key content knowledge/skills with members of their "home team." They then compete against members of other teams and bring the points they earn back to their home team. The home team with the highest score at the end is the winner.

The type of competition that students engage in is entirely up to you. Two options appear below.

- *Skills Competition:* Pairs of students square off in a "skills competition" (e.g., solving ten math problems or completing twenty verb conjugation exercises). Students correct their work using a teacher-provided answer sheet and earn points for correct answers. The student with the most points is awarded five team points to bring back to his or her home team. The other student is awarded three team points. In the case of a tie, both students receive four points. Offer a one-point bonus for perfect scores.

- *Study Showdown:* Students work with their home teams to review big ideas and important details about a given topic. They list their ideas on "showdown sheets" (one per student), compare sheets with someone from another team, and earn a point for each item their opponent doesn't have. Be sure to moderate the initial idea-generating sessions so that students focus on important-to-know facts and details rather than trivial ones. Because students receive points for ideas their competitors don't have, they might be tempted to record anything and everything—important or not—on their showdown sheets.

Since the goal is to maximize team points, students should use the initial practice session to make sure that everyone on their home team is prepared for competition. To keep the competition fair and confidence high, have students compete against individuals of similar ability levels.

🌑 Teacher Talk

➜ Many teachers report that these structures have changed their minds about cooperative learning. For example, a high school English teacher told us she was ready to give up on cooperative learning for two reasons: (1) regular requests from students to work alone and (2) freeloading, in which the group lets one or two students do all the work. This teacher wrote to tell us, "Divide and Conquer resolves the 'I would rather do it alone' request because you simply cannot work alone. And Sign Off (especially when you allow time for students to consider each member's contribution and encouragement of others) is a simple way to eliminate freeloading. There is great power in asking students to use their signatures as their word."

My name: _____ Date: _____

My team members' names: _____

Activity or assignment: _____

Team-O-Graph, version 1

CRITERIA FOR SUCCESSFUL GROUP WORK	Not Really	Sort of	Yes!
I participated and helped my team succeed.	☹	😐	🙂
Everyone else participated and helped the team succeed.	☹	😐	🙂
I listened quietly when others were speaking.	☹	😐	🙂
Everyone took turns speaking.	☹	😐	🙂
I stayed focused on my work.	☹	😐	🙂
Everyone stayed focused on his or her work.	☹	😐	🙂
We worked well as a team.	☹	😐	🙂

What did I do to help my team succeed?

How could my team have done even better?

My name: _____   Date: _____

My team members' names: _____

Activity or assignment: _____

Team-O-Graph, version 2

Review the criteria for successful group work *before you begin working* on the given assignment or activity. Keep the criteria in mind *as you work*. Use the criteria to rate your own and your entire team's performance *after you finish working*.

CRITERIA FOR SUCCESSFUL GROUP WORK	Not really	Somewhat	Mostly	Definitely
I made a major contribution to my team's success.	1	2	3	4
Everyone else made a major contribution to our success.	1	2	3	4
I stayed on task.	1	2	3	4
Everyone else stayed on task.	1	2	3	4
I learned the required material.	1	2	3	4
Everyone else learned the required material.	1	2	3	4
I sought out help if I needed it, and I accepted help gratefully.	1	2	3	4
Everyone who needed help asked for it and accepted it well.	1	2	3	4
I helped and supported my teammates.	1	2	3	4
All of my teammates helped and supported each other.	1	2	3	4
I gave people feedback about their work, ideas, and progress.	1	2	3	4
Everyone else on the team gave people feedback as well.	1	2	3	4
I treated everyone the way that I'd want to be treated.	1	2	3	4
Everyone treated others the way they'd want to be treated.	1	2	3	4

Some things my group did well …

My greatest challenges when working with this group …

Ideas for improvement …

Community CIRCLE

What is it?

A discussion technique for establishing a classroom culture that promotes respect and active listening—and that empowers students to explore critical content collaboratively

What are the benefits of using this tool?

To establish a classroom that supports high levels of collaboration, teachers need to create a culture of conversation. But what does this mean? In a culture of conversation, students listen actively to one another, address each other with respect, and feel comfortable expressing their ideas and opinions. Community CIRCLE helps teachers establish this kind of culture so that students come to see themselves as a community of learners who explore content collaboratively. And because the tool helps make students' personal knowledge, experiences, and values the starting point for classroom conversations, it increases student engagement and personal commitment to the learning process.

What are the basic steps?

1. Establish the ground rules for the Community CIRCLE. Explain that all students should come prepared to share, listen carefully to their peers, and use one another's names when they speak.

2. Use the CIRCLE technique to run Community CIRCLE sessions:

Create a question or prompt that invites students to share their personal knowledge, experiences, or opinions about a specific topic.

Invite students to sit in a circle and share their responses. Encourage all students to participate.

Review key ideas by having students summarize each other's responses. Ask students to use their classmates' names when summarizing. ("Gabe said he thought that ...")

Compare responses. Help students identify similarities and differences among their ideas.

Look for patterns. Help students find big ideas, make generalizations, and draw conclusions.

Extend the thinking and learning process. You can do this by assigning a synthesis task or connecting Community CIRCLE responses to upcoming learning. ("Let's see how our ideas about friendship compare to those in the next book we'll be reading.")

Note: The goal is to have many students share many specific ideas by drawing on their prior knowledge and experiences. Analyzing these specifics, finding commonalities, and developing generalizations then become the collaborative charge of the class.

3. Teach or review positive discussion behaviors (e.g., listening carefully, disagreeing respectfully, asking questions, addressing classmates by name) before initiating a Community CIRCLE. Assess and acknowledge students' use of these behaviors throughout the CIRCLE process.

4. Make Community CIRCLE a regular part of your classroom culture, both by using it consistently and by encouraging students to use the same basic process when working in small groups (i.e., share and review ideas, compare ideas and look for patterns, form generalizations and conclusions).

How is this tool used in the classroom?

✔ To engage students in discussing critical concepts and content collaboratively

✔ To develop a regular and comfortable forum for students to share their ideas and experiences

✔ To help students connect their prior knowledge and experiences to classroom content

✔ To help students become active listeners and respectful contributors

EXAMPLE 1: A middle school teacher uses the Community CIRCLE process to help her students discover the relationship between attitude and achievement. Here's what each step looks like:

Create a prompt that invites students to share personal knowledge, experiences, or opinions.

The teacher uses the following prompt to get students thinking about their personal experiences with the attitude-achievement relationship: "Think of a time when your attitude has either helped or gotten in the way of your success. How did your attitude affect your success?" To prepare students for the sharing process, the teacher has students jot down their ideas on paper before joining the circle.

Invite students to sit in a circle and share their responses.

Students arrange their chairs in a circle and begin sharing. Everyone is required to participate.

Review key ideas by having students summarize each other's responses.

Students restate or summarize their classmates' ideas, making sure to refer to each other by name.

Compare responses.

With the teacher's help, students identify similarities and differences like these:

• "Taryn's and Carlos's experiences seem similar. Both spoke about how a coach helped them improve their attitude and how their improved attitude helped them get better at their sport."

• "Joe and Amy had very different opinions. Amy didn't believe that her attitude affected her performance in class, but Joe was convinced that his did. He supported his belief with several specific examples, like how when he made an effort to have a more positive attitude about math, he actually started doing better in math class."

Look for patterns.

The teacher challenges students to develop generalizations about attitude that are rooted in their collective experiences. After some discussion and debate, students agree to these two generalizations: (1) Your attitude can affect your performance. (2) It's better to have a positive attitude than a negative one.

Extend the thinking and learning process.

The teacher asks students to read the classic American poem "Casey at the Bat" and look for evidence that supports and/or refutes their generalizations about attitude.

EXAMPLE 2: A high school history teacher presents this prompt at the end of a unit on World War I: "For what purposes, and under what conditions, should our country deploy its armed forces?" After students share and defend their positions, they work to reach a consensus on some common principles. Over the course of the year, students revisit and refine these principles as they evaluate the United States' decision to participate in other military engagements.

EXAMPLE 3: A primary-grade teacher uses Community CIRCLE to begin a unit on healthy eating. She starts by asking students if they like to eat candy and junk food. She then poses this question: "What would happen if we only ate junk food?" After students share their various ideas, the teacher helps them summarize responses, compare their ideas, and draw these three conclusions: (1) Too much junk food can make you sick. (2) Healthy foods like fruits and vegetables are good for our bodies. (3) We need to eat many different kinds of foods to grow.

As students learn about nutrition and healthy eating over the course of the unit, they come back to their conclusions and decide if anything they have learned helps them support their conclusions. At the end of the unit, students create a picture book that teaches simple guidelines for healthy eating.

🌑 Teacher Talk

➔ To help students get in the habit of sharing, you can set up a practice circle and use simple questions like "What's your favorite food?" or "What do you like to do in your free time?" Another option is to use forced-choice questions like "Cats or dogs?" or "Chocolate or vanilla?" Getting all students used to sharing prepares them for higher-level questions later on.

➔ Remember that the ultimate goal of Community CIRCLE isn't to have students share for the sake of sharing. It's to use students' personal knowledge, experiences, and opinions as a framework for discussing and learning critical content. For this reason, be sure to have a concrete purpose or learning goal in mind when you initiate a Community CIRCLE conversation. Keep this purpose or goal in mind as you craft your initial prompt, guide the conversation, and develop your synthesis task.

➔ You can promote more interactive and thoughtful conversations by encouraging students to jot down their ideas before joining the circle. Younger students can use pictures rather than words.

➔ Teachers often think that "sharing tools" are just for primary or elementary teachers. Not so! Because Community CIRCLE discussions can be designed around just about any topic, they can work in any classroom. Examples 1–3 and the sample prompts below show how the tool works across grade levels and content areas.

➔ If you're not sure where to begin, consider prompts that invite students to

- *Explore a critical theme or concept.* For example:
  — What does it mean to be brave?
  — What do scientists do? How do they think and behave? What does it mean to be a scientist?

- *Analyze and/or weigh in on a challenging decision.* For example:
  — Why do you think the mouse decided to leave home? Was his decision a good one?
  — Was President Truman right to use the atomic bomb? Explain your reasoning.

- *Analyze causes and/or effects.* For example:
  — What makes a class engaging? What kinds of classes or teachers get you excited to learn?
  — What if you couldn't use fractions? How might your life be different?

- *Activate and consolidate prior knowledge.* For example:
  — We are about to learn about Lewis and Clark's expedition west. Based on what you know about the United States at this time, what challenges do you believe Lewis and Clark faced?

Interaction in an Instant

What is it?

A set of pairing and grouping techniques that can be used on the fly to engage students in talking to and learning from their classmates

What are the benefits of using this tool?

Not all group-learning activities need to be formal processes; sometimes teachers just need simple ways to get students talking to, interacting with, and learning from one another. Interaction in an Instant provides seven simple-to-implement techniques that create energy in the classroom and promote positive interactions among students. The techniques do more than ask students to talk to one another; they get students engaged in the learning-by-talking process, and they keep students focused on important content. The Interaction in an Instant techniques also help ensure that students talk to and learn from many different students, not just close friends or students who sit near them.

What are the basic steps?

1. Familiarize yourself with the Interaction in an Instant techniques described on pages 76–78.

2. Select the technique that best meets your instructional objectives.

3. Review the technique with students to make sure they are clear about their roles.

4. Implement the technique in the classroom. Monitor students as they work to ensure that they're staying on task and participating productively.

5. Invite students to share what they learned about the content as well as their reactions to the selected technique.

How is this tool used in the classroom?

✔ To enhance student learning via the use of well-designed pairing and grouping techniques

✔ To foster interaction and collaboration in the classroom

✔ To increase the sense of community among students

Interaction in an Instant Techniques

Think-Pair-Share

Think-Pair-Share (Lyman, 1981) allows students to test and refine their ideas with a partner before sharing them with the class or committing them to paper. To use the technique, simply pose a question, prompt, or problem and instruct students to

> THINK through a response or solution on their own

> PAIR up with another student to discuss, compare, and refine their ideas

> SHARE their responses with the class or summarize their responses in writing

Think-Pair-Share is very versatile in the sense that it can be used at any stage of the instructional process (before, during, or after a lesson/unit) and for a variety of different purposes, including activating prior knowledge, reviewing critical content and skills, defining essential attributes, and prompting original or analytical thinking. The sample prompts below reflect these and other uses.

- What do you know about dinosaurs?
- What makes something "art"?
- Was the Civil War inevitable? Why or why not?
- Which of these two math problems is solved incorrectly? How can you tell?
- What do you think the poet was trying to say here? How would you interpret these lines?
- How many ways can you color in exactly half of a ten-by-ten grid?
- What do you predict will happen if we raise the height of this ramp?
- What do you believe were the three most important events in Helen Keller's life? Why?
- What conclusions can you draw from this data table?

Give One, Get One

Give One, Get One encourages the free flow of ideas and the generation of multiple responses through a rapid series of student-student interactions. Use the technique when you want students to think divergently or come up with many valid responses to a single question/prompt. For example:

- What are the attributes of a good friend?
- Why are plants important to us and our world?
- What are some reasons that people move from one place to another?
- Where are fractions used in the real world?
- What could someone do to improve his or her cardiovascular health?
- Can you name at least seven different styles of music?
- What are some effective strategies for promoting student engagement?

Tell students how many total responses you want them to gather, and give them time to generate two or three on their own. Then, instruct them to meet with another student, *give one* of their responses to their partner, and *get one* in return. Clarify that students shouldn't huddle in groups (pairs only!) or share multiple responses. Instead, they should get only one response from each partner and meet with as many partners as it takes to collect the required number of responses. (If two paired students have identical responses, they should work together to generate a new one.) Conclude by helping students share, summarize, or further explore the responses they collect.

Physical Barometer

Physical Barometer creates instant interactions by requiring students to take positions on multisided issues, discuss and refine those positions with like-minded classmates, and attempt to win over classmates who hold different positions. To use this technique, pose a question or statement that allows students to select from three or more possible positions. For example:

- Where do you stand on the issue of using animals for scientific research? Do you strongly support it, support it, disapprove of it, or strongly disapprove of it?

- We have learned the critical attributes of tall tales, and we have read three different tall tales. Which of the tales we read do you believe would be the best one for teaching a younger student the critical attributes of a tall tale?

- What is your position on the controversy surrounding the proposal to build a big-box store where the Northvale Farm used to be? Do you support the development of the store, oppose it, or are you not sure?

Once the varying positions that students can take are clear, ask students to go to a physical space that represents their position. For example, the front of the room could represent "support," the back of the room could represent "oppose," and the middle could represent "not sure." Instruct students to work with classmates who share their position to develop and fine-tune a defense of that position. Students in each group should get a chance to make their case and to try to sway members from other groups to change positions and join their group. Students who switch groups should explain what convinced them to change their minds.

Clock Partners

This technique makes the student-pairing process quick and easy, while also ensuring that students do not gravitate to the same learning partners over and over again. To use the technique, distribute copies of the Clock Partners sheet on page 79 and ask students to "make appointments" with twelve different students—one for each hour on the clock. When two students agree to make an appointment with each other, they must both fill in each other's names on their Clock Partners sheet at the agreed-upon hour. For example, in Zoe's Clock Partners sheet (shown at the right), Zoe made an appointment with Enzo to be her one o'clock partner; consequently, Enzo wrote Zoe in as his one o'clock partner (not shown).

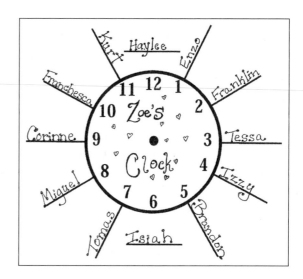

Once students complete their Clock Partners sheets, they can attach their sheets to the inside of their notebooks for safekeeping and ease of access. Then, whenever it comes time for students to pair up, all you need to do is tell them which clock partner to work with, and they can pair up immediately. ("For this activity, you'll be working with your five o'clock partner. Find your partner and get to work!") By rotating around the clock, you can ensure that students work with many different partners instead of always pairing up with the same close friends or neighbors.

Numbered Heads Together

This well-known technique (Kagan & Kagan, 2015) uses a simple grouping structure to ensure that each member of a group understands the content that has been taught. To use the technique, number the students in each group, up to four. (If one group is smaller than the others, have number three answer for number four as well.) Ask students a recall or comprehension question, or present a problem to solve. Provide time for students to write their responses individually and then discuss as a group. Remind students that every member of the group must be able to answer the question/solve the problem. If you call out number two, for example, then student two from each group responds. Repeat with additional questions/problems.

Mix-Pair-Share

This technique (Kagan & Kagan, 2015) is a great way to get students up and moving as they are processing new information. Pose a question and call, "Mix!" Students walk quietly around the room until you say, "Pair!" Students stop where they are and pair up with the closest student. Student pairs then share their responses to the question. Students can meet and share responses with new partners each time you call out "Mix!" and "Pair!"

A variation on this technique is Inside-Outside Circle (Kagan & Kagan, 2015), in which students face each other in two concentric circles, each with an equal number of students. Students on the inside circle face a partner on the outside circle. When asked to share a response or an idea, inside students share first, then outside students share. With each new question or prompt, the inside circle rotates so that a new set of partners is formed. On each successive rotation, the student who shares first (inside/outside) should be reversed.

Talking Chips

This protocol (Kagan & Kagan, 2015) ensures that all students in a group participate during group discussions. It also develops students' ability to listen to one another and respond thoughtfully during these discussions. To use this technique, divide students into groups of four or five. Each student should get one or two chips or counters (poker chips work well). The groups are given a prompt or question to discuss. To contribute to the discussion, a student must use a chip. When students run out of chips, they are no longer allowed to speak until the other members have used all their chips. If there is more to discuss, students should collect their chips and continue using them to contribute to the discussion.

Clock Partners

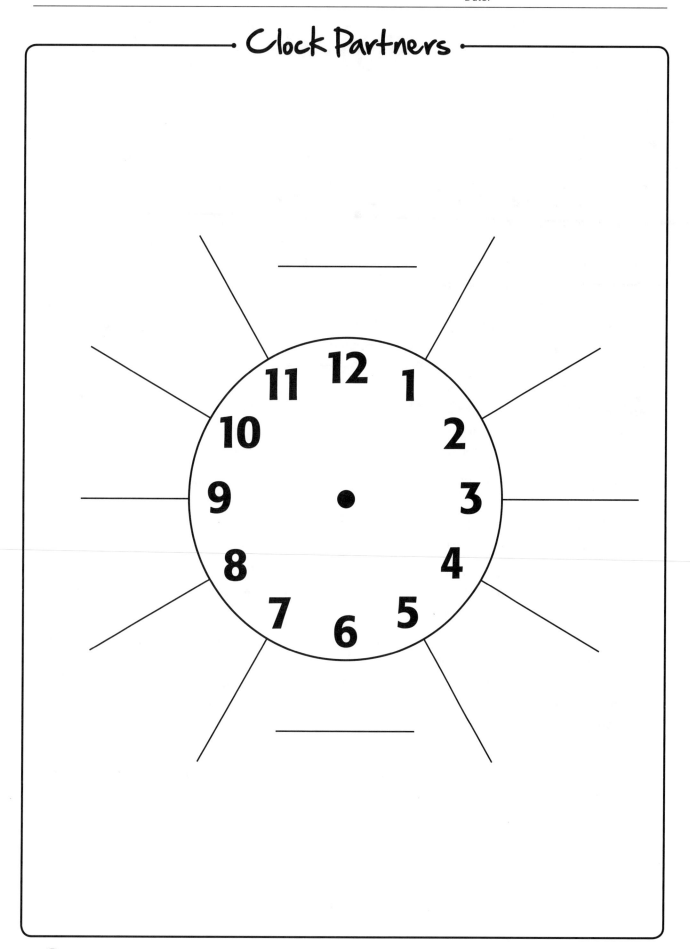

Jigsaw

What is it?

A cooperative learning technique that develops students' research and communication skills by challenging students to become experts and teachers in particular aspects of classroom content

What are the benefits of using this tool?

Daniel Vasgird, director of research integrity and compliance at West Virginia University, states, "You have to walk into any research project with an understanding that collaboration is going to be needed. It is extraordinarily rare to find a publication in almost any discipline in which there is a single author" (Holgate, 2012). This field-wide trend toward collaborative research and collective understanding means that our work in enhancing cooperative learning ought to be married to the work of developing students' research skills. Jigsaw (Aronson et al., 1978) is a tool that's ideally suited to this task. It gives students the opportunity to conduct focused research with their peers, practice group communication skills, and teach what they learn to a team of fellow learners.

What are the basic steps?

1. Select a topic that you want students to research. Break the topic up into three to five subtopics, and assemble resources that students can use to develop expertise in each subtopic.

2. Break students up into three- to five-member Home Teams. Explain that each team member will learn about one subtopic and teach what he or she learns to the Home Team.

    Tip: Provide, or help students develop, an organizer that facilitates the collection and sharing of the information to be learned. (See Example 1 and Teacher Talk for ideas.)

3. Assign the students in each Home Team to a different subtopic. Have students leave their Home Teams and form Expert Groups by meeting with students from other Home Teams who are responsible for the same subtopic.

4. Instruct Expert Groups to use the provided resources to research their subtopic and then develop a plan for teaching what they learn to their Home Teams. Provide assistance as needed.

    Tip: To facilitate independent research and collaborative skills, have students first conduct their research individually, then work with their Expert Groups to determine the most important information and develop a plan for teaching the content to their Home Teams.

5. Have students rejoin their Home Teams. Ask experts to share what they learned about their respective subtopics with their Home Team. Remind Home Teams that their goal is to make sure that all team members have a big-picture understanding of the topic.

6. Lead a follow-up discussion on key content points and the Jigsaw process.

7. Assign a task, test, or set of questions that assesses understanding of the content as a whole.

How is this tool used in the classroom?

✔ To foster individual accountability and positive interdependence during cooperative work

✔ To develop students' research and communication skills

✔ To help students acquire and construct content knowledge together

EXAMPLE 1: A high school history class is learning about the Harlem Renaissance. The teacher is using Jigsaw to help students answer an essential question: What can artists teach us about historical movements? The teacher explains that each student in a four-member Home Team will be responsible for becoming an expert on a different Harlem Renaissance artist. For each artist, the teacher has prepared a set of readings and multimedia resources (e.g., audio files, poems, prints of paintings), along with a research organizer (shown at the right) with four common elements that all experts must research.

When students leave their Home Teams to join their Expert Groups, the teacher reminds them to research their artist and discuss their findings. Expert Group members must agree that every member has collected the critical information and develop a plan for teaching what they learn to their Home Teams.

Artist _Duke Ellington_	Artist _Billie Holiday_
Inspiration/influences:	Inspiration/influences:
Most famous works:	Most famous works:
Key themes:	Key themes:
Historical/artistic significance:	Historical/artistic significance:

Artist _Langston Hughes_	Artist _Jacob Lawrence_
Inspiration/influences:	Inspiration/influences:
Most famous works:	Most famous works:
Key themes:	Key themes:
Historical/artistic significance:	Historical/artistic significance:

After the experts have returned to and presented their findings to their Home Teams, the teacher asks students to identify any commonalities or themes across all four artists. Students use what they have learned to reexamine the original essential question, now with greater specificity (What do these artists teach us about the Harlem Renaissance?).

EXAMPLE 2: An elementary teacher uses a hands-on approach to Jigsaw by guiding Expert Groups through simple experiments that help them understand the nature of sound. To conduct their research, Expert Groups work at one of three learning stations and collect information from their experiments on specially designed research organizers (see the organizer for Station One at the right):

- At Station One, students experiment with a buzzer, listening to it from every direction (above, below, left, right).

- At Station Two, students experiment with a tuning fork, striking it in the air, in water, and next to a ping-pong ball on a string.

- At Station Three, students experiment with a plastic ruler by holding it down on a table, letting the end hang off at different lengths, and snapping the ruler to create vibrations.

Research Organizer for Station One

1. Does sound travel in all directions?
   ___ Yes ___ No

2. How do you know?

3. How can you explain what you learned to your Home Team?

Teacher Talk

➜ Graphic organizers are a big help to students when conducting research, as shown in Example 1. Organizers are also helpful when students reconvene in their Home Teams, giving students a way to record what each team member reports and a visually organized view of the topic as a whole. A matrix organizer (shown at the right) is ideal for synthesizing all students' research during student reporting, with the subtopics across the top and research questions down the left.

RESEARCH QUESTIONS / TYPE OF BRAKING SYSTEM	Disc Brakes	Drum Brakes	Anti-Lock Braking System (ABS)	Emergency/ Parking Brake
What are the key components?				
How do they work to stop the vehicle?				
What are the most common repair issues?				

➜ For both Home Teams and Expert Groups, aim for heterogeneous groupings, and mix things up by having students work with different students throughout the year. The more students have opportunities to work with and learn from one another, the better.

➜ To make sure students work productively in their Expert Teams, try one of these techniques:

• *Sign Off:* This technique (see p. 68) ensures individual accountability by requiring all members of the Expert Group to sign off on the group's research. However, students can only sign off if they agree that all group members (1) have contributed, (2) have encouraged other group members, and (3) understand the content well enough to present it to their Home Teams.

• *Test Rewards:* If you administer a test or quiz, reward Expert Groups based on the class's overall performance. If the class scores highest on the questions related to a particular subtopic, give a bonus to the members of the Expert Group who researched and taught that subtopic.

➜ There are many ways to design the research component of a Jigsaw lesson. Here are a few ideas:

• For relatively quick Jigsaw lessons contained within the classroom, assemble relevant resources ahead of time and make sure there are enough copies/resources for all Expert Group members.

• To make the research more authentic, challenge students to conduct independent research. When students meet in their Expert Groups, they can use the time to identify relevant resources and develop a research plan. Then, after they conduct the research on their own, students can meet again in their Expert Groups to compare and refine their findings. Note that this option takes longer to complete, as students will likely be conducting research outside the classroom.

• Allow students to use experiments and hands-on activities to gather key information, as shown in Example 2.

• Don't get stuck on print resources. Look for ways to incorporate pictures and diagrams, 3D models, data charts, video and media, and computer simulations.

PART II

Tools for Helping Students Develop Understanding

Cues, Questions, and Advance Organizers

The beginning seems to be more than half of the whole.

—Aristotle

Using cues, questions, and advance organizers at the beginning of a lesson or unit focuses learning on the important content to come. Such an approach can motivate students by tapping into their curiosity and interest in the topic. In addition, using higher-order questions can help students deepen their knowledge by requiring the use of critical-thinking skills.

—Ceri B. Dean, Elizabeth Ross Hubbell, Howard Pitler, and Bj Stone,
Classroom Instruction That Works (Second Edition)

The category of instruction identified in *Classroom Instruction That Works* (Second Edition) as cues, questions, and advance organizers is a category that emphasizes beginnings. More specifically, the category highlights how teachers can create powerful beginnings to their lessons and units—beginnings that grab students' attention, focus learning on the content to come, and help students activate relevant background knowledge. These kinds of beginnings go by many names in education literature, including *hook*, *anticipatory set*, and *set induction*, among others. What the authors of *Classroom Instruction That Works* (Second Edition) show is that regardless of the names we use, great openings to lessons and units can be designed in a variety of ways: by using direct cues, by posing well-crafted questions, or by setting up learning with a range of organizer types.

In this chapter, we present nine tools for putting cues, questions, and organizers to work in the classroom. These tools reflect Dean et al.'s (2012) advice about how to use these strategies to the greatest effect. Specifically:

- Focus students' attention on what's most important in the content to come.
- Don't be afraid to be direct—sometimes, using explicit cues to preview content is the best approach.
- Pose questions that go beyond basic recall.
- Use a variety of types of advance organizers, including expository advance organizers, narrative advance organizers, graphic advance organizers, and skimming as an advance organizer.

These are the nine tools:

1. **Hooks & Bridges** is a lesson-opening technique that uses thought-provoking questions or activities to activate students' background knowledge and help students connect their background knowledge to the upcoming learning.

2. **Vocabulary Knowledge Rating (VKR)** uses a visual organizer to preview the vocabulary terms that students will encounter during an upcoming unit; students then use the organizer to rate and track their growing understanding of those terms as the unit progresses.

3. **Anticipation Guide** uses an advance organizer to preview upcoming content, activate prior knowledge, and spark engagement; the organizer contains content-driven statements that students take positions on, both before and after the lesson is delivered.

4. **From Topics to "Top Picks"** helps students build a strong framework for learning by previewing upcoming topics; it helps teachers design more engaging lessons by providing information about the topics students find most interesting.

5. **Questioning in Style** identifies four different styles of questions that can be used to activate, deepen, and assess student learning.

6. **Before, During, After (BDA)** uses a three-step process to help students develop high-quality responses to classroom questions—whenever those questions are posed during the lesson.

7. **Start with a Story** shows teachers how stories (a type of advance organizer) can be used to capture student interest and set the scene for new learning.

8. **S-O-S Graphic Organizers** presents a variety of graphic organizer types and explains how using these organizers before, during, and after a lesson can serve to enhance student learning.

9. **Power Previewing** prepares students to get more out of what they read by having them skim assigned texts before reading those texts for real.

Note: While this chapter focuses primarily on setting the stage for upcoming learning, some of the chapter's nine tools—especially Questioning in Style; Before, During, After; and S-O-S Graphic Organizers—aren't specifically "beginning of instruction" tools; they're designed to be used at different points in an instructional sequence.

Hooks & Bridges

What is it?

A lesson-opening technique that uses engaging questions or activities ("hooks") to spark student interest and activate background knowledge; students' responses are then connected ("bridged") to the purpose or content of the upcoming lesson

What are the benefits of using this tool?

For the most part, the *Classroom Instruction That Works* (Second Edition) category called cues, questions, and advance organizers is about setting the stage for future learning. Three key elements that are critical to the success of this setting-the-stage process are (1) getting students engaged and interested, (2) activating students' background knowledge, and (3) connecting students' initial thinking to the learning to come so that students can use their background knowledge as a foundation to build on. Hooks & Bridges is a tool designed to put all three of these elements in place in the classroom. The tool explains how to use interest-grabbing questions and activities as hooks to capture student interest and spur student thinking. Once students share their knowledge and experiences, the teacher creates a connection, or a bridge, between students' responses and the lesson.

What are the basic steps?

1. Think about the topic and learning goal(s) of an upcoming lesson or unit.

2. Design an engaging question or activity (a hook) that you can use to introduce the overall topic and/or a specific learning goal. See the bulleted list on page 88 for general ideas; see pages 88–89 for concrete examples.

   Note: A well-designed hook should capture students' interest, get students thinking about the relevant content, and help students activate prior knowledge.

3. Present your hook at the outset of the lesson or unit. Invite students to think about it and then share their responses.

   Tip: Give students time to think before asking them to respond. To help students deepen their thinking, ask them to write down their initial responses and then have them share with a partner or small group before sharing with the class.

4. Collect and summarize students' responses.

5. Connect the question or activity that students just completed (the hook), along with students' responses, to the content and/or learning goals of the lesson you're about to teach. This connection is called a "bridge."

6. Incorporate hooks and bridges into your lesson plans as often as possible. To maximize engagement and stimulate different types of thinking, use different types of hooks for different lessons rather than falling back on the same type of hook every time.

How is this tool used in the classroom?

✔ To preview content, activate prior knowledge, and increase engagement before a lesson

Teachers from different grade levels and content areas use Hooks & Bridges to introduce lessons and units in a way that gets students engaged. In our experience, the hooks that work best in the classroom do one or more of the following things:

• Present a CHALLENGE

• Spark CURIOSITY (for example, by presenting a mysterious event or puzzling data)

• Stimulate DEBATE

• Appeal to STUDENTS' INTERESTS

• Invite SPECULATION (What if ___? What/why might ___? What do you predict will happen?)

• Involve PHYSICAL MOVEMENT

• Inspire CREATIVE THINKING

• Ask students to make personal or real-world CONNECTIONS

• Trigger an EMOTIONAL RESPONSE

Below are examples showing what some of these types of hooks look like (and how teachers bridge their hooks to the relevant content).

EXAMPLE 1: A hook that appeals to STUDENTS' INTERESTS

A teacher tried to capitalize on her students' enthusiasm for sports by using the hook-and-bridge combination below to open a lesson on angles.

HOOK: After showing students a video of basketball phenom LeBron James hitting an amazing three-point shot, the teacher replayed the video a second time, hit pause as LeBron was in the act of shooting, and asked students how many angles they could find in his body. Students then came up to the screen one by one to point out the angles they identified.

BRIDGE: This week, you'll learn some new vocabulary terms that will help you describe, name, and compare the different kinds of angles that you identified. You will also learn how to measure those angles using a protractor.

EXAMPLE 2: A hook that invites SPECULATION

The hook-and-bridge combination below, which was used to introduce a lecture on the fall of the Roman Empire, asks students to speculate about possible causes of a hypothetical event.

HOOK: Imagine that you jumped into a time machine, traveled one hundred years into the future, and found that the United States was no longer the great superpower that it is today. What might have happened? Develop some possible explanations.

BRIDGE: Believe it or not, you just identified many of the factors that were responsible for the decline and fall of the Roman Empire hundreds and hundreds of years ago. Today, we'll take a look at some of these factors in more detail.

EXAMPLE 3: A hook that inspires CREATIVE THINKING and involves PHYSICAL MOVEMENT

An English teacher used the hook-and-bridge combination on the next page to spark a discussion of blood- and water-related imagery in *Macbeth*.

HOOK: How is guilt like a stain? Generate two responses on your own. Then use the Give One, Get One technique (p. 76) to add four more ideas to your list.

BRIDGE: Let's keep this simile in mind as we continue our discussion of *Macbeth*. As you read the first scene of Act V, ask yourself whether Lady Macbeth's original assessment ("A little water clears us of this deed") was an accurate one. Can guilt be washed away so easily?

EXAMPLE 4: A hook that asks students to make personal CONNECTIONS

A primary-grade teacher opened a lesson on how and why leaves change color with the hook-and-bridge combination below.

HOOK: How do the changing seasons affect your life? Do they affect the way you dress? The activities you do? Anything else?

BRIDGE: Have you ever noticed that trees' lives are affected by the seasons as well? You have? That's great because today we are going to be talking about some of the different ways that trees respond to the changing seasons.

EXAMPLE 5: A hook that sparks CURIOSITY

Before beginning a lesson on communicable diseases and how students can minimize the risk of becoming sick, an elementary teacher strategically dusted common surfaces in the classroom with glitter. She then began the lesson with the hook-and-bridge combination below.

HOOK: I want everyone to look closely at their own hands. How many of you can find any specks of glitter on your hands? How about on your clothes or your hair? Look closely for any signs of glitter you can find. So now for the big question: Why do so many students have glitter on them?

BRIDGE: You've done great detective work to figure out that some of the surfaces in our classroom have glitter on them. And because the glitter was in common areas, lots of students came in contact with it and spread it around. This is a lot like the germs that can cause communicable diseases. And that's what we'll be learning about today.

🎧 Teacher Talk

➜ Here are some questions to help you design and implement high-quality hooks and bridges:

- What key idea, concept, or information do you want students to understand as a result of your hook?

- Will students have relevant background knowledge or experience to draw on?

- What will you need to do to set up the hook? Will students need a video, visual aid, story, reading, demonstration, or other source of information to make the hook work?

- Is the hook engaging? Will it capture students' attention?

- What do you expect to hear in students' responses? How will you guide their thinking to broaden their responses?

- How will you summarize students' responses?

- How will you connect students' responses to the learning to come? What particular angle or way in do you want to use for the bridge?

Vocabulary Knowledge Rating (VKR)

What is it?

A technique (adapted from Blachowicz, 1986) that introduces students to critical vocabulary terms before instruction begins and that trains them to assess and improve their understanding of those terms as the unit unfolds

What are the benefits of using this tool?

Using cues and advance organizers at the outset of an instructional sequence "focuses learning on the important content to come" (Dean et al., 2012, p. 51). With this increased focus, students can pursue new learning with greater purpose and with a way to monitor their evolving understanding ("What content do I know well? What content is outside my current understanding?"). Vocabulary Knowledge Rating, or VKR for short, focuses students' attention on the most important content of all—the critical concepts and academic vocabulary terms that anchor learning units. Students review the terms and rate their knowledge of each one at the start of the unit to provide a baseline of their understanding. They then rate their knowledge again at the end of the unit to see how their understanding has grown.

What are the basic steps?

1. Record the critical vocabulary terms for an upcoming unit on a Vocabulary Knowledge Rating Organizer (p. 93).

   Note: If specific people, places, or things (proper nouns like Iroquois, Peru, or Nobel Prize) are critical to the content that you're teaching, be sure to include them on the organizer.

2. Introduce the terms to students by having students see, hear, and say them (*look* at the terms on their organizers, *listen* to the terms as you read them aloud, *say* the terms as a class).

3. Explain that these are the terms students will encounter and need to master during the upcoming unit.

4. Instruct students to assess and indicate their familiarity with each term by circling the appropriate number on the four-point scale. Have them add up their points to get their initial (pre-instruction) vocabulary knowledge rating.

5. Stop at various points throughout the unit to have students reflect on how their understanding of the terms has grown and changed.

   Optional: Ask students to recalculate their vocabulary knowledge ratings.

6. Ask students to reassess their understanding of each term at the end of the unit. Have them compare their final vocabulary knowledge ratings with their initial ones.

7. Help students reflect on and celebrate their progress. Encourage them to develop plans for shoring up their understanding of terms they haven't yet mastered.

How is this tool used in the classroom?

✔ To activate and assess students' prior knowledge of critical vocabulary terms

✔ To have students monitor their understanding of key terms over time

✔ To have students reflect on their learning at the end of instruction

EXAMPLE 1: The VKR Organizer below was completed by a student at the start of a unit on fractions. This student reassessed his knowledge of these same terms again at the end of the unit (not shown).

LIST OF TERMS	I've never seen or heard of this term.	I've seen or heard of this term, but I don't know what it means.	I know this term, but I can't fully explain it in my own words.	I can explain this term in my own words and give an example of it.
fraction	1	2	③	4
numerator	1	2	③	4
denominator	1	2	③	4
proper fraction	①	2	3	4
improper fraction	①	2	3	4
equivalent fractions	1	②	3	4
mixed numbers	①	2	3	4
whole	1	2	3	④
part	1	2	3	④

Initial vocabulary knowledge rating __22__ Date: __3/12__

Final vocabulary knowledge rating _____ Date: _____

EXAMPLE 2: A first-grade teacher uses this simpler three-column VKR Organizer with her students. She also uses emojis for each level of the scale.

VOCABULARY WORD	I don't know what this word means.	I think I know what this word means.	I definitely know what this word means!
character	1	2	3
setting	1	2	3
events	1	2	3
conflict	1	2	3
resolution	1	2	3

🌐 Teacher Talk

➔ To help students see their progress clearly, have them use different colored pens—or different VKR forms—to do their initial and final ratings. This will also make it easier for them to distinguish and tally their before and after scores.

➔ If you want, add a definition/explanation column to the basic VKR Organizer. Use this column to have students define the terms in their own words at the end of the unit.

➔ To avoid vocabulary overload, limit the terms that you include on your VKR Organizer to concepts and terms that are central to your content. Consider grade level as well (select fewer terms for younger students).

A simple technique to help you identify concept/terms that are worthy of the most instructional time is a Content Priority Pyramid (Silver Strong & Associates, 2007). To use this tool, conduct a brief content analysis during unit planning. List all the vocabulary terms in the unit, and then organize them into three categories: essential, important, and nice to know. Depending on the number of terms, you may opt to omit the nice-to-know words from the VKR Organizer. In any case, the categories will help you determine how much instructional emphasis should be placed on various terms. The Content Priority Pyramid below shows how a teacher categorized the terms associated with a unit on plants and their role in the world's ecosystems.

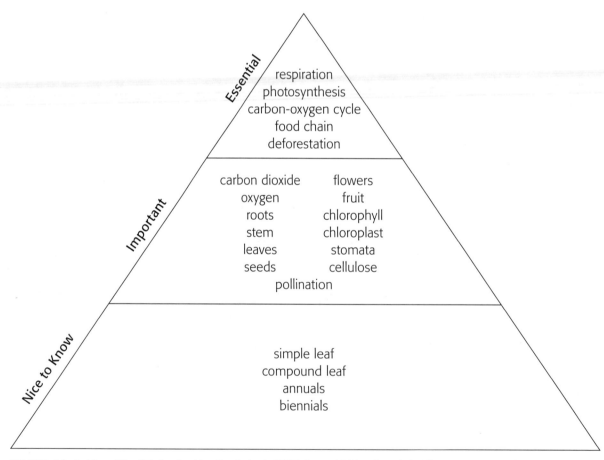

SOURCE: Adapted from *Word Works: Cracking Vocabulary's CODE*, Second Edition (p. 34), by Silver Strong & Associates, 2007, Ho-Ho-Kus, NJ: Thoughtful Education Press. © 2007 Silver Strong & Associates. Adapted with permission.

Name: _____   Date: _____

Lesson/unit topic: _____

Vocabulary Knowledge Rating Organizer

INSTRUCTIONS: Indicate your familiarity with each term by circling the appropriate number. Add the numbers together to get a vocabulary knowledge rating. Assess your progress by comparing your initial rating with your end-of-unit rating.

Term	I've never seen or heard of this term.	I've seen or heard of this term, but I don't know what it means.	I know this term, but I can't fully explain it or give an example of it.	I can explain this term in my own words, use it in context, and give an example if appropriate.
	1	2	3	4
	1	2	3	4
	1	2	3	4
	1	2	3	4
	1	2	3	4
	1	2	3	4
	1	2	3	4
	1	2	3	4
	1	2	3	4
	1	2	3	4
	1	2	3	4
	1	2	3	4

Initial vocabulary knowledge rating: _____ Date: _____   Final vocabulary knowledge rating: _____ Date: _____

Anticipation Guide

What is it?

A pre-learning tool used to preview content, activate students' prior knowledge, and get students to take positions on upcoming topics

What are the benefits of using this tool?

Agree or disagree: *Removing carbohydrates from your diet is a good long-term weight loss strategy.* Are you thinking? Chances are that you are because the simple act of agreeing or disagreeing with a thought-provoking statement rouses the mind to life. Anticipation Guide, which is based on the work of Harold Herber (1970), is a tool that taps directly into this brain-awakening power. By providing students with a set of statements about the learning to come, Anticipation Guides activate students' prior knowledge and help students get a pre-learning grasp on the content. By requiring students to take a position on each statement, the tool promotes a spirit of inquiry, as new learning becomes an active search for information that supports students' positions. And by asking students to review the statements after learning and decide anew whether they agree or disagree, Anticipation Guides teach students to reflect on how their thinking has grown or changed.

What are the basic steps?

1. Identify a lesson, reading, video, or other important chunk of content that you want students to understand deeply.

   Note: Anticipation Guides can also be used to preview a unit, as shown in Example 1.

2. Generate a list of statements about the content of the lesson or learning chunk. Statements can be true, false, or open to interpretation/designed to provoke debate.

3. Ask students to read the statements carefully, make sure they understand them, and decide whether they agree or disagree with each statement. Remind students that they are not expected to have "correct" responses; they should take their best guesses based on what they know.

4. Survey students and probe their responses for the reasoning behind their positions.

   Note: Surveying responses and encouraging students to explain their thinking provides a wealth of pre-assessment data about students' knowledge of the content and reasoning skills.

5. Conduct the lesson.

6. Have students review their positions. Ask them if their initial positions have changed or been reinforced. Encourage them to justify their positions using relevant information from the lesson.

7. Use students' responses to evaluate both their understanding of what they've learned and their ability to support a position with evidence.

How is this tool used in the classroom?

✔ To provide students with a preview of the learning to come

✔ To encourage students to use their prior knowledge to take positions on new content

✔ To increase engagement in and curiosity about an upcoming lesson

EXAMPLE 1: An elementary teacher is about to begin a unit on communities and wants students to think deeply about what a community is and how their own community affects their daily lives. After a brief introduction, the teacher presents an Anticipation Guide (below) and reviews all of the statements with students. Both before and after the lesson, students decide if they agree or disagree with the statements and explain why.

Before the lesson		Statements	After the lesson	
Agree	Disagree		Agree	Disagree
		Communities make our lives better.		
		Communities and neighborhoods are the same.		
		Evansville is a unique community.		
		All communities have similar characteristics.		
		Events from the past have shaped our community today.		

EXAMPLE 2: A high school sociology teacher challenges her students to design and conduct a research study on a topic that interests them. As part of the unit, students learn about questionnaire design and how to construct questionnaires that meet the standards of authentic research in the social sciences. Before learning about the design principles of sociology questionnaires, students respond to and discuss the statements in this Anticipation Guide:

Before the lesson		Statements	After the lesson	
Agree	Disagree		Agree	Disagree
		It is easy to tell when a questionnaire question is biased.		
		A good questionnaire question should always isolate the topic or issue that respondents should consider.		
		It is difficult to keep our personal assumptions and opinions from influencing the questions we design.		
		Words like *regularly*, *often*, and *rarely* are too imprecise to use in a questionnaire.		
		The order of the questions in a questionnaire is irrelevant.		

EXAMPLE 3: In addition to including statements for students to take positions on, a middle school math teacher also includes a few pre-assessment questions to help him better gauge students' background knowledge. He uses these modified Anticipation Guides to help him make informed decisions about how to adapt instruction based on patterns in students' responses. Below is a modified Anticipation Guide that the teacher used to begin a lesson on probability.

Before: Agree or Disagree	Statements	After: Agree or Disagree
	1. The probability of an event occurring will always fall between 0 and 1, where 0 = not possible (0%) and 1 = certain (100%).	
	2. If a baseball player has a career batting average of .300, you can safely predict that he will get 3 hits in his next 10 at bats.	
	3. You can safely predict that the probability of getting snow in the Sahara Desert in July is 0.	
	4. Rolling dice and/or flipping coins are ways of finding the theoretical probability of an event occurring.	
	5. If you roll two six-sided dice, the chances of getting an even number are the same as the chances of getting an odd number.	

Before the lesson: Respond to items 6 and 7

6. Describe events that correspond to the probabilities below the boxes.

0	0.5	1

7. Which shape do you have the highest probability of landing on in the spinner? What is the probability of landing on the shape you chose?

After the lesson reflection: Which, if any, of your responses (statements 1–5) did you change after the lesson? Explain your reasoning for changing your responses. Would you change any of your answers to items 6 and 7? If so, why?

From Topics to "Top Picks"

What is it?

Inspired by Tomlinson's (2001) Interest Questionnaire, this tool helps students build a framework for learning by previewing upcoming topics; the tool also increases engagement by helping teachers assess and capitalize on student interests

What are the benefits of using this tool?

When kicking off a new unit, capturing students' interest is just as important as activating prior knowledge, since students learn better when they're interested in what they're studying. Unfortunately, with all of the competing demands that we face, student interest sometimes takes a back seat. The good news is that assessing students' interests relative to the content we're teaching doesn't need to be a difficult process. All that's required is a simple ranking system ("Rank these topics from most to least interesting") and time for students to assess their interest in the various unit topics. Even better news is that this tool does more than assess student interest—it also provides specific recommendations for capitalizing on and growing student interest in academic content.

What are the basic steps?

1. Make a list of the topics you plan to cover during an upcoming unit. Introduce the topic list to students and invite them to rank the topics from most to least interesting.

   Tip: Try to make topics more interesting by giving them creative titles. See Example 1 for a model.

2. Review the results of this student-interest survey. Use what you learn to inform and enhance classroom instruction. Specifically,

   - Look for ways to accommodate students' interests when designing lesson plans and assessment tasks. See the Six Ways to Accommodate Students' Interests box on page 99 for suggestions.

   - Encourage students to broaden their interest horizons by trying to make less interesting topics more appealing. See the Six Ways to Broaden Students' Interests box on page 99 for suggestions.

3. Repeat the survey at the end of the unit so that you and your students can see how (or if) their interests have changed.

How is this tool used in the classroom?

✔ To assess students' interests and use those interests to inform instructional decisions

✔ To help students build a big-picture framework of the learning to come

EXAMPLE 1: The social studies teacher who designed the interest survey below made an effort to carry the interest concept throughout his unit. He aimed to engage student interest by generating creative names for the unit topics (see Part 1 of the survey) and by setting up visually appealing learning centers where students could go to learn about each topic. He also tried to broaden students' interests by using a fun format (role-playing) to make the topic voted least interesting (Life as a Sailor) seem more exciting.

EXAMPLE 2: At the start of a gymnastics unit, a physical education teacher asked her students to rank the various events (balance beam, floor, etc.) from most to least interesting. As the unit progressed, she encouraged students to reevaluate their interests and devote the bulk of their practice time to their top three choices. Students were told that their end-of-unit grades would be largely determined by their performance in those same three events.

EXAMPLE 3: A first-grade teacher used the Shared Interest Groups variation described on page 99 to deepen her students' grasp of critical story elements. After introducing a particular story element (e.g., setting), she put different books on tables around the room, had students examine the books, and asked them to sit at the table with the book that seemed most interesting. The students at each table then read their selected books and discussed whatever story element they had been learning about ("The setting in our group's book is …").

STUDENT INTEREST SURVEY
The Age of Exploration

Next week, we'll start learning about the Age of Exploration. Before we begin, I am interested in finding out what you already know about this topic *and* what you're interested in learning. Please help me by completing this three-part survey.

PART 1: The topics in this unit are listed below. Please rank them from most to least interesting (1 = most interesting, 9 = least interesting).

If there are any topics that you wish we'd cover, go ahead and add them to the list!

___ *1492: The Time Was Right!*

___ *Christopher Columbus: Does the Man Make the Times, or Do the Times Make the Man?*

___ *All the Hot New Technology Trends*

___ *The Competition to Claim New Lands*

___ *Life as a Sailor: A Hard Way to Make a Living*

___ *The Conquistadors: A Tale of Bravery and Treachery*

___ *The First Expedition around the World*

___ *Through the Eyes of Native Americans: A Very Different Perspective*

___ *Explorers or Exploiters: What's Their Legacy?*

___ *Other:* _____

PART 2: Do you already know anything about the Age of Exploration? If so, please tell me about it on the back.

PART 3: Reevaluate your responses at the end of the unit to see how much you've learned and whether your interests have changed.

🌑 Teacher Talk

➜ The idea isn't to teach the topics students are interested in and skip the rest; the idea is to use students' interests to make instruction more engaging and effective. The teacher who created the survey in Example 1 covered all nine survey topics; she simply used students' interests to decide where to begin, which topics to emphasize, and which topics to make more interesting.

➜ To make this tool do double duty, design your survey to assess students' background knowledge as well as their interests; use the survey in Example 1 (see Part 2) as a model.

Six Ways to Accommodate Students' Interests

✓ Build choice into activities and assessment tasks so that students can work on things that interest them. ("Which of the dance styles we studied do you like best? Choreograph an original piece in that style.")

✓ Create enrichment centers where students can go to learn more about topics that interest them.

✓ Allocate more instructional time to topics that students select as their "top picks."

✓ Begin your unit with whatever topic students deem most interesting. ("Since most of you picked 'gunslingers and outlaws' as your top choice, we'll start there.")

✓ Develop—or invite students to develop—projects related to their interests.

✓ Organize students into Shared Interest Groups so that they can discuss, explore, or report on topics of interest with like-minded classmates. (The Shared Interest Groups variation is explained in more detail below; it's also illustrated in Example 3.)

Six Ways to Broaden Students' Interests

✓ Create interesting and provocative names for the topics you plan to teach. Use the survey in Example 1 as a model.

✓ Connect your content to students' interests, hobbies, and personal experiences.

✓ Present less interesting topics in more engaging and interactive ways (e.g., use a hands-on activity instead of a sit-still-and-listen lecture).

✓ Give students the option to acquire content knowledge that *doesn't* interest them in a way that does. ("Review the list of learning targets for the arteries/veins portion of our circulatory system unit. Then decide how you want to learn the relevant material. You can read your textbook, browse the Internet, dissect a frog, or watch a video.")

✓ Let students demonstrate their learning in a way that appeals to them. ("Summarize what you learned by building a model, creating a podcast, or writing a descriptive paragraph.")

✓ Pair up students with different interests. Challenge them to change each other's opinions.

Variation: Shared Interest Groups

The purpose of establishing Shared Interest Groups (Silver, Strong, & Perini, 2007) is to let students explore material that interests them with classmates who share their interests. To establish the groups, present students with a choice of books to read, topics to investigate, activities to complete, or problems to solve. Let them sample the different options (e.g., skim the first page of each book or read a one-sentence summary of each topic), choose the option that interests them, and work on their selected task with students who made the same choice. Whenever possible, have students discuss their choices as a class before breaking off into groups. ("Why does this interest me? Why did I pick this as opposed to that?") These kinds of discussions can give you insight into students' likes and dislikes. They can also serve to expand students' interests. ("Hmmm … that topic sounds more interesting than I thought. Maybe I should switch groups.")

One way to use this variation is to have students select their favorite topic from a student-interest survey and research that topic with like-minded classmates. These "expert groups" can then be called on during the course of the unit to provide insight into the topics they've pursued.

Questioning in Style

What is it?

A tool that identifies four different styles of questions that can be used to activate, deepen, and assess student learning

What are the benefits of using this tool?

Because no one style of question will appeal to all students or give us a complete picture of what students know and understand, it's important to vary the kinds of questions that we pose in our classrooms. This tool helps us broaden our questioning repertoires by identifying four different styles of questions that we should be asking at the beginning of—and throughout—our instructional sequences.

What are the basic steps?

1. Familiarize yourself with the four different styles of questions described below.

   RECALL questions ask students to *remember* and *describe* (facts, formulas, definitions, procedures).

   REASONING questions ask students to *think analytically* (interpret, explain, justify with evidence).

   CREATING questions ask students to *generate* similes, predictions, solutions, alternatives, etc.

   RELATING questions ask students to *connect* with the content on a personal level.

2. Familiarize students with the four different styles of questions. Explain that each type of question will require them to use a different but equally valuable style of thinking.

   Tip: Model the process for students by thinking aloud as you analyze different styles of questions, determine what kind of thinking each requires, and develop your response.

3. Generate all four styles of questions about a topic or text that you plan to teach (use the Question Stem Menu on p. 104 as a reference). Use the planning form on page 105 to record your questions.

   Tip: Think about questions that you could ask at different stages of your lesson (before, during, and after).

4. Pose some or all of these questions during an upcoming lesson. Adjust instruction based on the responses that you receive.

   Note: It's critical to get *all* students (not just the usual hand-raisers) involved in answering your questions. One way to achieve this goal is to have everyone jot down a response on paper before inviting anyone to share.

5. Survey students at the end of the lesson to determine which styles of questions (recall, reasoning, creating, relating) they're most and least comfortable answering. Help them develop the skills they'll need to answer all four styles of questions successfully.

How is this tool used in the classroom?

✔ To pose different types of questions at all stages of an instructional sequence

✔ To activate, develop, and assess relevant content knowledge

✔ To differentiate instruction and engage all learners

The examples that follow show how different styles of questions can be used to enhance or assess learning at various points in an instructional sequence. The words that tip you off to each question's style have been italicized for your reference.

EXAMPLE 1: A world history teacher uses Questioning in Style to design different types of questions and activities that will activate students' prior knowledge and help students build a strong conceptual framework at the beginning of new units. She designed the questions below to kick off a unit on the Renaissance. Each question, along with relevant resources, was posted at a learning station. Groups of students rotated around to each station, where they could develop new responses or expand on ideas left by previous student groups.

RECALL QUESTION	RELATING QUESTION
Examine this map. Notice the trade routes between Europe and the East as well as population density in areas of Europe. *List* at least two *facts* about population and/or trade during this time.	Renaissance thinkers believed in the "ideal" man and woman. *What do you think* would be the characteristics of the ideal person today?
REASONING QUESTION	**CREATING QUESTION**
"Renaissance" means "rebirth." Look at these three paintings from the Middle Ages and *compare* them to the three Renaissance paintings. If art is a reflection of the times, what can you *infer* about how people's ideas were changed or "reborn" between the Middle Ages and the Renaissance?	Leonardo da Vinci was the ultimate "Renaissance Man." Among his many accomplishments, da Vinci developed prototypes for modern inventions. Take a look at da Vinci's sketches for a helicopter and a parachute. Now imagine that you've found another of da Vinci's sketches for an invention. *How might* it look? *Create* a *sketch*.

EXAMPLE 2: Here's how a high school math teacher used the learning objectives for a lesson on arithmetic and geometric sequences to develop relevant questions in all four styles:

LEARNING OBJECTIVES
• Students will be able to define and visually represent arithmetic and geometric sequences.
• Students will be able to identify key similarities and differences between arithmetic and geometric sequences.
• Students will be able to assess their own learning process.

RECALL QUESTION	RELATING QUESTION
Define an arithmetic sequence in your own words. *Define* a geometric sequence in your own words.	Think about *your own* learning process for this lesson. *Would you say your* learning has been more arithmetic or geometric? Why do *you feel* this way?
REASONING QUESTION	**CREATING QUESTION**
Compare an arithmetic sequence with a geometric sequence. What are two *similarities*? What are two *differences*?	*Create* two icons—one to *represent* arithmetic sequences and one to *represent* geometric sequences. What makes your icons good *representations* of each type of sequence?

EXAMPLE 3: A first-grade teacher poses different styles of questions during story time to keep her students engaged, check their understanding of what she's read, and target core reading standards. Some of the questions that she developed for William Steig's *Sylvester and the Magic Pebble* are shown below.

RECALL QUESTION	RELATING QUESTION
• Can you *retell* what happened so far in your own words?	• *If you were Sylvester*, would you use the pebble again?
REASONING QUESTION	**CREATING QUESTION**
• Does the author want us to feel happy or sad when we read this story? What *evidence* in the story can you use to *support* your choice?	• *Can you think of another* (better) wish that Sylvester could have made to escape from the lion?

Variation: Other Questioning Frameworks

Varying the types of questions we ask students is an important instructional goal, whether we use Questioning in Style or not. In fact, there are a variety of frameworks that teachers use to design better questions, from Webb's Depth of Knowledge model to Bloom's Taxonomy. The questioning framework below, presented in *Classroom Instruction That Works* (Second Edition), highlights two types of questions that engage higher-order thinking.

Question Type	Description	Examples
Inferential	Requires students to call up prior knowledge to address missing information in relation to events, things, people, actions, or states of being	• *Events:* Take a look at this drawing of a Lenni Lenape Gamwing Festival. During what season do you think this festival took place? What evidence supports your answer? • *Things:* What do you think catapults were used for? How do they work? • *Actions:* We have learned how to add and subtract fractions. But what do you think will happen when we multiply fractions together? Will they get bigger or smaller? • *States of being:* Why do volcanoes sometimes erupt? What's going on underneath the surface?
Analytic	Builds critical thinking skills, including analyzing errors, constructing support, and analyzing perspectives	• *Analyzing errors:* Is there anything in the commercial that might be misleading? If so, how is it misleading? • *Constructing support:* Agree or disagree—caring for an animal is more difficult than caring for a plant. What evidence can you use to support your position? • *Analyzing perspectives:* What is the author's rationale for calling for no new development on Lake Kemah? What other perspectives are there, and what's the reasoning behind them?

Another well-known questioning framework is found in the reading strategy called Question-Answer-Relationships, or QAR (Raphael, 1986). QAR teaches students how to identify and answer four types of questions:

• "Right there" questions are answered directly in the text; students need to find and state the answer.

   For example: What are the self-evident truths presented in the Declaration of Independence?

- "Think & search" questions have answers that are found in the text but require students to gather the relevant information from different parts of the text.

  For example: What do the authors argue is the purpose of government?

- "Author & me" questions have answers that are not found directly in the text; students combine their background knowledge with text information to develop a response.

  For example: In what ways does the Declaration of Independence affect your safety and happiness?

- "On my own" questions have answers that are not found in the text; students must use background knowledge to construct a response.

  For example: What are some issues we are experiencing today that relate to the Declaration of Independence?

🔘 Teacher Talk

➔ Before using this tool for the first time, assess the "stylishness" of your *existing* questioning repertoire by recording how many of each style of question you ask during a given class period. Notice any patterns? If you favor certain styles over others, aim for a more balanced approach.

➔ Prepare students to be successful by modeling the kinds of thinking and responses that different question types require (e.g., show them how to respond successfully to a comparison question).

➔ Style-based questions can be used for a number of different purposes (e.g., to hook students' interest, help students access their prior knowledge, encourage reflection)—and at all stages of the instructional process. The ultimate goal is to pose different styles of questions throughout your lessons/units.

A Unit Blueprint Organizer like the one below can help you achieve this goal. Use it to map out specific questions that you can ask to meet different purposes during different phases of an upcoming unit. Here is how a math teacher did this for a unit on long division:

PURPOSE OF INSTRUCTION	QUESTIONS THAT ADDRESS THIS PURPOSE	STYLE
Establish purpose, spark interest, activate prior knowledge.	How can you make a complex problem easier to solve?	Reasoning
Present and help students engage with/acquire the content.	Watch as I solve these two problems on the board. What are the steps in long division? Describe them.	Recall
Help students review, practice, and deepen their learning.	What happens if you change or add a digit to the divisor or dividend? Experiment. Notice any patterns?	Creating
Challenge students to demonstrate and apply their learning.	Two of the long-division problems on the board are incorrect. Can you locate and explain the errors?	Reasoning
Help students reflect on and celebrate their learning.	How did you feel about long division at the start of the unit? How do you feel now?	Relating

Question Stem Menu: Four Different Styles of Questions

RECALL QUESTIONS

ask students to *remember facts and procedures*:

✓ Recall facts and formulas

✓ Observe and describe

✓ Locate, organize, or sequence

✓ Perform procedures/calculations with accuracy

✓ Define, restate, or summarize

Sample question stems:

- Who? What? When? Where?
- What do you know or remember about __?
- Can you list the key points/facts/details from __?
- What are the characteristics or properties of __?
- Can you put these __ in order based on __?
- What happened first? Second? Third?
- Can you show me how to __?
- Can you describe __?
- Can you define, retell, or restate __?
- Can you locate or give an example of __?
- Can you calculate __?

RELATING QUESTIONS

ask students to *relate on a personal level*:

✓ Share their feelings, reactions, and opinions

✓ Draw connections to their own lives

✓ Assist or advise other people

✓ Put themselves in someone else's shoes

✓ Consider personal preferences and values

Sample question stems:

- How did you feel about __? React to __?
- Where do you stand on __?
- What do you think of __'s choice?
- What was most/least __ (interesting, difficult, etc.)?
- How is __ relevant to your own life? To society?
- Have you experienced something like __ before?
- How would you advise this person or character?
- How might this look from the perspective of __?
- If you were this person or character, how would you feel? What would you do?
- Which of these __ is most important to you?

REASONING QUESTIONS

ask students to *reason, analyze, and explain*:

✓ Compare and contrast

✓ Explain, reason, or understand why

✓ Give reasons, evidence, and examples

✓ Analyze, interpret, evaluate, or conclude

✓ Classify or categorize

Sample question stems:

- What are the key similarities and/or differences?
- Are __ and __ more similar or different? Why?
- What are the causes and/or effects of __?
- Why __? What is the reason for __? Explain.
- How would you support, prove, or disprove __?
- Do you agree or disagree with __? Why?
- Does __ make sense? Explain your reasoning.
- What do you think __ means? Why?
- What can you conclude or infer from __?
- What are the central ideas or themes?
- What connections or patterns do you see?
- What larger category/concept does __ belong to?

CREATING QUESTIONS

ask students to *create and explore possibilities*:

✓ Speculate (what if?), hypothesize, or predict

✓ Generate and explore alternatives

✓ Create or design something original

✓ Represent concepts visually/symbolically

✓ Develop and explore similes

Sample question stems:

- What if __? What might happen if __?
- How might __?
- Can you make a prediction about __?
- How many ways can you __?
- Can you think of another __ (explanation, solution, ending, strategy, hypothesis)?
- What other perspectives should we consider?
- Can you create or invent an original __?
- Can you devise a plan/procedure to __?
- What comes to mind when you think of __?
- How can you represent __ visually or symbolically?
- How is __ like a __?

Lesson or unit topic: _____

Questioning in Style Planning Form

RECALL QUESTIONS

ask students to *remember facts and procedures*:

✓ Recall facts and formulas

✓ Observe and describe

✓ Locate, organize, or sequence

✓ Perform procedures/calculations with accuracy

✓ Define, restate, or summarize

My questions:

RELATING QUESTIONS

ask students to *relate on a personal level*:

✓ Share their feelings, reactions, and opinions

✓ Draw connections to their own lives

✓ Assist or advise other people

✓ Put themselves in someone else's shoes

✓ Consider personal preferences and values

My questions:

REASONING QUESTIONS

ask students to *reason, analyze, and explain*:

✓ Compare and contrast

✓ Explain, reason, or understand why

✓ Give reasons, evidence, and examples

✓ Analyze, interpret, evaluate, or conclude

✓ Classify or categorize

My questions:

CREATING QUESTIONS

ask students to *create and explore possibilities*:

✓ Speculate (what if?), hypothesize, or predict

✓ Generate and explore alternatives

✓ Create or design something original

✓ Represent concepts visually/symbolically

✓ Develop and explore similes

My questions:

Before, During, After (BDA)

What is it?

A tool that helps students develop high-quality responses to classroom questions—whenever those questions are asked

What are the benefits of using this tool?

How often do teachers ask higher-order-thinking questions but get lower-level-thinking responses? One reason for this disconnect is that good responses depend on what teachers and students do before a question is posed and after an initial response is developed. Before, During, After outlines a three-phase thinking process that helps to increase student engagement and depth of thinking during classroom questioning. The three phases are preparing students to think BEFORE the question, posing the question in a way that invites students to explore possible responses (DURING), and processing student responses through probing, paraphrasing, and the use of varied classroom participation techniques (AFTER).

What are the basic steps?

1. Develop a question that you want students to think about deeply.

    Note: It is important to have a clear purpose for your question: Why are you asking it? What do you hope students will learn/discover by exploring it? How will you assess student responses?

2. Prepare students for deep thinking BEFORE posing the question by providing context and piquing student interest. See Teacher Talk for tips on how to provide context and increase interest.

3. Pose the question to the class. Make sure all students understand the question, and provide wait time DURING the process to encourage students to think about possible responses.

4. Make students' covert thinking overt by having students generate their initial thoughts on paper.

    Tip: Have all students set aside a dedicated thinking journal or learning log at the beginning of the year as a place to collect and record their thoughts.

5. Allow students to share and compare their initial thoughts with a partner. Encourage students to listen to each other's responses carefully, look for similarities and differences in their thinking, and generate additional thoughts or select the best idea.

6. Invite students to share their ideas as a class. Call on a wide variety of students to ensure high levels of participation.

7. Use probing questions, paraphrasing, and participation techniques to help students evaluate and expand their thinking AFTER they share their initial responses.

    *   *Probe:* What is your evidence? How do you know that's so? And you think that because?
    *   *Paraphrase:* Do I hear you saying …? Do you mean …?
    *   *Participation techniques:* How many people agree? Who has a different point of view?

How is this tool used in the classroom?

✔ To train students to think deeply before, while, and after responding to questions

✔ To make the questioning process active

✔ To deepen responses through probing and participation techniques

EXAMPLE: A high school English class is reading Shakespeare's *Romeo and Juliet*. The teacher uses the BDA process to help students think about and discuss a soliloquy in which Juliet expresses her love for Romeo.

BEFORE: The teacher begins by asking students if they know what the word *naïve* means and if any of them has ever been accused of being naïve. After drawing on students' experiences, she reads Juliet's soliloquy aloud. Then, she poses two related questions: "Is Juliet naïve? Do you agree or disagree that this soliloquy reveals that Juliet is naïve?"

DURING: The teacher gives students time to think and jot down their initial ideas in their learning logs. Students compare their ideas with a neighbor. In pairs, students must use textual evidence to decide whether they agree or disagree with the premise that Juliet is naïve.

AFTER: The teacher initiates a whole-class discussion in which students share and justify their ideas using the text.

Teacher: So what do we think?

Student 1: I agree with the statement. Juliet is naïve.

Teacher: What evidence in the text leads you to believe that?

Student 1: Well, it's the way she talks. It's so gushy.

Teacher: How many of you agree?

Student 2: I agree. It sounds like an obsession, like she's a teenager with a bad crush.

Teacher: Can you give me an example?

Student 2: "Take him and cut him out in little stars,

And he will make the face of heaven so fine

That all the world will be in love with night

And pay no worship to the garish sun."

Teacher: Does anyone disagree with the idea that Juliet is just an infatuated teenager?

Student 3: I disagree. I mean, just listen to the way she can express herself. Her ability to express herself is incredible. It's not young-sounding to me.

Teacher: Interesting. What language in particular are you referring to?

🔆 Teacher Talk

→ To better prepare students for the question, provide background information or a context that will make the question more meaningful and interesting when you pose it.

Sample language: Have you ever heard of a mixed blessing? It means that something is both positive and negative at the same time. Take cars, for example. They get us where we want to go whenever we want. But they also create huge amounts of pollution, and car accidents cause thousands of deaths every year. Today, we'll be exploring a different mixed blessing: fracking.

→ To increase student interest in your question, consider how you can use the "Eight Cs of Engagement" (Silver & Perini, 2010) to make your question especially intriguing. Some of the Cs, along with questions that engage these Cs, include

- **C**URIOSITY: Have you ever wondered why some animals hibernate and others don't? What's going on? Why do some animals hibernate?

- **C**ONTROVERSY: Should street artists like Banksy be studied alongside masters like Monet and Picasso?

- **C**REATIVITY: What if Thomas Edison had never lived? How would your life be different?

- Personal **C**ONNECTIONS: Have you ever rebelled against something? When is rebellion justified?

→ Posing a question is different than asking a question. Posing is an invitation to explore possible ideas and responses. To help emphasize this point in the classroom, explain to students that the root of the word *question* is *quest*. A quest is a journey, a search for truth. Instead of questioning, invite the class to go "questing."

→ Pausing several seconds after asking a question to give students time to think before responding and to refine their thinking is called wait time. Research indicates that when students have more time to think about their responses before they actually respond, they tend to participate more in class, think more deeply, and generate more thoughtful responses (Rowe, 1972; Tobin, 1987). Of course, it's not just the wait time that counts; it's also what students do with the time. By inviting students to write down their initial thoughts, you help them get their ideas out in the open; by allowing them to share their ideas with another student, you help them test and refine their ideas—and gain new perspectives.

→ The probing and participation prompts/questions below enhance student discussions. Notice that they encourage thinking rather than looking for correct answers.

- Share your thinking.
- What are your ideas?
- Can you give me an example?
- That's an interesting way to think. How did you arrive at that idea?
- What's behind your idea? Can you explain your reasoning?
- Does anyone have a different idea?
- How many agree? How many disagree? Who's unsure?

Start with a Story

What is it?

A tool that provides a range of ways to use narrative advance organizers (in the form of stories) to frame content, build intrigue, and prepare students for new learning

What are the benefits of using this tool?

All throughout history, humans have used stories to engage and teach. Why? Because stories, with their sensory language, attention to details, and focus on human experiences and activities, light up the brain, activating multiple regions at once (Paul, 2012). It is with this unique power in mind that the authors of *Classroom Instruction That Works* (Second Edition) recommend the use of narrative advance organizers, or stories, to engage students' interest and activate their prior knowledge at the outset of a learning experience (Dean et al., 2012). Start with a Story provides teachers with a variety of ways to use stories to capture students' attention, build deeper understanding, and prime students for the learning to come.

What are the basic steps?

1. Review a lesson or unit you're about to teach. Ask yourself the following questions: How can I prepare students for the learning to come? What elements, concepts, themes, or ideas might I want to introduce or preview before I begin teaching?

2. Think about a story that would help you introduce or preview the elements/themes you identified in Step 1. Among other things, you might select a personal story, a real-world story, a short story or fable, or an allegory (see the examples on pp. 110–111 for ideas).

3. Present the story to students.

   Note: If you're using the story to preview a series of ideas or events that you want students to retain (see, for example, the allegory in Example 5), you may want to have students jot down or sketch those ideas as you present.

4. Help students process the story. Depending on your goals, processing might involve anything from reviewing the story's message to extracting key ideas to speculating about the story's relevance to the upcoming lesson.

5. Connect the knowledge/understandings that students gained in Step 4 to the upcoming lesson.

How is this tool used in the classroom?

✔ To capture student interest

✔ To activate students' prior knowledge

✔ To provide a foundation that students can build future learning upon

The examples below illustrate some of the many different ways teachers can "start with a story."*

EXAMPLE 1: Start with a fable

A second-grade teacher uses Aesop's "The Four Oxen and the Lion," which teaches the importance of teamwork, to prepare students for a cooperative learning lesson. Students listen to the fable, explore its central lesson, and discuss how they might apply this lesson to the activity they're about to begin.

EXAMPLE 2: Start with a real-world story

A STEM teacher opens a unit called "Why Do Things Break—And What Can Engineers Do About It?" by showing students a video of the Kansas City Hyatt skywalk collapse, which killed over a hundred people. The teacher's goal in using the Hyatt disaster as his opening "story" is to get students interested in what they're about to learn by helping them appreciate the dire, real-world consequences that a simple engineering error can have.

After students watch the video, the teacher asks them to speculate about what went wrong. He then bridges the story of the Hyatt collapse to the upcoming unit by telling students that they'll work in teams to figure out what happened, why it happened, and what engineers can do to ensure that tragedies like it don't happen in the future.

EXAMPLE 3: Start with a personal story

To help his students understand the real-world relevance of a skill he's about to teach them (calculating the area of an irregular trapezoid), a math teacher tells them a personal story about the time he decided to build a stone patio in his backyard. He explains that knowing how to calculate the area of the patio was critical, so that he didn't waste money buying more stone than he needed or buy too little and have to go back to the store for more. To bridge the story to the content of the lesson, the teacher puts a sketch of his patio on the board and uses that sketch to explain and model how to calculate the area of an irregular trapezoid.

EXAMPLE 4: Start by having students share personal stories

Prior to beginning a lesson on the great female pharaoh Hatshepsut, an elementary teacher asked students to think of a time in their own lives when they accomplished something that others said they couldn't. After students share their personal stories, the teacher helps them look for big ideas and then bridges those ideas to the learning to come: "We have some great ideas about what it's like to accomplish something when people think we can't. Today, we'll be learning about a great pharaoh who overcame unbelievable odds to accomplish great things for her people. During the lesson, let's pay attention to how our experiences relate to Hatshepsut's."

EXAMPLE 5: Start with an allegory

Over the years, a high school history teacher has found that allegories are great vehicles for helping students get a handle on complex concepts and topics. Before beginning a lesson on the Protestant Reformation, she uses the allegory on the next page to familiarize students with key players and

---

*The lessons in Examples 3 and 5 are adapted with permission from the work of Dean et al. (2012, p. 59) and Heather Rippeteau of Manhattan/Hunter Science High School in New York City, respectively.

principles. Notice how the characters in the allegory represent the key players in the Reformation (Papa Cy = Papacy; Brother Marty = Martin Luther)—and how the plot presents the story of the Reformation, but in a simple way that's easy to follow. Because students are able to follow the story, they are able to follow the actual lesson once the teacher presents it. Having a simple framework into which they can slot the actual content makes that content easier for them to remember and retrieve.

Papa Cy was a great father; all of his children admired and obeyed him.

Every night after dinner, Papa Cy would sit down with all of his family and tell them stories from a book that only he was allowed to read.

The family was captivated by Papa Cy and wanted his affection.

The most devoted family members would give Papa Cy gifts at the end of each dinner to earn his affection.

One night at the end of dinner, Brother Marty, who rarely gave Papa Cy gifts, asked him why he gave all of his attention to those who gave him gifts when there were other children who needed attention.

The brothers and sisters were shocked! How could one of them question their Papa Cy? The devoted gift-givers defended Papa Cy, but Brother Marty pressed on: "Don't those of us who do not have gifts to give still deserve your attention? Are we not still your children? Shouldn't we focus on being good family members more than on giving gifts?"

Brother Marty continued asking questions: "We all love the stories in the book, but why can't anyone else read it to the family?"

As he kept asking questions, some of the children stopped defending Papa Cy and began to agree with Brother Marty. They moved to Brother Marty's side of the dinner table.

With the support of some of his siblings, Brother Marty made a list of changes that he thought the family should make to improve their relationships—no more exchanging affection for gifts, more attention from Papa Cy for all children, and everyone gets a chance to read from the book.

Papa Cy still had the support of many of his children who did not agree with Brother Marty's way of thinking. So Brother Marty and some of his siblings left to build a new home based on Brother Marty's ideals.

🌐 Teacher Talk

➡ Be sure you're not telling stories for the sake of telling stories. The stories you select should be linked to your content and have a clear purpose (e.g., generating interest, activating background knowledge, previewing upcoming topics, or highlighting real-world applications).

➡ Opening a lesson by having students share personal stories is a great way to promote engagement and get students personally connected to the content they're about to learn. Giving students "think of a time" frames (see Example 4, p. 110) is an easy way to help them access relevant background knowledge (e.g., "Think of a time when you used fractions to settle a dispute" or "Think of a time when being precise made a difference").

➡ When searching for stories, don't limit yourself to traditional print sources; the Internet is chock full of story-driven video clips that can help you set up learning for just about any lesson or unit.

S-O-S Graphic Organizers

What is it?

A tool that shows how using graphic organizers before, during, and after instruction can save our students from drowning in a sea of information

What are the benefits of using this tool?

Many students feel overwhelmed in our classrooms because they don't know what's important to pay attention to or how information fits together to form a big picture. Providing students with an "organized conceptual framework" (Dean et al., 2012, p. 51) in the form of a graphic organizer can help, but only if we use organizers strategically. S-O-S Graphic Organizers outlines a three-phase process for maximizing the use of organizers in the classroom: The teacher **S**hows students how the information they're about to learn is structured *before* instruction begins, students **O**rganize the information they acquire *during* learning, and students use their organizers to review and **S**ummarize key points *after* learning.

What are the basic steps?

1. Review the content for a lesson you're about to teach. Think: What do I want students to know and understand? What are the key topics/concepts/details? What is the overarching structure of the material I plan to present (e.g., topic/subtopic, chronological sequence, cause/effect)?

2. Create or select a graphic organizer (see pp. 116–117 for options) that reflects the structure you identified in Step 1. Customize the organizer as needed to fit your content. Then, add a title or focusing question that will help students understand what they're expected to learn.

   Note: Graphic organizers can be designed around texts or activities as well as presentations.

3. Prepare students for the learning to come by walking them through the organizer. **S**how them how the presentation will be structured, the kinds of information you want them to focus on, and the way(s) the organizer highlights relationships between individual chunks of information.

4. Present the content one chunk at a time. Instruct students to record key points in the appropriate sections of their organizers. This will help them **O**rganize the information that they acquire.

   Tip: Teach students to take accurate, complete, and concise notes by modeling the process for them. Take notes on a blank organizer as you present, and have students either transfer your notes to their organizers *or* take their own notes, compare their notes with yours, and revise as needed.

5. Pause after presenting each chunk of information—and then again at the end—to help students review and process the information on their organizers. Posing different styles of questions about that information (see the Questioning in Style tool, pp. 100–105, for details) is a great way to do this.

6. Have students **S**ummarize what they learned using their completed organizers as a guide. Explain that their summaries should reflect the same general structure as their organizers (e.g., if their organizer introduces, compares, and contrasts two things, so should their written summary).

How is this tool used in the classroom?

✔ To provide students with a strong conceptual framework for upcoming learning

✔ To focus teaching and learning on the most important ideas

✔ To model and help students develop good note-taking behaviors

✔ To promote retention and understanding of critical content via questioning and summarizing

EXAMPLE 1: A middle school math teacher created the Topic-Subtopic Organizer shown below to accompany a presentation she planned to deliver about the family of three-dimensional solids known as polyhedrons. Her goal was for students to develop a strong conceptual understanding of the polyhedrons they'd be studying before they learned how to calculate surface area and volume.

What Are Polyhedrons and What Do They Look Like?

Polyhedrons
Definition:

Prisms	Pyramids
Definition:	Definition:

Triangular Prisms	Rectangular Prisms	Triangular Pyramids	Rectangular Pyramids
Critical attributes	Critical attributes	Critical attributes	Critical attributes
Real-world examples	Real-world examples	Real-world examples	Real-world examples
Sketch	Sketch	Sketch	Sketch

The teacher walked students through the organizer before beginning her presentation, calling their attention to the types of polyhedrons they'd be learning about and how those polyhedrons are related to one another and classified. She explained that students would be expected not just to understand these important relationships but also to sketch each solid accurately, identify its critical attributes, and provide real-world examples.

The teacher stopped regularly during her presentation to let students record the relevant information in their organizers. She then encouraged them to check their notes against hers and make any necessary corrections before moving on.

For homework, the teacher asked students to review their organizers and to use them to write a summary of what they learned. She explained that their summaries should reflect not just the notes they took about each individual solid but also the relationships that exist between the various solids they learned about. She also reminded them to use their organizers as a guide when structuring their summaries. ("Introduce and explain the largest family of solids first: the polyhedrons. Next, discuss the two types of polyhedrons you learned about—prisms and pyramids. After that …")

Finally, to ensure that students addressed all the vocabulary terms from the organizer in their summaries, she instructed them to underline those terms in their summaries. The summary that one student developed using his completed organizer as a guide is shown here:

<u>Polyhedrons</u> are <u>3D</u> solids with faces that are all polygons. There are many different kinds of polyhedrons, but two common types are prisms and pyramids.

A <u>prism</u> is a type of polyhedron with two identical and parallel polygon bases. The shape of those bases determines the type of prism you have—for example, a triangular prism or a rectangular prism. A <u>rectangular prism</u> has two rectangular bases and six total faces. Things like bricks and a Rubik's Cube are rectangular prisms. <u>Triangular prisms</u> have two triangular bases and five total faces. A triangular tent is shaped like a triangular prism.

Another type of polyhedron is the <u>pyramid</u>. Pyramids are 3D solids that have one base and triangular faces. The shape of the base determines the type of pyramid you're talking about, be it a rectangular pyramid or a triangular one. <u>Rectangular pyramids</u> look like the Egyptian pyramids. They have one base shaped like a rectangle and four sides shaped like triangles. <u>Triangular pyramids</u> have a triangular base and three triangular sides. Four-sided dice are examples of triangular pyramids.

EXAMPLE 2: A third-grade teacher recognizes that students often think spiders are insects, and he wants to help them understand the difference. To do this, he asks them to research similarities and differences between spiders and insects on the Internet—and to collect their notes on a Top Hat Comparison Organizer. (One student's completed organizer is shown at the right.) He shows students how the organizer has places for recording similarities and differences—and explains that they should record comparable types of information in the same row when completing the differences section. (See, for example, how *6 legs* and *8 legs* appear across from each other in the organizer.)

For homework, he challenges students to write a comparison paragraph that summarizes what they learned. Because many of his students struggle to write coherent summaries from scratch, he scaffolds the process by giving them this simple comparative writing frame to use as a model:

How Are Insects and Spiders Similar and Different?

DIFFERENCES

Insects — 6 legs, 3 body parts -head -thorax -abdomen; Many have antenae for feeling and smelling; some have wings; can't spin webs

Spiders — 8 legs, 2 body parts -head -thorax; No antenae; No wings; Many spin webs

SIMILARITIES — Both have exoskeleton - skeleton on the outside. Both lay eggs. Both can be posionous

---

I am comparing _____ and _____ .
Although _____ and _____ are different, they are alike in some important ways. For example, _____ and _____ both _____ . There are also some interesting differences between _____ and _____ .
For example, _____ .
[Concluding sentence] _____ .

EXAMPLE 3: Prior to having students read a textbook passage about the Cuban Missile Crisis, a teacher used the Episode Organizer below to review the essential elements of any important historical event (time, place, causes/effects, important players, individual incidents, etc.). She reminded students to pay attention to each of these elements while reading and then make notes in the appropriate boxes of their organizers. After checking their organizers against hers and making any necessary revisions, students used their completed organizers to help them summarize the key elements from the original passage in their own words.

The What, Why, and How of the Cuban Missile Crisis

Sequence of specific incidents

EXAMPLE 4: After realizing that none of the standard graphic organizer structures would meet her needs, a primary-grade teacher got creative and designed an organizer from scratch (see below). She used this organizer to show students how they could make a basic sentence more interesting and beautiful by adding different kinds of descriptive words. ("In the same way we add different kinds of flowers to a garden to make it more interesting and beautiful, we can make basic sentences more interesting and beautiful by adding different kinds of descriptive words—things like adjectives, adverbs, and prepositional phrases.") She reviewed the different parts of speech on the organizer and their functions within a sentence. She then showed students how to "grow" fabulous sentences using the organizer as a guide. For homework, students grew sentences of their own.

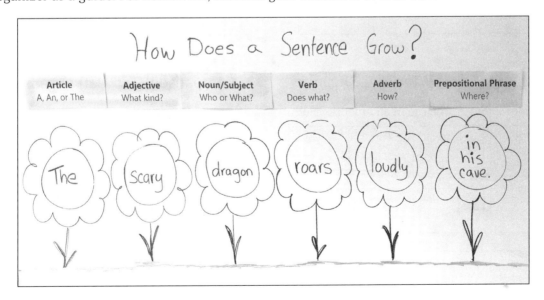

A Potpourri of Graphic Organizers

Topic-Subtopic Organizer

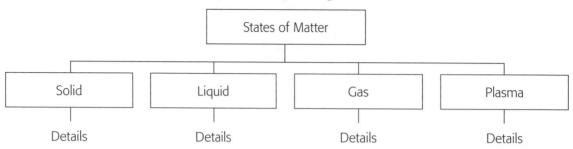

States of Matter

| Solid | Liquid | Gas | Plasma |

Details   Details   Details   Details

Matrix Organizer

	Impressionism	Post-Impressionism	Expressionism
Themes			
Stylistic Innovations			
Major Artists			
Key Works			

Story Maps

Version 1

Horton Hears a Who by Dr. Seuss

| Characters | Setting |

| Beginning | → | Middle | → | End |

Version 2

"The Birth-Mark" by Nathaniel Hawthorne

Someone…	Somewhere…
Wanted…	But…
So…	Then…
Therefore…	Finally…

Time Sequence / Timeline Organizer

Harriet Tubman: The Life of an American Hero

Date	Date	Date	Date
Event	Event	Event	Event
Significance	Significance	Significance	Significance

Comparison (Top Hat) Organizer

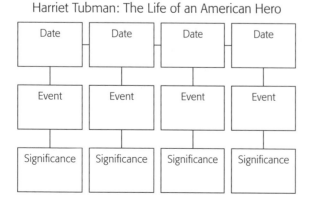

Key Differences

| Surface Area | Volume |

Similarities

Episode Organizer

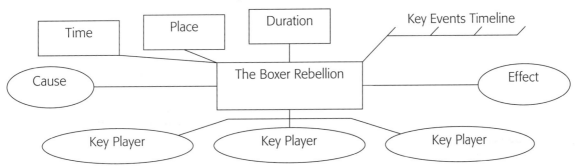

Time · Place · Duration · Key Events Timeline

Cause · The Boxer Rebellion · Effect

Key Player · Key Player · Key Player

Chronological Sequence Organizer

How to conduct a hair strand test

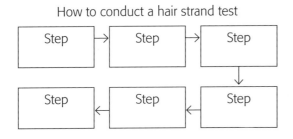

Step → Step → Step

Step ← Step ← Step

Principle/Generalization Organizer

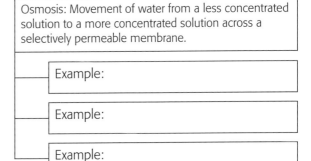

Osmosis: Movement of water from a less concentrated solution to a more concentrated solution across a selectively permeable membrane.

Example:

Example:

Example:

Concept Definition Map

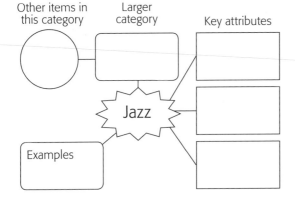

Other items in this category · Larger category · Key attributes

Jazz

Examples

Cycle Organizer

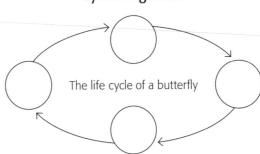

The life cycle of a butterfly

Cause/Effect Organizer

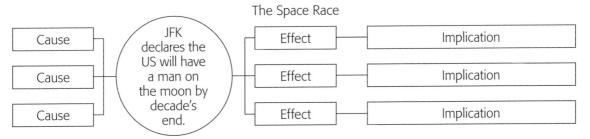

The Space Race

Cause · Cause · Cause

JFK declares the US will have a man on the moon by decade's end.

Effect — Implication
Effect — Implication
Effect — Implication

Note that Cause/Effect Organizers can be designed to focus on the causes behind an event, the effects of the event, or both, as in this example.

🔆 Teacher Talk

➔ Students are more likely to appreciate and use a tool well when they understand its purpose—particularly if that purpose is to help them. For this reason, it's worth taking the time to tell students how using graphic organizers before, during, and after instruction will benefit them.

Sample language: Organizers help you determine what to pay attention to by highlighting the big ideas BEFORE instruction begins. They give you an organized framework for taking notes DURING instruction. And they make it easy to review and summarize key points AFTER instruction.

➔ This tool supports a number of recommendations from different chapters in *Classroom Instruction That Works* (Second Edition). Specifically, it supports these recommendations:

- Introduce graphic organizers before a lesson, for the purpose of previewing and preparing students for the learning to come (Chapter 4, p. 51).

- Use graphic organizers as a means of having students represent and organize information both linguistically and nonlinguistically (Chapter 5, pp. 66–67).

- Model the process of good note taking by providing teacher-generated notes for students to look at and learn from—and note-taking templates that call students' attention to important information (Chapter 6, pp. 90–91).

- Help students understand and use the critical elements of common organizational structures (e.g., topic/subtopic) to summarize important information (Chapter 6, p. 83).

➔ Don't feel boxed in by the organizer structures featured on pages 116–117. If none of those structures meets your needs, design an organizer from scratch as the teacher in Example 4 (p. 115) did.

➔ Use your organizer to outline your presentation before delivering it. This will help you present your material in an organized way that's aligned to the organizer. It will also let you determine whether your organizer needs to be modified in any way before using it. (Do you need to add/remove/reorganize boxes? Insert headings or titles for clarity? Make other changes?)

➔ Keep students oriented during a lesson or presentation by referring to the organizer as you go. ("Now, let's look at the second type of reptile on our organizers.") Help students see how individual bits of information fit together by using appropriate organizing and connecting words. In a presentation about a sequence of events, for example, you might use words like *first*, *next*, and *after that*. If you were comparing two items, words like *similarly* or *in contrast* might help.

➔ Knowing how to use graphic organizers isn't something that comes naturally. For this reason, it's important to familiarize students with the various organizer structures on pages 116–117 (What kind of information is each one designed to collect? What kinds of relationships does each one highlight? What topics/types of material might each kind of organizer lend itself to?) and practice using them as a class before asking students to take notes on the organizers independently. Dean et al. (2012) advise using familiar content when introducing each type of organizer "so students can focus on learning to use the graphic organizer without having to worry about new content" (p. 67).

Power Previewing

What is it?

A tool that prepares students to better handle rigorous texts by teaching them to skim those texts in advance using specially designed visual organizers

What are the benefits of using this tool?

Skimming a text is a practical, but often overlooked, technique for preparing students for new learning. When used well in the classroom, skimming helps students activate prior knowledge, organize information, and build a conceptual framework that can support new learning (Dean et al., 2012). Power Previewing is a tool that teaches students how to skim a text strategically by searching for textual cues, making predictions, and determining how a text is structured. The tool also helps students become more proficient readers, as reading research consistently shows that the best readers preview texts actively before reading (Pressley, 2006).

What are the basic steps?

1. Distribute copies of the Power Previewing Organizer for nonfiction texts (p. 122).

   Note: This tool was designed with nonfiction texts in mind, but you can use it with works of fiction as well. See Teacher Talk for details; see page 123 for a fiction-specific organizer.

2. Use sample texts (e.g., articles, textbook passages) to explain and model the Power Previewing steps outlined below. Thoroughly review the "where to look for important information" section of the organizer so that students know where to look and what to pay attention to while skimming.

   Prowl for clues: Look for important information as you skim through the text.

   Pencil in key information: Record what you learn about the text's content and organization.

   Pry open your memory: Ask yourself if anything in the text looks or sounds familiar.

   Personalize the preview: Identify aspects of the text that you find interesting or challenging.

   Predict what the text will be about: Use what you learn by skimming to make some predictions.

3. Have students use their organizers to preview a text that you or they select. Intervene as needed to help them make the most of the previewing process. Among other things, you can

   - Ask guiding and focusing questions (e.g., "Do you see any recurring themes in this section?").
   - Suggest strategies for addressing specific challenges (e.g., vocabulary strategies if challenging terms are the issue or strategies for figuring out what's important enough to write down).
   - Encourage students to check their predictions when they read the text "for real."

4. Help students reflect on and learn from the previewing process. See Teacher Talk for ideas.

5. Remind students to use the Power Previewing strategy on their own, not just when you say so. To facilitate the process, post the Power Previewing steps in the classroom and give students copies of blank organizers to keep in their notebooks.

How is this tool used in the classroom?

✔ To help students use skimming as a way to preview new learning

✔ To develop active and engaged readers who understand and enjoy what they read

EXAMPLE: The organizer below highlights the different kinds of information that a student might notice and comment on while previewing a nonfiction text (e.g., how the text is organized, recurring terms/ideas, themes with ties to previous units, items in illustrations and sidebars).

Where to look for important information:

- Titles, headings, and subheadings
- Opening paragraphs or introduction
- First and last sentence of each paragraph
- Summary paragraphs or lists of key points
- End-of-chapter or start-of-chapter questions
- Bold, italicized, and underlined information
- Circled, boxed, or highlighted information
- Graphs, figures, tables, charts, and maps
- Pictures, cartoons, and photographs
- Captions and figure legends

What are you previewing? What is it about (topic)?

A textbook chapter about Mesopotamia

How is the text structured or organized?

The chapter has three sections:
1) Sumer
2) Akkad and Babylon
3) Contributions and inventions

What else did you notice or learn while skimming? What information and ideas seem to be important?

- *There is a timeline with major periods in Mesopotamia.*
- *There is a focus on key figures: Gilgamesh, Sargon II, and Hammurabi.*

Does anything look familiar or relate to something you've seen, read, learned about, or experienced?

- *The subsection on city—states reminds me of Ancient Greece.*

What seems interesting?

- *The section on inventions seems interesting because it seems like some major inventions like the wheel and the calendar were invented by the Mesopotamians.*

What seems confusing or challenging? Do you know any strategies that can help you address these challenges?

- *There are a lot of unusual names to remember. I think I'll add the names to my glossary!*

What predictions can you make and why? (Check and mark the accuracy of your predictions as you read.)

- *I predict that the Mesopotamians had a strong military and conquered other people because several section headings are about the Mesopotamian military.*

🎯 Teacher Talk

➔ Help students understand the rationale for using this tool by initiating a conversation about the benefits of skimming through (previewing) a text before actually reading it.

- Begin by having students describe the purpose of previews they are likely to be familiar with (e.g., movie previews, preseason sports previews, fashion previews in magazines).

- Ask students why it might be useful to preview texts before reading.

- Summarize and/or add to students' ideas. You might, for example, point out that knowing how a text is organized can make the information easier to understand and remember—or that generating predictions and personal connections can make reading more interactive and enjoyable.

➔ Don't assume the Power Previewing steps are self-explanatory. Explain and model each one thoroughly, making sure to think aloud as you work your way through sample texts. Continue modeling the previewing process until students are clear about how to find important information and complete their organizers on their own.

➔ In the beginning—or when using the tool with younger students, struggling readers, or English language learners—preview texts as a class and use guiding questions to focus students' attention on what's important. For example, "Does anything on this page look like something we've seen before?" or "Do you notice any words that look different than the others? Why might the author have done that?" Once you've flipped through the entire text, review the questions on the organizer as a class. Have students speak their answers aloud or write (or draw) them on the organizer.

➔ Having students highlight the important information that they find while prowling and/or turn in their organizers at the end of the lesson can help you identify individuals who need extra help.

➔ Help students reflect on and learn from the previewing process (Step 4) using questions like these: How did you prowl? What did you learn by previewing? How did previewing affect what you paid attention to while reading? Did previewing make the text more enjoyable or easier to understand? Might it be useful to preview texts on your own? Why or why not?

➔ Previewing the structure and organization of a text can be as helpful as previewing the content. For this reason, it's a good idea to familiarize students with common text structures (e.g., problem-solution, comparison, argument, chronological sequence) and encourage them to prowl for those structures as they skim. Reviewing "tip-off words" that signal different kinds of text structures (e.g., *first*, *second*, and *finally* for a chronologically or sequentially structured text) can help.

➔ If you want students to preview works of fiction instead of nonfiction texts, give them fiction-specific organizers. Use the organizer on page 123 as is, or modify it as needed to fit your selected text type (e.g., illustrated versus not illustrated, chapter book versus no chapters). Offer students guidance about what to focus on while skimming fiction (e.g., elements like illustrations and chapter titles rather than end-of-chapter questions and summary paragraphs). You might ask younger students to do a "picture walk" (look at a book's illustrations, describe what they notice, and make predictions based on what they see). You might have older students skim a few paragraphs to get a sense of an author's writing style or use chapter titles to make predictions about overall plot or theme.

Name: _____   Date: _____

Power Previewing Organizer (nonfiction)

Where to look for important information:

- Titles, headings, and subheadings
- Opening paragraphs or introduction
- First and last sentence of each paragraph
- Summary paragraphs or lists of key points
- End-of-chapter or start-of-chapter questions
- Bold, italicized, and underlined information
- Circled, boxed, or highlighted information
- Graphs, figures, tables, charts, and maps
- Pictures, cartoons, and photographs
- Captions and figure legends

What are you previewing? What is it about (topic)?

How is the text structured or organized?

What else did you notice or learn while skimming? What information and ideas seem to be important?

Does anything look familiar or relate to something you've seen, read, learned about, or experienced?

What seems interesting?

What seems confusing or challenging? Do you know any strategies that can help you address these challenges?

What predictions can you make and why? (Check and mark the accuracy of your predictions as you read.)

Power Previewing Organizer (fiction)

What to look at as you skim:

- Title and author
- Front and back cover
- Pictures
- Opening lines or paragraphs
- Chapter titles
- Text that looks "different"
  (for example, a different size or style)
- Anything else that stands out

What are you previewing? What is its title?

Who is the author?

What did you see or notice while skimming?

Did anything look familiar or interesting?

What do you think this reading will be about? What do you think might happen?

Check your ideas after you finish reading.

| *Tools for Classroom Instruction That Works* | © 2018 Silver Strong & Associates | Visit www.ThoughtfulClassroom.com/Tools to download this page.   123

Nonlinguistic Representations

Thank God I have the seeing eye, that is to say, as I lie in bed I can walk step by step on the fells and rough land seeing every stone and flower and patch of bog and cotton pass where my old legs will never take me again.

—Beatrix Potter

The ultimate goal for using these strategies is to produce nonlinguistic representations of knowledge in the minds of students so they are better able to process, organize, and retrieve information from memory.

—Ceri B. Dean, Elizabeth Ross Hubbell, Howard Pitler, and Bj Stone,
Classroom Instruction That Works (Second Edition)

Early in the play *Hamlet*, Shakespeare coins what is perhaps the single best phrase for the ability to create mental images:

> *Hamlet:* My father—methinks I see my father.
> *Horatio:* O, where, my lord?
> *Hamlet:* In my mind's eye, Horatio.
> (1.2.193–195)

Of course, the mind's eye has great value beyond allowing melancholy princes to imagine their dead fathers, which is why the authors of *Classroom Instruction That Works* (Second Edition) highlight the importance of teaching students to "represent knowledge as imagery" (Dean et al., 2012, p. 64). Citing the work of brain researcher John Medina (2008), they go on to tell us that nonlinguistic strategies "are powerful because they tap into students' natural tendency for visual image processing, which helps them construct meaning of relevant content and skills and have a better capacity to recall it later" (Dean et al., 2012, p. 64).

In terms of student achievement, the effects of teaching students how to use nonlinguistic representation to deepen and advance their learning are clear. A 2010 McREL study analyzing relevant research associated the use of nonlinguistic representation in the classroom with a positive effect size of 0.49, or roughly a 19 percentile point gain in student achievement (Beesley & Apthorp, 2010). To achieve these benefits, the authors of *Classroom Instruction That Works* (Second Edition) suggest that teachers do the following:

- Teach students how to use graphic organizers to represent knowledge.
- Engage students in hands-on learning experiences like making models and using manipulatives.
- Invite students to create mental pictures of what they're learning. (Remember that mental pictures can and should include not just images, but also sensory details, physical sensations, and feelings.)
- Give students opportunities to represent their learning using drawings, symbols, or technology.
- Allow students to use their bodies (e.g., through role-playing or physically representing concepts) as a way to build understanding kinesthetically.

For the first recommendation above (using graphic organizers), we refer you to the S-O-S Graphic Organizers tool in Chapter 4 (pp. 112–118). To help you put the remaining four recommendations to work in your classroom, we present these four tools:

1. **Do, Look, Learn** uses a three-phase process to ensure that hands-on classroom experiences and activities that use models or manipulatives lead to deep and meaningful learning.

2. **Mind's Eye** teaches students how to create powerful mental images before reading—and use those images to engage deeply with the text.

3. **Split Screen** uses a simple note-taking format that enables students to represent their learning by creating images and reinforcing those images with words.

4. **Visualizing Vocabulary** helps students build a deep understanding of new vocabulary terms by challenging them to create or find images to represent words' meanings.

Do, Look, Learn

What is it?

A three-step process that enhances student learning during kinesthetic activities, hands-on experiences, and activities that involve models and manipulatives

What are the benefits of using this tool?

Many students (and many adults) will be quick to tell you that they learn best by doing. But as the authors of *Classroom Instruction That Works* (Second Edition) point out, hands-on learning experiences can carry a risk: "Many times, students are so enamored with the materials and the experience…that paying attention to the content or concepts they need to learn becomes secondary" (Dean et al., 2012, p. 68). Do, Look, Learn is a technique designed to help focus students' attention squarely on the learning during activities that feature DOING (e.g., making physical models, using manipulatives, or participating in kinesthetic activities such as role-playing and acting out concepts). The tool is also designed around the recognition that there is much more learning to be gained after the activity is over. That's why the tool encourages students to LOOK back on the activity, discuss their insights, and ask the most important question of all: "What did I LEARN as a result of this experience?"

What are the basic steps?

1. Identify the learning objectives you intend to address through the learning-by-doing process.

   Example: If the learning-by-doing process asks students to physically represent key vocabulary terms, an important objective would be for students to demonstrate understanding of the critical attributes of each term.

2. Decide what type of activity you will use to facilitate learning and how students will work to complete the activity (e.g., individually, in pairs, in small groups).

   Note: Do, Look, Learn works well for activities that involve physical models, manipulatives, and kinesthetic activities like role-playing. See Examples 1–4 for various uses of the tool.

3. Introduce the activity to students. Make sure that they are clear on what they are expected to do, the learning objective of the activity, and the information you want them to collect (e.g., observations, similarities, personal reactions, areas of confusion).

4. Have students DO the activity. Help keep students focused on the content and learning objectives by walking around, listening in, and providing coaching as needed.

5. Have students LOOK back on the activity by giving them time to think about and collect their observations and experiences and then share their insights with their team or the class. Encourage students to listen to each other's responses carefully and look for similarities and differences.

   Note: Depending on your goals and content, you may want students to stop at several points during the activity to look back on what they did, rather than just at the end.

6. Encourage students to draw conclusions/explain what they have LEARNED from the activity.

How is this tool used in the classroom?

✔ To ensure that hands-on activities lead to deep and meaningful learning

✔ To help students reflect on and build deep learning from the learning-by-doing process

EXAMPLE 1: Hands-on group learning

A teacher wants his students to experience what it means to work effectively as a team, so he uses an adaptation of a classic group-learning activity called Broken Squares (adapted from Pfeiffer & Jones, 1974). Students work in teams of five, and each team receives fifteen jumbled pieces of paper that together form five squares. Each team member gets three of the fifteen pieces. The goal is for each team to make five equal squares, one in front of each member. The rules are as follows:

1. There is absolutely no talking.

2. Team members can give any other team members any of their pieces of paper.

3. Pieces of paper can only be given to another team member one piece at a time.

4. To give a piece of paper to a team member, the giver must place the piece in front of the recipient. Under no circumstances may the giver place the piece into the recipient's square or show the recipient where to put the given piece.

5. No team member may take a piece of paper from another team member. The only way to receive a new piece of paper is to be given it by another team member.

After all teams have completed the task, the teacher hands out a data collection sheet for students to record what happened during the activity and how they felt during it. The teacher invites students to share their experiences, which he records on the board. To synthesize the learning, the teacher asks students to take out their learning logs and write about what they have learned from the experience and what it takes to work effectively in a group.

EXAMPLE 2: Acting out/physically representing vocabulary terms

An American history class is learning about the events that led up to the American Revolution. The teacher wants to help her students deepen their comprehension of these events, so that they can distinguish these events from one another and explain the cumulative effect they had over time. She breaks students into pairs and gives each pair one of the following terms to study:

The Treaty of Paris, 1763	Committees of Correspondence, 1772/1773
The Currency Act, 1764	The Tea Act, 1773
The Stamp Act, 1765	The Boston Tea Party, 1773
The Quartering Act, 1765	The Intolerable Acts, 1774
The Townshend Acts, 1767	The First Continental Congress, 1774
The Boston Massacre, 1770	The Battles of Lexington and Concord, 1775

Student pairs must develop a way to act out or physically represent their given term so that the class will understand what it is, its causes, and its effects on the relationship between the colonists and the British. (Students use a graphic organizer to collect this information.) Once all the terms have been presented, students look back on and discuss the impact the events had on the colonists' desire for independence. The teacher then has them review, synthesize, and demonstrate what they learned about the individual events and their cumulative impact by responding to the following writing prompt: "How was the lead-up to the American Revolution like a dripping faucet?" (Students are instructed to include at least eight of the original terms in their responses—and in a meaningful, not superficial, way.)

EXAMPLE 3: Role-playing

A first-grade class acts out stories to help students build a deep understanding of key literary elements. For today's read-aloud, the teacher stops at key points in the story and asks different groups of students to demonstrate through role-playing what the characters are like, the problem the main character faces, and how the character solves the problem. After the role-play, the teacher helps students look back on the story elements they acted out and use them to develop a simple retelling of the story.

EXAMPLE 4: Using/creating models

A middle school math teacher wants her students to discover the relationship between two-dimensional shapes and three-dimensional shapes. She also wants them to figure out on their own—rather than simply memorize formulas—how the surface area of three-dimensional shapes is calculated. In groups of three, students work together to figure out how a cereal box (a rectangular prism) can be cut and opened into six flat rectangles and how a carton of salt (a cylinder) can be cut and opened into one rectangle and two circles. Once each group has completed the task, the teacher challenges students to use what they learned from the activity and what they know about finding the area of two-dimensional shapes to see if they can calculate the surface area of the three-dimensional shapes they have cut open. As students work, the teacher walks around to listen in on each group's thinking and provide help where needed. To help students apply what they have learned, the teacher presents student groups with a final challenge: Using graph paper, scissors, and tape, they must create, assemble, and calculate the surface area of three different three-dimensional shapes—a triangular prism, a rectangular pyramid, and a triangular pyramid.

🌑 Teacher Talk

→ You can help students focus on and record the most critical information by providing a graphic organizer.

→ To maximize the power of reflection during the LOOK phase, make sure students take a moment to collect their thoughts, notes, and/or feelings before they begin sharing. Remind them to hold off on making conclusions (the LEARN phase) until all information is shared.

→ When doing group activities like the one in Example 1, it can be helpful to designate one member of each group as an observer, whose job it is to observe and make notes about (rather than participate in) the activity.

Mind's Eye

What is it?

A pre-reading tool that encourages students to generate mental pictures and use them to read more actively; the tool is adapted from work by Brownlie and Silver (1995) and Pressley (1979)

What are the benefits of using this tool?

The ability to create mental pictures is a key to reading comprehension (Wilhelm, 2012). One way to help students build this skill is "by providing details that enable students to incorporate sounds, smells, tastes, and visual details as part of the overall mental picture" (Dean et al., 2012, p. 70). Mind's Eye is a tool that provides such details by focusing students' attention on the most sensory, most evocative, and most important words in the texts they read—and empowering students to turn those words into mental images. In addition to teaching students to picture a text in their minds, this tool also invites students to make and test predictions, generate questions, and develop personal connections—all proven strategies for improving comprehension (Gambrell, n.d.).

What are the basic steps?

1. Select five to twenty-five key words from a work of fiction (e.g., short story, fable, book chapter) or literary nonfiction (e.g., excerpt from a biography, autobiography, or memoir).

   Note: Words should reveal information about key aspects of the text (e.g., plot, setting, theme) and contain visual or other sensory information that will help students picture the text in their minds.

2. Ask yourself whether the words you've selected, and the order you plan to read them in, will allow students to create relevant images and make quality predictions. If not, revise your list.

3. Read each word aloud slowly, adding emphasis, sound effects, or emotion if appropriate. Ask students to close their eyes and try to picture the story in their minds as you read the words. Encourage students to adjust their mental images as needed after each new word is read.

4. Have students use the images they created to help them complete one or more of the tasks below. Instruct them to record their responses on a Mind's Eye Organizer (p. 133) and then share and compare ideas with their classmates. Students can
   - Draw a picture of the story
   - Record questions they have about the story
   - Make predictions about the story
   - Describe feelings or personal connections that their images brought to mind

5. Ask students to read the actual text. Tell them to look for answers to their questions, assess the accuracy of their pictures and predictions, and revise those pictures/predictions as needed.

6. Pose questions that ask students to reflect on the *content* of the text (e.g., How is this similar to the previous fable we read? What is the moral?) and on the Mind's Eye *process* (e.g., How did this activity affect your understanding of the text? Your interest in reading it? Your ability to recall it?).

How is this tool used in the classroom?

✔ To teach students how to create mental pictures

✔ To preview content, activate thinking, and increase student engagement before reading

✔ To familiarize students with active-reading strategies that boost interest and comprehension

EXAMPLE 1: A third-grade teacher used the Mind's Eye technique to help her students interact with and make predictions about Barbara Cooney's *Miss Rumphius* before they began reading it. The key words that she selected and a sample of one student's work are shown below.

> KEY WORDS: grandfather, artist, stories, library, books, sailing ship, faraway places, tropical islands, beaches, coconuts, mountains, jungles, lions, house by the sea, friends, crazy, seeds, flowers, beautiful, happy

Mind's Eye Organizer

Name of text: Miss Rumphius	Author: Barbara Cooney
PICTURE	**FEELINGS or PERSONAL CONNECTIONS** I feel peaceful. There are many words that make me feel peaceful like beaches, library, happy, and beautiful.
QUESTIONS Did some people believe that Miss Rumphius was crazy? Why did they think that?	**PREDICTIONS** I think Miss Rumphius will go sailing and see faraway places like tropical islands and jungles. Or maybe she will imagine these places by reading about them in the library.

EXAMPLE 2: A high school English teacher used Mind's Eye to have students preview and explore a pivotal chapter in Charles Dickens' *A Tale of Two Cities* (Book 2, Chapter 7). The key words that the teacher selected are shown below. Various students' responses to the four Mind's Eye prompts (picture, questions, predictions, feelings) are shown on the next page.

> KEY WORDS: handsomely dressed, haughty, carriage, horses, narrow streets, recklessness, common people, escaping, screaming, loud cry, child, killed, shrieked, desperation, eyes, watchfulness, purse, coin, pay, contemptuous, "Go on!", woman, knitting

Picture

Questions

- Who was killed? Was it a child?
- Did a reckless driver kill a child?
- Who is knitting and why?

Predictions

- A well-dressed and wealthy person will drive a carriage through the narrow streets.
- Someone will drive a carriage recklessly and kill a child.
- The conflict between common people and wealthy people that Dickens has been setting up will reach a breaking point.

Feelings or Personal Connections

- I feel anxious from these words.
- It feels ominous. Words like *screaming*, *cry*, *shrieked*, *desperation*, and *killed* all seem to indicate that bad things will happen.
- The conflict between the common people and the wealthy people seems like it will be a big part of this chapter. This reminds me of some of the protests about income inequality that have been happening around the world.

🌑 Teacher Talk

→ If students are new to making mental images, model and help them practice this skill before asking them to use it independently. Sketch the images that you'd create from a set of key words (explain your sketches) or review and give students feedback about the sketches that they create.

→ When selecting key words, feel free to include words that aren't in the actual text but that you feel would enhance students' grasp of that text (e.g., words that reflect key concepts or themes). If students were reading a book that had courage as a major theme, for example, it might be worth including the word *courage* on your word list even if it didn't appear in the specific section of text you were having students read.

→ Explain that constructing mental images, making and testing predictions, asking questions, and developing personal connections can help students get more out of texts they read on their own—and encourage students to use these strategies independently. Prepare students for success by modeling each strategy using one or more sample texts. Spend extra time explaining how you create images ("I stop after each section or page and …") and make informed predictions.

Name: _____ Date: _____

Text: _____ Author: _____

Mind's Eye Organizer

PICTURE	FEELINGS or PERSONAL CONNECTIONS

QUESTIONS	PREDICTIONS

Split Screen

What is it?

A tool that empowers students to process and encode new learning using both words and images

What are the benefits of using this tool?

As brain researcher John Medina (2008) reminds us, "the more visual the input becomes, the more likely it is to be recognized—and recalled" (p. 233). So what if we could capitalize on this primacy of visual information while also making learning more active and more personally meaningful for students? With Split Screen, we can. The tool asks teachers to think of the content they are teaching or the texts students are reading as chunks of information. It invites students to actively process each chunk by making "split screen" notes, with words on one side and relevant images on the other.

What are the basic steps?

1. Divide the content (or text) you plan to present into two to seven meaningful chunks. You might, for example, divide a lecture on the Navajo into sections on social structure, art, customs, etc.

2. Distribute a Split Screen organizer (p. 138), or have students make their own. Teach students how to take notes using simple pictures/icons rather than words. Explain that the goal isn't to draw every last bit of information but rather to draw simple images that capture big ideas and details.

   Note: Before asking students to take "picture notes" on their own, model the process repeatedly, allow students to practice as a class, and observe/provide feedback about their performance.

3. Present (or have students read) a single chunk of content. Instruct students to think about the most important ideas before they begin drawing. Enforcing a ten- to thirty-second "no drawing period" is one way to ensure that they complete this stop-and-think step.

   Note: Remind students that they are not creating complex works of art—just simple sketches.

4. Have students pair up to compare pictures, guess what each other's images represent, and discuss the big ideas that they were trying to capture in their sketches.

5. Invite students to explain their sketches in the right-most column of the organizer. ("Summarize the big ideas and important details that your sketches represent in your own words.")

6. Examine students' notes, or have students share their ideas with the class. Check that students got key ideas and details correct. Reemphasize and/or expand on important points, and correct any misconceptions. Encourage students to revise their sketches and explanations as needed.

7. Repeat Steps 3–6 until all chunks of information have been presented and processed. Assign a task that requires students to review, synthesize, and summarize the key ideas from their notes.

How is this tool used in the classroom?

✔ To help students capitalize on the power of visualization when learning new content

✔ To teach students a note-taking strategy that improves comprehension and recall

✔ To make classroom learning more active, engaging, and personally meaningful

EXAMPLE 1: High school students with a construction specialization in their school's career and technical education program are learning how to pour a proper concrete footing. Before they begin the application phase of the lesson, the teacher explains why footings sometimes fail and how to ensure that theirs don't. As the teacher explains the root causes behind footing failure, students create a set of Split Screen notes by visually representing the main causes of and solutions for failed footings and by turning their images into key points and important reminders for pouring footings.

Topic: _Why footings fail – and how to make sure they don't!_

	Sketch	Big Ideas and Important Details
1	↑ ↑ ↑	Water in soil freezes into thin sheets called ice lenses. Ice expands almost 10%. Ice lenses below the footing push it up.
2	– – – – – No frost here!	When frost pushes up a footing, it's called frost heave. To prevent frost heave, always follow local code to make sure the footing is below the frost line.
3	① smooth! ② ③	Other ways to stop frost heave: 1) Use waxed cardboard tubes when you pour footings. Ice lenses can't cacth the sides. 2) Flare out the bottom of the footing. 3) Mound soil around the posts to direct water away.

EXAMPLE 2: A second-grade teacher uses Split Screen to help students enhance their comprehension of the texts they read. Because the teacher recognizes that identifying big ideas can be difficult for young readers, she scaffolds the process by reviewing each section of the text and working as a class to identify the big ideas before students begin drawing. One student's Split Screen notes for a reading that explains why snakes shed their skin appear below.

Topic: Snake skin

	Sketch	Big Ideas and Important Details
1	befor / after skin / skin	snake skin does not grow the snakesheads so it can keep on growing
2	befor / after	tiny animals called parisites eat the snake the snake sheads to get rid of the parisites
3		Snakes shead many times as they get older

EXAMPLE 3: A history teacher used this tool to help students discover, summarize, and remember the key points about the great accomplishments of the Inca civilization (a section of the textbook that they had read and discussed as a class). One student's partial notes are shown below. The synthesis task (not shown) asked students to review their notes, decide which accomplishment of the Inca civilization was the most impressive, and defend their choice.

Section	Sketch	Big Ideas and Important Details
1: Government Cuzco		I drew a star with a C to represent the capital of Cuzco. I drew people with arrows going back to Cuzco to show that the Incas had a strong central government that collected taxes in the form of labor.
2: Technology Inca calendar		I drew two circles divided into twelve parts to show that the Incas developed calendars. One calendar was based on the position of the sun and the other on the position of the moon.
3: Religion		

🌀 Teacher Talk

➔ Most students won't be familiar with this way of recording information, so modeling, practicing, and talking students through the process are critical. Among other things,

- Reassure students that they don't have to create complex works of art—just simple sketches.

- Clarify expectations by helping students compare effective and less effective sketches (simple ones that capture main ideas/details versus overly detailed ones that illustrate every last bit of information).

- Prepare students for success by introducing key themes and mapping out possible images/icons in advance (this is especially helpful for abstract concepts). For example, "Today we're going to talk about the American colonists' fight for independence. What kind of icon might we use to represent a war? How about the concept of independence? Who has an idea?"

➔ You may want to help students understand what's important to pay attention to and record by introducing the overall topic and key ideas/sections in advance. You or students can record these ideas on the left side of the organizer as shown in Example 3.

➔ While we have chosen to place this tool in Chapter 5 (Nonlinguistic Representations), it would go equally well in Chapter 6 (Summarizing and Note Taking). More specifically, Split Screen directly supports the *Classroom Instruction That Works* (Second Edition) recommendation to teach students to generate "combination notes" (Dean et al., 2012, p. 93) that include both words and pictures.

Name: _____   Date: _____

Topic or text: _____

Split Screen

	Sketch	Big Ideas and Important Details
1		
2		
3		

Visualizing Vocabulary

What is it?

A technique that helps students master critical vocabulary by asking them to process important terms both nonlinguistically (students find or create images to represent each term) and linguistically (students explain why their image is a good representation of the term)

What are the benefits of using this tool?

One of the simplest—and most powerful—ways to enhance students' understanding and retention of important vocabulary terms is to tap into the power of "dual coding" (Clark & Paivio, 1991; Paivio, 2006). When students dual code information, they store it in two different ways—through language and through images—thus making the memory stronger. What's more, by asking students to find or create images to represent their own understanding, this tool makes learning personally meaningful, which "can be especially helpful when students are learning new vocabulary words and terms" (Dean et al., 2012, p. 71).

What are the basic steps?

1. Identify an important term that you want students to process deeply using dual coding.

   Note: You may choose to use this tool for multiple terms as well (see Example 2 and Teacher Talk).

2. Explain to students the importance of dual coding—how using both words and images to process new vocabulary makes learning deeper and leads to better retention.

3. Introduce the term to students. Allow them to write down the definition of the term and, if needed, to ask questions that will help them build a solid understanding of the term's meaning.

   Tip: Encourage students to write the definition in their own words, either in addition to or instead of the textbook definition.

4. Have students create or select (e.g., via image libraries) a personally meaningful image or set of images to represent the term. Remind students that their images can be literal (a direct representation of the term) or conceptual (an icon or symbol).

5. Have students write a simple explanation of their image. Remind students that their explanations should tell why the image is a good representation of the term.

6. *Optional:* Allow students to share their images and explanations in pairs, small groups, or with the entire class. If you include this step, give students the chance to refine or add to their images and definitions if they choose.

7. Encourage students to use their definitions, images, and explanations as a study guide.

How is this tool used in the classroom?

✔ To help students develop a deep understanding of vocabulary terms

✔ To make direct vocabulary instruction personally meaningful for students

EXAMPLE 1: A second-grade teacher uses Visualizing Vocabulary throughout the year, especially when students encounter abstract concepts that she wants them to concretize. Here is how one student used the tool to express his understanding of the term *freedom*:

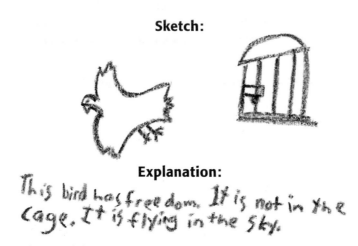

Freedom is the right to do what you want.

Sketch:

Explanation:

This bird has freedom. It is not in the cage. It is flying in the sky.

SOURCE: From *Word Works: Cracking Vocabulary's CODE,* Second Edition (p. 34), by Silver Strong & Associates, 2007, Ho-Ho-Kus, NJ: Thoughtful Education Press. © 2007 Silver Strong & Associates. Reprinted with permission.

EXAMPLE 2: A middle school math teacher integrates Visualizing Vocabulary into his instructional sequences by providing students with a specially made student glossary at the beginning of the year. Whenever a new term is introduced, students create a new entry by recording the textbook definition of the term. Then, as students learn more about the term, they add to their entries by developing their own definition of the term, creating relevant images, and explaining the reasoning behind their images. An excerpt from one student's glossary is shown below.

Term	Textbook Definition	My Definition	Visualization	Explanation
Triangular Region	The union of a triangle and its interior.	A triangle plus its inside area		The inside is colored in to remind me that a triangular region also includes the interior.
Polygonal Region	The union of a finite number of nonoverlapping triangular regions in a plane	A set of connected triangles that don't overlap and that create a new shape		The triangular regions are all connected (union) but don't overlap.

EXAMPLE 3: A fourth-grade teacher likes to use Visualizing Vocabulary in a cooperative learning setting to help students learn to think through important content together. For a unit on the water cycle, the teacher posted the following terms on the class word wall: *precipitation, condensation, evaporation, water vapor, pollution, ground water, water table,* and *renewal.* For each term, groups of four students were asked to develop a definition of the term in their own words, an image to represent the term, and an explanation of their image. Before posting their work on the word wall, all four group members had to sign off on all elements of the work (definition, image, explanation). Once all groups' work was on the word wall, the class conducted a "word-wall walk" by getting up and reviewing all of the groups' definitions and images. During the walk, student groups were given the choice of the following for each term:

- Select the definition/image that you think is best and tell why.
- Create a new "super definition" by stealing and combining elements of different groups' work.

 Teacher Talk

→ Not all nonlinguistic information needs to be visual. Indeed, the authors of *Classroom Instruction That Works* (Second Edition) point out that we can also enhance students' understanding of terms and concepts by asking students to act the terms out or represent them physically (e.g., hold up two hands with an equal number of fingers up to represent the concept *equation*). To see how one teacher helped students build deep understanding of important terms through physical representation, see Example 2 in the tool called Do, Look, Learn (p. 128).

→ Some teachers wonder, How many terms is too many to visualize in this way? When using Visualizing Vocabulary, think about your overall instructional goals. If you are looking for students to develop a deep conceptual understanding of a unit's core concepts, you may want to reserve Visualizing Vocabulary for those select concepts. To learn more about how to identify core concepts, see the Teacher Talk section of the Vocabulary Knowledge Rating tool (p. 92).

On the other hand, you may want to have students tap into the power of dual coding for all of the terms in your unit and use Visualizing Vocabulary whenever students encounter new terms. If you choose to use Visualizing Vocabulary this way, consider providing or having students create a simple glossary, as the teacher in Example 2 did. A glossary gives students a set place to record, define, and visualize new terms as the unit progresses. The glossary then becomes a powerful study guide where students can check in on and review their emerging understanding of new terms.

Summarizing and Note Taking

It is my ambition to say in ten sentences what others say in a whole book.

—Friedrich Nietzsche

Whether they are in a college class, take on-the-job training, or simply watch a how-to video for a home-repair project, today's learners will be well prepared to distill vast amounts of information into manageable chunks of knowledge when they know how to use tools that allow them to save, sort, and capture key points or ideas they want to explore in detail later.

—Ceri B. Dean, Elizabeth Ross Hubbell, Howard Pitler, and Bj Stone,
Classroom Instruction That Works (Second Edition)

Based on a series of Pulitzer Prize-winning articles, Ron Suskind's *A Hope in the Unseen* tells the true story of Cedric Jennings, who attends Brown University after graduating from one of the lowest-performing high schools in the country. When Cedric realizes that he is falling behind in classes that require him to take a significant amount of notes, a professor gives him this bit of advice: "Don't be a lecture-hall stenographer" (Suskind, 1998, p. 336).

What Cedric's professor recognizes is that many students believe they need to capture every last bit of information that they encounter in the classroom. For these students, the odds of academic success are slim because their learning typically doesn't take hold. Big ideas and tiny details all swirl together in one undifferentiated mass of information.

So what should we do? The response should be clear enough based on the name of this chapter: We need to teach students how to summarize information down into manageable forms, and we need to teach students how to take notes that enhance understanding and recall. These two strategies—summarizing and note taking—belong together because "they both require students to distill information into a parsimonious and synthesized form" (Dean et al., 2012, p. 78). In addition, both have demonstrable effects on student learning, with effect sizes of 0.90 for note taking and 0.32 for summarizing (Beesley & Apthorp, 2010). These effect sizes translate into percentile gains of 32 points and 13 points, respectively.

And yet, as important as note taking and summarizing are to students' success, the fact is that both are under-taught in many classrooms. Teachers often assume that note taking and summarizing are intuitive (i.e., that students just know how to do them). In reality, note taking and summarizing don't come naturally to most students; they are skills that need to be explicitly taught, modeled, and practiced. This chapter presents six tools for helping students develop their note-taking and summarizing skills. These tools are consistent with research and recommendations from *Classroom Instruction That Works* (Second Edition), including the recommendations to

- Provide students with concrete steps and strategies for developing summaries
- Teach students to use summarization in conjunction with other cognitive strategies
- Familiarize students with a variety of formats for taking notes
- Model the note-taking process for students (e.g., by providing teacher-prepared notes and note-taking templates)
- Provide opportunities for students to revise their notes and use them for review

What are the six tools?

1. **AWESOME Summaries** teaches students how to craft high-quality summaries by spelling out concrete guidelines for them to follow.

2. **4-2-1 Summarize** presents a collaborative strategy for helping students summarize key points from a lesson, reading, or other information source.

3. **Reciprocal Teaching** prepares students to deepen their comprehension of assigned texts by using summarization and other expert-reader strategies.

4. **Three Ways of Webbing** familiarizes students with a note-taking format known as "webbing"; it also shows them how they can use the webbing technique for three distinct purposes.

5. **Window Notes** makes students aware of four different types of notes they can make—and gives them a window-shaped organizer for jotting their notes down.

6. **Review & Revise** teaches students that notes should be updated, revised, and used as a review tool—not taken, tossed in a notebook, and forgotten about.

Note: The S-O-S Graphic Organizers tool from Chapter 4 (pp. 112–118) is another great tool for developing note-taking and summarizing skills. Like the tools from this chapter, it's consistent with the recommendations from *Classroom Instruction That Works* (Second Edition) about how to build these critical skills—specifically, the recommendations to teach students a variety of note-taking formats, to provide students with teacher-prepared notes to use as models, and to make information easier for students to summarize by helping them see how that information is structured.

AWESOME Summaries

What is it?

An acronym-based tool that helps students write better summaries by giving them concrete guidelines to follow

What are the benefits of using this tool?

Authors Jane Hill and Kirsten Miller (2013) capture the key challenge of summarizing in a nutshell: "Students know that they need to summarize to condense information, but they don't always have a good method for doing so" (p. 99). This tool provides students with a good method for summarizing by teaching them an easy-to-remember acronym that captures the critical attributes of effective summaries as identified by Wormeli (2005). It also shows students how to analyze and evaluate summaries so that they truly understand what those critical attributes mean in practice.

What are the basic steps?

1. Distribute copies of the AWESOME Summary Checklist on page 147.

2. Explain (and use concrete examples to illustrate) the attributes of an AWESOME summary as defined on the checklist. You may want to focus on one or two attributes at a time, particularly with younger students.

3. Help students internalize the attributes of an AWESOME summary by having them use their checklists to evaluate specific examples. Here are some options:

- Give students examples of high-quality summaries (provide the original passages as well). Help them determine how each example satisfies the criteria in the AWESOME acronym.

- Give students high-quality and low-quality summaries of the same passage. Help them compare the two summaries using the AWESOME criteria, decide which one is better, and explain why.

4. Test students' grasp of the AWESOME criteria by asking them to revise an existing summary.

- Give students a short passage, along with a summary of it that fails to meet one or more of the AWESOME criteria. (Create the summary from scratch or use an existing one.)

- Have students revise the summary using the acronym as a guide and explain their revisions.

- Use students' responses to decide whether additional instruction is needed before moving on.

5. Challenge students to use what they've learned to summarize a passage that you give them.

6. Remind students to consult the AWESOME criteria both before they begin working (to remind them what they're aiming for) and after they're done (to evaluate their work). Encourage them to revise their summaries as needed based on their evaluations, either on their own or with a partner.

7. Use the AWESOME criteria to give students specific feedback about their completed summaries. For example, "What you've written is 100% *accurate*, but I'm not sure you've included *enough information*. Would someone who hasn't read the passage understand it based on your summary?"

How is this tool used in the classroom?

✔ To help students generate high-quality summaries of information they've seen, read, or heard

✔ To give students concrete criteria for evaluating and improving existing summaries

🌓 Teacher Talk

➜ Since students often have trouble determining which details are essential enough to include and which are minor enough to be eliminated, it's important to model and practice this skill regularly. Teach and model strategies that you yourself use, or familiarize students with the rule-based summarizing process outlined in *Classroom Instruction That Works* (Second Edition) (Dean et al., 2012, pp. 80–83). In rule-based summarizing, students use the following four rules to help them decide what information to keep and what to omit:

- Remove material not essential to understanding.
- Remove repetitive information.
- Replace lists of specific items (e.g., "softball, soccer, and lacrosse") with a general word that describes them (e.g., "sports").
- Look for a topic sentence or create a topic sentence if there is none.

➜ To adapt the tool for use with younger students, you can change the acronym so it covers fewer attributes. For example, teach students to "create summaries that MOM would be proud of" by asking themselves, "Did I retell the **M**ain points or parts? In the right **O**rder? And in **M**y own words?" You can also read passages aloud and have students draw rather than write their summaries.

➜ The AWESOME Summaries acronym can be used in a variety of ways. Students can focus on specific attributes from the acronym, or they can focus on all the attributes in AWESOME. In addition, students can use the acronym to write their own summaries or to evaluate and revise existing ones. The table below provides examples of summary tasks that reflect these various uses.

Task type / Focus	Writing a summary	Evaluating and revising a summary
Focus on specific attributes *Note:* Focus attributes are highlighted in italics.	SAMPLE TASK: Write a summary of this passage. Include *enough information* to capture the essence of the original text, but don't include unnecessary details. Remember that a good summary should contain the *essential ideas only.*	SAMPLE TASK: Review the summary of the passage you just read. Identify and remove any unnecessary details so that the summary contains the *essential ideas only.* Be prepared to justify your cuts during an in-class discussion.
Focus on all attributes	SAMPLE TASK: Write a summary of the passage we just read. Consult the criteria on the checklist, both as you write and after you're done. If you fail to satisfy any of the criteria in your first draft, revise your draft to make it better. Submit the checklist along with your final draft. If you've done your job, every box should be checked off!	SAMPLE TASK: Pretend that you are the teacher. Give the student who wrote this summary two specific suggestions for improvement. The suggestions you provide can focus on any of the criteria from the acronym. For example, "The sequence of ideas in your summary doesn't match the sequence of ideas in the original. Can you fix that?"

AWESOME Summary Checklist

BEFORE: Consult this checklist before you begin writing your summary so that you know what crafting a good summary looks and sounds like.

☐ Is the information in my summary **A**CCURATE?

☐ Has the length of the original material been **W**HITTLED DOWN significantly?

☐ Did I include **E**NOUGH INFORMATION to capture the essence of the original material?

☐ Is the information in my summary logically organized and **S**EQUENCED?

☐ Did I give an **O**BJECTIVE (free from personal opinions) summary of the original material?

☐ Did I summarize the original material in **M**Y OWN WORDS?

☐ Does my summary contain the **E**SSENTIAL IDEAS ONLY? Did I eliminate unnecessary details?

AFTER: Which criteria on the AWESOME Summary Checklist above does your summary meet? Check all that apply. Are there any criteria that your summary did not meet or could meet better? Do you need to revise your summary?

4-2-1 Summarize

What is it?

A collaborative process that teaches students how to identify important ideas and generate focused summaries that are supported with relevant details

What are the benefits of using this tool?

One of the biggest challenges that students face when developing summaries is deciding what information is important to include and what is less essential. 4-2-1 Summarize helps students hone this critical skill by having them work with their classmates to identify key points. It also gives us insight into how well students have understood what they've read and learned by having them synthesize and summarize the key points in writing.

What are the basic steps?

1. Ask students to record the FOUR most important points from a reading, lecture, or other learning episode on a 4-2-1 Summarize Organizer (p. 150).

   Note: Before using this tool, discuss and model strategies that students can use to identify important information within a text or presentation. ("When looking for important information, remember to check out section headings, topic sentences, and summary paragraphs.")

2. Ask students to share and compare their ideas with a partner and come to an agreement about the TWO that are most important. Explain that they can pick and choose from their original ideas, combine their original ideas, and/or add ideas that were missing from their original lists.

3. Pair up the pairs. Have each group of four reach a consensus about the ONE most important idea.

4. Invite students to share their most important ideas (and the strategies that they used to arrive at those ideas) with the class. Help them refine or refocus these main ideas if needed.

5. Choose (or let students choose) one of these main ideas to write about. Have them synthesize and summarize what they learned about this idea/topic in a written paragraph. Encourage them to use some or all of the ideas they generated during Steps 1 and 2 as supporting details.

6. Use students' paragraphs to assess their content knowledge (did they get the key points?) and/or summarizing skills.

7. Address any deficiencies in content knowledge or summarizing skills.

How is this tool used in the classroom?

✔ To have students summarize the key ideas from a lecture, text, or other learning experience

✔ To check students' understanding of material they've read or learned about

✔ To assess students' ability to identify main ideas and support them with details/examples

✔ To help students learn to distinguish essential information from non-essential information

EXAMPLE: Here is the organizer that a fifth grader completed after reading an article on endangered tigers. Notice that in negotiating the key ideas down from four to one, this student and his partners kept some of his original ideas (*There are fewer than 3200 tigers left on Earth*), combined some of his original ideas (*Tigers are getting killed and their habitat is being destroyed*), and wrote one idea—the final main idea—from scratch (*Tigers will go extinct if we don't do something about it*).

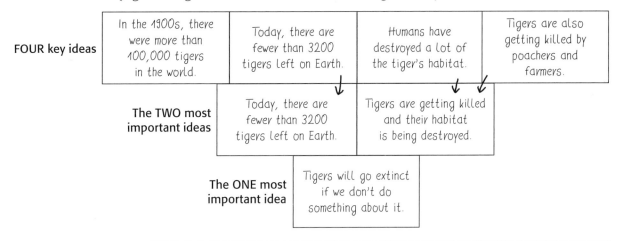

Summary paragraph: What did I learn by reading this article?

Tigers are in big trouble. If we don't do something about it, they will go extinct. Last century, there were over 100,000 tigers in the world. Today, there are fewer than 3200. Tigers need lots of space and the places where they live are getting destroyed by humans. In the last ten years, about half of their habitat has been destroyed. Another problem is that tigers are getting killed by poachers. Killing the tigers is illegal, but the poachers do it anyway because they want to sell tiger skin and tiger claws and tiger teeth for money. Thinking about a world with no more tigers makes me sad. If we don't do something about this problem, kids 100 years from now might not even know what a tiger is.

Variation: 4-2-1 Freewrite

Have students freewrite about their main ideas instead of writing formal summary paragraphs. The goal is to have them get everything they know or feel about the topic (thoughts, questions, reactions) down on paper without worrying about the quality or correctness of their writing.

Name: _____   Date: _____

Topic or text: _____

4-2-1 Summarize Organizer

FOUR key ideas

The TWO most important ideas

The ONE most important idea

Summary paragraph:

Reciprocal Teaching

What is it?

A tool that teaches students four concrete strategies for improving comprehension: summarizing, questioning, clarifying, and predicting

What are the benefits of using this tool?

Dean et al. (2012) remind us that we can maximize the benefits of summarizing by teaching students to use it in concert with other strategies. The Reciprocal Teaching technique, based on the work of Palincsar and Brown (1985), does just that by teaching students to use summarizing, along with three other expert-reader strategies, to deepen their comprehension of a text. As students become more familiar with the Reciprocal Teaching strategies, they learn to apply them collaboratively (as part of a discussion team) and, ultimately, on their own.

What are the basic steps?

1. Talk to students about why texts can be difficult to understand. Explain that expert readers use specific strategies to help them monitor and improve their understanding of what they're reading— and that you're going to teach, and help students practice using, four of those strategies.

2. Introduce the strategies using the descriptions below and the handout on page 154. Explain what each strategy entails and model it thoroughly, using short and simple text passages.

   - *Summarize:* Summarize the main point(s) or big idea. Leave out minor points and details.
   - *Generate questions:* Generate checking-for-understanding questions about key points and ideas.
   - *Clarify:* Identify—and work to clarify—elements that don't make sense or you don't understand.
   - *Predict:* Use both your existing knowledge and clues in the text to predict what will come next.

3. Train students to use the strategies. Alternate using—and having students use—the strategies to lead a discussion of a simple text passage. Provide concrete suggestions for improvement. Continue these training sessions until students can execute the strategies with a basic level of competence.

   Tip: Incorporate the sample language from the handout on page 154 into your dialogue. Encourage students to do the same.

4. Transfer the responsibility for leading these types of discussions to students. Organize students into teams of four, and have them use the strategies to discuss and advance their understanding of assigned passages. Listen in as they work. Provide coaching and assistance as needed.

   Note: Each team member can tackle a different *strategy* ("I'll summarize this section; you generate questions about it …") or a different *passage* ("I'll lead the discussion of this section, using all four strategies. You'll lead the discussion of the next section …").

5. Help students learn to use the strategies more expertly and automatically by having them continue practicing in class. But emphasize that the ultimate goal is for students to use the strategies on their own, so that they get more out of texts they read independently.

How is this tool used in the classroom?

✔ To help students develop summaries of the texts they read

✔ To teach students four reading comprehension strategies that lead to deep understanding

✔ To engage students in rich, structured discussions about the texts they read

EXAMPLE 1: A fourth-grade teacher has been using Reciprocal Teaching throughout the year to help her students use the tool's four strategies more expertly and automatically. Prior to assigning a passage about Bent's Fort in Colorado, she assigns the members of each four-person team a different strategy (summarizing, questioning, clarifying, or predicting). As they read, students prepare for the upcoming discussion by making notes that reflect their assigned strategies. During the discussion, students use their notes to help them lead their portion of the discussion. The notes that one team's summarizer, questioner, clarifier, and predictor developed are shown below.

Summarizer's Notes

This section was mostly about Bent's Fort and how it was an important part of Colorado history. Bent's Fort was built right beside the Santa Fe Trail. It was important because it provided water, furs, food, and supplies that travelers needed as they moved through the area.

Questioner's Notes

Where was Bent's Fort located?

Why was Bent's Fort important?

When was Bent's Fort founded?

What was the purpose of Bent's Fort?

Who traveled to Bent's Fort?

How did trappers and traders travel to and from Bent's Fort?

Clarifier's Notes

I didn't know what the word "outpost" meant, so I looked it up in the dictionary and in my textbook.

I didn't understand the author's explanation of why the fort "went out of business." Perhaps one of the other sections will clarify this. If not, I can look online for more information.

Predictor's Notes

Based on the title of the next section, I think that section will tell us more about the kinds of people who stopped in at the fort.

EXAMPLE 2: A middle school English language arts teacher has come to recognize just how important modeling and practice are to ensuring that students master the strategies and procedural elements associated with Reciprocal Teaching. So she uses the tool called Procedural PRO (pp. 171–174) to teach students the procedure and roles associated with Reciprocal Teaching. Here's what this looks like in the classroom:

To **P**resent the procedure and strategies, she

- Models all four strategies using a portion of a simple and familiar story—*Jack and the Beanstalk*
- Shows a video of a Reciprocal Teaching team using the strategies to discuss a text

To help students **R**ehearse, she

- Uses fishbowl sessions in which different groups of students practice engaging in a Reciprocal Teaching discussion while the rest of the class observes and offers feedback

To facilitate student **O**wnership of the process, she

- Builds weekly reading sessions around Reciprocal Teaching, so students use it regularly
- Reminds students to use their Reciprocal Teaching Strategies handout to guide their work
- Encourages students to use the strategies independently

🎧 Teacher Talk

➔ Before using this tool, prepare students to use the strategies successfully. Teach them concrete approaches for summarizing (see, for example, rule-based summarizing on p. 146), show them how to develop big-idea questions rather than trivial ones, familiarize them with a variety of what-to-do-when-stuck strategies (e.g., consult a dictionary or find a simpler text about the same topic), and point out the kinds of textual clues that can help them make predictions.

➔ Modeling and practice are essential to the use of this tool in the classroom. Here are some tips to make modeling and practice especially effective:

- When you think you have modeled well enough, model one more time!
- Use videos of students engaging in Reciprocal Teaching to help students develop a clear sense of how each strategy is used (see, for example, http://nccc.mcrel.org/reciprocalteaching*).
- Help students get used to the strategies by having them apply the strategies to personal experiences, familiar stories, or movies rather than complex texts. ("Can you summarize what you did on Saturday?" "What do you predict we'll do in class tomorrow and why?")
- Try using fishbowl modeling and practice sessions like the teacher in Example 2 did.
- Remind students to refer to their Reciprocal Teaching Strategies handout before, during, and after reading.
- Practice using texts that students are already familiar with and/or that are below students' reading levels so that students can focus more of their effort on mastering the strategies.
- Provide additional support when students work in teams (Step 4) by allowing summarizers, questioners, clarifiers, and predictors to meet in "corner groups" (students from other groups with the same role) before meeting with members of their Reciprocal Teaching team. The students in each corner group should work together to add to or refine their summaries/questions/predictions or to clarify areas of confusion.

*The *Reciprocal Teaching in Action* videos were created by McREL for the North Central Comprehensive Center, a program funded by the US Department of Education under cooperative agreement S283B120018; the views expressed in these videos do not necessarily reflect the position of the US Department of Education, and no official endorsement should be inferred.

Reciprocal Teaching Strategies

 SUMMARIZING

If you're asked to summarize, you should say what the passage is about. Keep it short. Describe the big ideas only.

Language that might help you:

- This section is about __.
- The main point is __.
- The most important thing this section tells us is __.
- The author wants us to understand that __.
- So far, we've learned that __.
- If I had to sum up the key points in one sentence, I'd say __.
- The most important person, place, or thing is __. The most important idea about this person, place, or thing is __.

CLARIFYING

If you're asked to clarify, you should find words, ideas, or passages that confuse you and work to clarify them.

Language that might help you:

- Something that confused me was __.
- I didn't understand __, so I __.
- Here's what I think this means: __.
- I tried to figure this out by __.
- How can I figure out what this means?
- Here's something I'd like to clarify . . .
- Are there any words whose meanings I need to check?
- Does this reasoning make sense? Why or why not?

GENERATING QUESTIONS

If you're asked to generate questions, you should develop questions about important information from the passage.

Language that might help you:

- Who/what/when/where __?
- How __?
- Why __?
- What if __?
- In what ways __?
- Would/should/could __?
- Why is this important to know?
- What's the reason/explanation for __?

MAKING PREDICTIONS

If you're asked to make predictions, you should use what you know and clues in the text to predict what will come next.

Language that might help you:

- I think the author will discuss __ because __.
- I think I will learn __ because __.
- I predict the next section will be about __ because __.
- I don't think this text will cover __ because __.
- A clue I found to support this prediction was __.
- Based on what I know about this topic, I predict __.
- A clue to what will come next is __.
- There isn't enough information to make a good prediction.

Rules for when reading with others:

1. Know your role. Which strategy or strategies have you been asked to use?

2. Read the assigned passage carefully. Use the appropriate strategy or strategies.

3. Make notes that will help you lead a discussion about what you read.

4. Lead a discussion about the passage. Use the provided starters / sample language to help you.

5. Get your classmates engaged by posing direct questions. For example, "Do you want to add anything to my summary?" "How might we clarify what this means?" "Do you agree with my prediction?"

6. Ensure that everyone participates. Everyone should lead a discussion and respond to other discussion leaders.

Three Ways of Webbing

What is it?

A tool that maximizes the power of the note-taking technique known as webbing by showing students three different ways that webbing can be used to advance learning

What are the benefits of using this tool?

A key benefit of webbing as a note-taking technique is that it is nonlinear, unburdening students from the formal structure of outlining and providing them with a way to organize their thoughts and ideas visually. Webbing can also help students see how information is structured by organizing big ideas and the details that support them into clear chunks. But students often struggle with the *how* and the *when:* How do I create a web? When is webbing especially useful? This tool helps students understand and master three distinct uses for webbing: to generate ideas, to collect information from a text or other information source, and to review/assess what they've learned. The tool also invites students to share and compare their webs with their classmates, which allows them to see relationships they might have missed and refine their webs accordingly.

What are the basic steps?

1. Review the different purposes for webbing described on pages 156–157. Develop a webbing task that's consistent with your content and lesson objectives.

2. Explain and model the basic webbing process. Align your modeling session to the task/goals you identified in Step 1 (e.g., if students will be collecting information from a text, model using a text)— but be sure to illustrate the following basic webbing principles in your modeling session:

   - Record the main topic (e.g., concept, event, problem) in the center of your paper and circle it.
   - Record subtopics around the central circle. Circle them and connect them to the central circle. (Young students can skip the subtopic circles and record details about the main topic instead.)
   - Add details or additional subtopics around each subtopic. Connect them to the web.
   - Continue adding branches and circles as needed to show additional relationships/details.

   Note: The central topic and/or subtopics can be framed as questions. See the Building the Great Wall of China example on page 157.

3. Call students' attention to the organizational structure of the web you created and how that structure is useful. ("See how the big ideas and the details that support them are organized into clear chunks? The chunks help us see how bits of information fit together.")

4. Present the task you created in Step 1. Provide guidance and feedback as students work on it.

5. Introduce and model the other uses of webbing over the course of the year.

6. Encourage students to use webbing independently by helping them appreciate the value of webbing ("Webs are great tools for collecting and organizing ideas—and for reviewing what you know") and recognize the kinds of tasks/learning experiences where webbing might help them.

How is this tool used in the classroom?

✔ To teach students how and when to use webbing

✔ To help students see big ideas, key details, and important relationships in the content

✔ To broaden students' note-taking repertoires

Three Purposes for Webbing

Webbing to generate ideas

Webs are ideal for recording the work of the mind as it generates ideas. Ask students to create this kind of "generative web" when you want them to collect their ideas as they think freely and divergently about a topic or problem.

The example below shows how a group of middle school students used this kind of webbing while brainstorming possible solutions to a challenge their teacher had posed: "How can you get thirty pennies to float using only aluminum foil?"

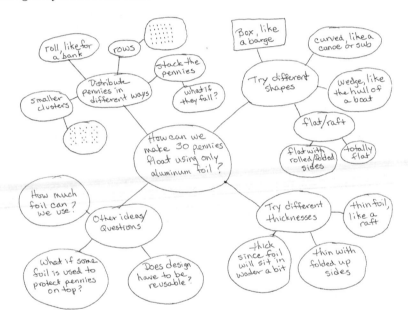

Generative webs are also great tools for assessing—and helping students activate—prior knowledge. Simply give students a central topic and ask them to jot down anything and everything they know about that topic. The example below shows how a second-grade teacher assessed her students' understanding of mathematics at the start of the year by having them web their responses to the question "What is mathematics?"

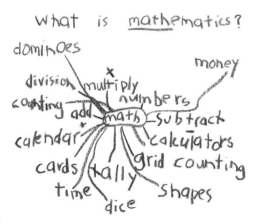

Webbing to collect information

Webbing can be a great help when taking notes while reading or collecting information from almost any source (e.g., video, podcast, painting). When students web to collect information from a text, teach them to look for the important subtopics within the text and to organize their webs around those subtopics. Subtopics can be recorded as is or converted into questions, as in the example below.

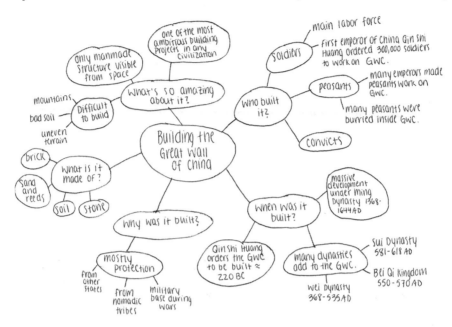

Webbing to review, assess, and/or apply learning

Students generate this type of web *after* a learning episode (e.g., reading assignment, lesson, or unit). Webbing after learning helps students solidify their understanding and create a record of their learning that clarifies—or helps them identify gaps in—that learning. A web used in this way serves as a kind of self-test: Can I recall the important information? Do I know how the information is organized into big ideas and supporting details? The web below was created by a student whose graphic design teacher asked students to build a web demonstrating their understanding of the key principles of design that they had learned in class. Students then used their webs as a guide for their final task: Create a home page that incorporates all four principles in its design.

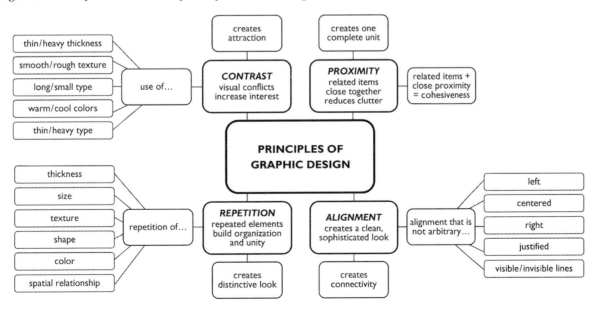

🐟 Teacher Talk

➔ If this is the first time students are creating their own webs, consider developing the web as a class, by collecting students' ideas and creating the web on the board or using a projection system.

➔ Primary-grade teachers often think that webbing is too complicated for their students, but that's not the case. To make webbing work with very young students, simply give them a single central topic (no subtopics) and instruct them to record everything they know about that topic around the central circle. The "What is mathematics?" web on page 156 shows what this kind of "starter web" will look like.

➔ Another way to scaffold the webbing process for younger students or students new to webbing is to give them subtopics rather than leaving it to them to generate subtopics on their own. This scaffolding process can be especially helpful when teaching students how to use webbing to collect information from a reading, as it makes the structure of the information clear and allows students to focus on relevant details while reading. For example, a fourth-grade teacher whose students were reading about the great children's author Roald Dahl scaffolded the webbing process by writing the key subtopics (framed as questions) into the web. In this way, she helped focus students' attention on the important information they needed to collect from the reading. All students needed to do was use lines and circles to add information from the text that helped answer each question.

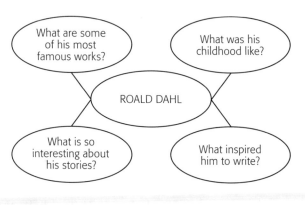

➔ There are many apps and programs that facilitate webbing via technology. Some sites to check out include bubbl.us, www.mywebspiration.com, and www.mindmeister.com.

Window Notes

What is it?

A tool that makes the note-taking process more engaging by encouraging students to record questions, personal reactions, and interesting connections in addition to facts

What are the benefits of using this tool?

Note taking is an essential part of classroom life, and it has a significant impact on student achievement (Dean et al., 2012). But ask most students (and most adults) about their experiences with taking notes and you'll probably get a shudder. Window Notes makes the process of taking notes more interesting for students by inviting them to jot down not just factual information but also questions, reactions, and connections they can make with what they're learning. Note that challenging students to generate different types of notes does more than enhance engagement; it stimulates active processing of the content in question, and it facilitates learning and retention as a result.

What are the basic steps?

1. Tell students that you want them to try making notes in a different way than usual—specifically, that you want them to generate notes that include the following four elements: (1) factual information, (2) questions, (3) feelings and reactions, and (4) connections that come to mind.

   Tip: Encourage students to record *any* connections that come to mind—for example, personal, real-world, literary, historical, or academic (i.e., connections to things they've learned in school).

2. Review the Window Notes organizer (p. 162) with students. Show them how it has a place for each of the four note types mentioned in Step 1, as well as guiding questions to spur their thinking.

3. Model the Window Notes process for students. Select a topic or text, and make all four types of notes about that topic or text on the organizer. Think aloud as you work.

4. Ask students to generate Window Notes about a specific topic, text, lecture, or other classroom presentation. They can use the Window Notes organizer on page 162, make their own organizers using the one on page 162 as a model, or express their thoughts orally (ideal for younger students).

   Tip: Before having students create content-related Window Notes, let them practice making Window Notes about a topic that's very familiar to them (e.g., a day in their life). Observe students as they work, and provide guidance or feedback as needed.

5. Invite students to share their notes with the class. Review key ideas and address students' questions if appropriate. Instruct students to add to or revise their notes as they see fit.

6. Encourage students to use the Window Notes technique independently, as a means of making the note-taking process more active, engaging, and personally meaningful. Facilitate the process by making blank Window Notes organizers readily available.

How is this tool used in the classroom?

✔ To promote note taking that includes facts, questions, feelings/reactions, and connections

✔ To make the note-taking process an active, engaging, and personally meaningful one

EXAMPLE 1: After reading a passage about the bee hummingbird aloud, a second-grade teacher invited students to generate Window Notes as a class. Students shared their ideas orally, and the teacher recorded them (shown below). Notice how the teacher made the four types of notes more distinct by using different symbols for each.

Facts	Feelings and Reactions
☑ The bee hummingbird is the world's smallest bird. ☑ They can fly forward, backward, and upside down. ☑ Hummingbirds are the only birds that can stay in place while they fly. This is called <u>hovering</u>. ☑ Bee hummingbirds beat their wings 80 times in a second.	☺ Bee hummingbirds are amazing! ☺ It must feel really cool to fly upside down. ☺ We want to learn more about bee hummingbirds.
Questions	**Connections**
? How do they fly upside down and backward? ? Why can't other birds hover?	✳ I saw a nature show on hummingbirds once. I remember that their wings move so fast that you can't see them flapping. ✳ It's probably called a bee hummingbird because it's tiny like a bee.

EXAMPLE 2: A high school student's notes from Maya Angelou's "Caged Bird" are shown below.

FACTS	FEELINGS & REACTIONS
· The poem goes back and forth between a free bird and a caged bird. · The free bird leaps and floats and flies and "claims the sky." · The caged bird's wings are clipped, and its feet are tired. · The poem is written in free verse.	The poem makes me feel sorry for the caged bird. It can't fly and longs to be free. I really like the way it repeats the verse about the caged bird singing of freedom. The song can't be stopped.
QUESTIONS	**CONNECTIONS**
Is the caged bird actually triumphant at the end?	The poem reminds me of a technique they sometimes use in movies where they keep cutting back and forth between two different characters.

EXAMPLE 3: Here are the notes a fourth-grade student made while watching a video on tornadoes:

FACTS	FEELINGS & REACTIONS
• Tornadoes are rotating columns of air. They go from a thunderstorm in the sky down to the ground. • They form when warm moist air hits cool dry air. • They can reach wind speeds of 300 miles per hour.	• Tornadoes are really scary! I didn't know how much damage they could cause!
QUESTIONS	CONNECTIONS
• How do they measure the wind speed inside a tornado? • Why don't tornadoes keep going? What makes them stop?	• I saw something about a tornado on TV when my parents were watching the news. Some of the people were crying because their houses had gotten blown away. • Tornadoes remind me of getting off to school. I am trying to do so many things and I am so rushed that it feels like I am spinning at 300 miles per hour!

🌑 Teacher Talk

➜ Because many students aren't used to being asked how they feel, particularly in a note-taking context, you may need to spend more time modeling and discussing what goes in the Feelings & Reactions quadrant of the organizer. One way to help is to give students a list of feeling stems that might help them—for example, "I really enjoyed ___," "I was impressed by ___," "I was surprised that ___," "I was inspired by ___," "I was confused about ___," or "I'm not sure how I feel about ___."

➜ While this tool is typically used to have students take notes on one specific text or presentation, it can also be used to help students reflect on and demonstrate what they've learned at the end of a lesson sequence or unit. When used in this way, students' completed organizers serve as a great tool for assessing students' learning, interests, open questions, and feelings about the topic or text.

➜ Help yourself (and your students) recognize that people have different note-taking preferences by surveying the class to see which of the four note types is each student's favorite. Explain that it's fine to have preferences, but that each note type has value—and, therefore, that students should aim to generate all four types of notes, even if some come less naturally to them.

➜ Help students appreciate—and encourage them to use—the Window Notes technique by identifying (or challenging them to identify) the value of each note type. Among other things, you might note that recording FACTS helps students extract and summarize key content, generating QUESTIONS allows students to express their curiosity, expressing FEELINGS & REACTIONS lets students connect with what they're learning on a personal level, and making CONNECTIONS encourages students to tap into their prior knowledge.

➜ To promote deeper understanding and retention of the material students took notes on, assign a task that requires students to review, summarize, and/or synthesize their understanding of that material.

➜ Some teachers may wonder if this technique is "fluffy." But, in reality, it promotes deeper understanding than traditional note taking. Why? Because making the four types of notes requires active processing and ensures that students are not simply copying, which can be done mindlessly.

Name: _____ Date: _____

Topic or text: _____

Window Notes

FACTS What did you learn?	FEELINGS & REACTIONS How did you feel about what you saw, heard, or read?
QUESTIONS What do you want to know or wonder about?	**CONNECTIONS** Can you make any connections to people, places, or things you know about? Or to experiences you've had?

Review & Revise

What is it?

A tool that trains students to view their notes as both a work in progress and a valuable learning tool

What are the benefits of using this tool?

What's the value of a good set of notes? When it comes time to study for a test, write an essay, or make a presentation, a set of high-quality notes can make a world of difference. But high-quality notes don't typically spring fully formed out of students' minds and onto the pages of their notebooks or laptop screens. That's why it is important to help students develop the habit of reviewing and revising their notes as their understanding of the content grows. Review & Revise teaches students a process (and gives them a set of guiding questions) that they can use to examine and improve their notes.

What are the basic steps?

1. Help students change their perception of notes from something that gets filed in a notebook and forgotten about to something that can help them. To do this, discuss ways students can use the notes they take (e.g., to help them review for a test, write a paper, or prepare a presentation).

2. Teach students that notes need to be added to, corrected, and improved over time. (The end-goal is a set of accurate, complete, and well-organized notes that students can study and use.) Explain that students should use the questions below to help them review and revise the notes they take.

   - Are there any errors or misunderstandings in my notes that I can identify and correct?
   - Do I need to add anything or elaborate on anything? Are there details that are worth adding?
   - Is there any redundant or unnecessary information that I can condense or delete?
   - Can I organize information into chunks—and give each chunk a descriptive heading?
   - Can I make important facts, terms, or sections stand out using underlining or other strategies?
   - Can I clarify anything by adding a sketch or diagram?
   - How can I highlight connections between individual bits of information?
   - Am I unclear about anything? Are there questions I need to ask or information I need to check?

   Tip: Train students to leave space when making their initial notes (e.g., skip lines, leave wide margins, insert space between chunks of information) so they'll have room for making revisions.

3. Prepare students to be successful by modeling the revision process repeatedly using sample sets of notes that you generate for this purpose. Think aloud as you work. (Ask yourself the questions from Step 2, identify issues that need attention, and explain what you do to address them.)

4. Have students practice using the questions from Step 2 to revise a set of notes that they take. Ask them to explain the changes they made, and give them feedback about their revisions.

5. Encourage students to use the Review & Revise process whenever they take notes. Remind them to review and use their revised notes, not file them in a notebook and forget about them.

How is this tool used in the classroom?

✔ To help students develop the habit of reviewing, revising, and using their notes

✔ To help students make their notes more meaningful and more useful

✔ To empower students to become more self-directed learners

EXAMPLE: A high school student divided her paper in half prior to taking notes on fats and cholesterol. She recorded her original notes in the left-hand column—and her additions and revisions on the right. This split-the-paper-in-half approach was one her teacher asked students to use when they first started practicing the Review & Revise technique. The teacher found that it allowed her to see the kinds of revisions students were making and give them feedback about their work.

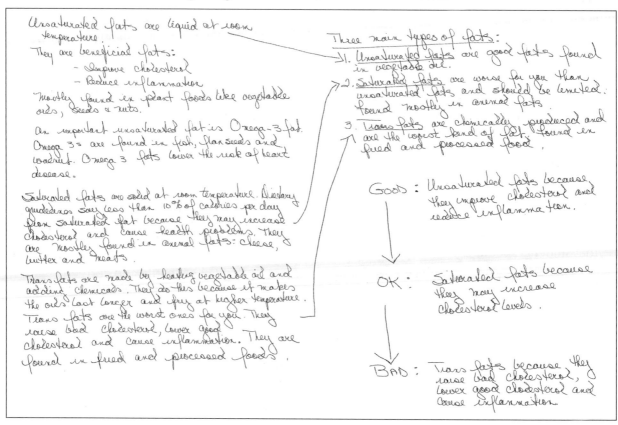

🌑 Teacher Talk

→ The process of taking and revising notes isn't just for older students. In fact, the skill should be taught to all learners. Even pre-readers can be taught to make picture notes and add to them or modify them as needed.

→ Initially, students may be resistant to the idea of revisiting and revising their notes. But the research couldn't be clearer about the benefits of this approach. As learning psychologist Tom Stafford (2014) tells us, "just looking at your notes won't help you learn them" (para. 17). Remind students that learning to come back to their notes and enhance them through revision is a skill that successful learners rely on.

Assigning Homework and Providing Practice

For the things we have to learn before we can do them, we learn by doing them.

—Aristotle

Practice is important for mastering skills, but, like homework, practice must have certain characteristics to produce the desired results.

—Ceri B. Dean, Elizabeth Ross Hubbell, Howard Pitler, and Bj Stone,
Classroom Instruction That Works (Second Edition)

We've all heard the saying "practice makes perfect," but is that cliché really true? The answer is *sometimes*. While it's true that practice can help students master important skills, "not all practice yields improved performance" (Dean et al., 2012, p. 102). And because "practice must have certain characteristics to produce the desired results" (p. 109), it's important for teachers to understand what effective practice looks like—both in class and at home—so that they can design their practice opportunities accordingly. The authors of *Classroom Instruction That Works* (Second Edition) help teachers acquire this knowledge by presenting concrete recommendations for maximizing the potential of homework and practice activities. Among other things, they advise teachers to do the following:

- Design homework and practice activities that are aligned with classroom learning objectives and that help students deepen content knowledge or master critical skills.
- Communicate the purpose of homework and practice activities to students.
- Provide feedback on homework and practice tasks.
- Establish multiple short and focused practice sessions that are spread out over time.

This chapter presents four tools for helping teachers put this important advice to work in their classrooms:

1. **From Homework to HOME Learning** helps students develop a more positive attitude toward homework by showing them how assigned tasks relate to class-

room learning targets and by putting them in charge of managing and making decisions about how to complete those tasks.

2. **Procedural PRO** reminds teachers that in order for students to master ("**O**wn") important procedures, it's critical to **P**resent those procedures directly, allow students to **R**ehearse those procedures repeatedly, and provide students with specific feedback about their performance.

3. **Repetition, Variation, Depth of Thought (RVD)** makes practicing critical content both engaging and effective by providing students with multiple opportunities to practice (**R**epetition), by **V**arying practice activities to prevent boredom, and by ensuring that practice activities promote **D**epth of thought.

4. **Graduated Difficulty** helps students get more out of classroom practice sessions by allowing them to practice at a level that's appropriate for them and get real-time feedback about their performance.

Note: Chapter 1 contains a number of feedback tools that can help you provide students with improvement-oriented feedback about their work. See, for example, Fine-Tune Your Feedback (pp. 29–32), PEERS (pp. 33–34), and Guiding & Grading Rubrics (pp. 35–40).

From Homework to HOME Learning

What is it?

A tool that teaches students the value of homework and helps them understand the decisions they need to make to produce quality work

What are the benefits of using this tool?

Too often, students see homework as an intrusion, as a chore that they need to complete as quickly as possible rather than as a learning experience. This tool puts the emphasis on the learning rather than the work. It helps students see how the tasks they complete at home support the learning targets they're working to achieve at school. It invites students to become active participants in assessing the impact of their homework on their achievement. And it changes the way students think about homework from "What's the point of this?" to "How did this help me learn?"

What are the basic steps?

1. Lead a discussion about the value of homework and its primary purpose: to promote learning. Explain that you'll call homework tasks *home learning tasks* to better reflect this purpose.

2. Present and describe students' home learning tasks for a given day or week, making sure to explain how the tasks support classroom learning targets. Have students record both the tasks and the learning targets on a HOME Learning Planner (p. 170).

3. Explain that you're going to put students in charge of managing and making decisions about how to complete the assigned tasks—specifically, that they will be responsible for deciding

   • **H**ow to complete their assignments (when, where, and for how long they'll work on them)
   • The **O**rder in which they'll complete their assignments
   • What **M**aterials they'll need to gather in order to complete the tasks successfully
   • How they'll **E**valuate their grasp of the content, their level of effort, and the quality of their work

   Tip: Show students how their HOME Learning Planners have space for recording their responses.

4. Discuss the value of making these kinds of decisions before starting to work on assigned tasks. Prepare students to make good decisions by discussing possible options and their consequences. ("How might doing your homework at the end of a packed day impact the quality of your work?")

5. Instruct students to fill in the HOME portion of the planner before beginning to work on the assigned tasks—and to complete the Reflection portion after they're done working.

6. Invite students to share what they learned from the assignment *and* from the decisions they made. ("So, might you do your homework without the TV on in the background next time?")

7. Teach students to ask themselves the "HOME questions" before tackling any assigned task.

How is this tool used in the classroom?

✔ To ensure that homework assignments support important learning objectives

✔ To teach students to make strategic decisions about how to approach and complete their work

✔ To help students and parents recognize the value of homework

EXAMPLE: A middle school student completed the planner below for one evening's assignments.

Tasks	Learning targets
1. Read the web article on kids and cell phones. Collect evidence for or against this statement: "There should be a mandatory minimum age to own a smartphone." →	I will be able to collect and use evidence to support a position.
2. Decision-based math: Complete as many time-distance-rate problems as needed to feel confident solving these problems. →	I will be able to solve for all three variables (time, distance, and rate) in time-distance-rate problems.

How: How will you complete these tasks?

When? *I will start after school and finish after dinner if I don't get done.*

Where? *At my desk*

How long will you spend? *I think these tasks will take a little more than an hour.*

Are there any distractions you'll need to avoid? *No music, no YouTube*

Order: In what order will you complete these tasks? Why?

I'll read first then reread to collect evidence.

I'll do math second.

I want to do the reading first right after school because that's when my attention level is highest.

Materials: What resources will you need to complete the tasks?

I need my tablet and ELA notebook.

I need my math textbook and math notebook.

Evaluation: How will you assess your performance (for example, your understanding of the content, effort level, or quality of work)?

For the reading task, if I can find evidence for or against the statement, I'll know I did a good job.

For the math task, when I can solve three problems in a row without mistakes, I will feel confident.

Reflection

How did the tasks enhance your learning? How did your decisions affect the quality of your work?

My decision to study at my desk instead of the kitchen table was a good decision. Blocking out distractions helped me focus on the reading and on finding evidence. I liked being able to make my own decisions about how many math problems to work on. I could actually see my skills getting better each time.

 **Teacher Talk**

→ Identifying the learning targets that home learning tasks support is not just for students' benefit—it's also an important reminder for you. Home learning tasks shouldn't be busywork, so make sure that the tasks you assign address classroom learning objectives in a meaningful way. If not, think about how you can revise assignments so that they better support important learning objectives.

→ By encouraging students to look back over their work—and their process for completing it—you help them recognize the control that they have over their work, which is essential to the development of self-management skills.

→ At the start of the school year, and especially with younger students, take some class time to model the decision-making process embedded in this tool. Using a sample assignment as a model, think aloud as you respond to each of the questions in the HOME acronym.

→ Feedback on homework, especially "in the form of comments rather than grades" (Dean et al., 2012, pp. 107–108), leads to better learning. Two tools in Chapter 1 are especially helpful for giving growth-oriented feedback to students. Fine-Tune Your Feedback (pp. 29–32) provides a set of research-based guidelines and feedback techniques to ensure that your feedback promotes learning and improvement. PEERS (pp. 33–34) uses a structured peer-feedback process that empowers students to review each other's work and help each other improve their performance.

→ By clearly spelling out how home learning assignments are connected to classroom learning targets, this tool can help overcome the negative perceptions that many students and their parents hold about homework. As such, it can be a valuable component of a school or district's homework policy. The letter below shows how a principal introduced the "home learning" concept and its benefits to parents.

Dear parents,

In our school, we refer to homework as "home learning" because the goal of the assignments that teachers send home is to promote learning. With your child's home learning assignments, you'll find a HOME Learning Planner that's designed to help your child

- See how the assigned tasks support important learning targets
- Make strategic decisions about how to complete home learning assignments
- Reflect on learning and the learning process

We encourage you to play a positive and active role in promoting learning at home by

HOME Learning Planner

Tasks	Learning targets

How: How will you complete these tasks?

When?

Where?

How long will you spend?

Are there any distractions you'll need to avoid?

Order: In what order will you complete these tasks? Why?

Materials: What resources will you need to complete the tasks?

Evaluation: How will you assess your performance (for example, your understanding of the content, effort level, or quality of work)?

Reflection (respond on the back)
How did the tasks enhance your learning? How did your decisions affect the quality of your work?

Procedural PRO

What is it?

A tool that uses direct instruction and guided practice to help students become pros at content-related procedures (e.g., multiplying fractions, conducting comparisons, calculating molarity)

What are the benefits of using this tool?

As educators, we're responsible for teaching students an enormous number of procedures over the course of their school careers. But just because we teach these procedures to our students doesn't mean that students actually get them—or get them well enough to execute them thoughtfully and independently. This tool presents a simple, three-phase process for teaching procedures more effectively. The three phases, which spell out the word *PRO*, highlight the gradual shift in responsibility that should come with teaching a procedure to students: (1) the teacher **P**resents the procedure, (2) the class **R**ehearses the procedure under the teacher's guidance, and (3) over time, students come to **O**wn (internalize and independently execute) the procedure.

What are the basic steps?

1. Identify a content-related procedure that you want students to master. Break the procedure into a series of manageable steps.

2. Ask students what it means to be a pro at something. Explain that you're going to use a simple, three-step process to help them become pros at the procedure you identified in Step 1.

3. Use the handout on page 174 to teach students (and yourself) what the PRO process entails. Help students notice how the PRO process gradually shifts the responsibility of executing the procedure from teacher to students.

4. **P**resent the selected procedure to students in a step-by-step manner.
   - Introduce the procedure and explain why it's important.
   - Explain and model the individual steps. Answer any questions that students might have.
   - Walk through the procedure as a class, completing one step at a time. Give students feedback about their performance after each step, and help them make any necessary corrections.

5. Give students multiple opportunities to **R**ehearse the procedure over time. Observe, coach, and give them feedback as they practice. The objective is to ensure that students are executing the procedure properly, while encouraging increasing independence over time.

   Note: You can have students practice as a class, in small groups or pairs, or independently.

6. Explain that the ultimate goal is for students to understand the procedure well enough to use it independently (**O**wn it).

7. Acknowledge students who follow individual steps, or the procedure as a whole, successfully. Identify students who still need help, and continue working with them until they, too, are pros.

How is this tool used in the classroom?

✔ To teach and help students internalize important content-related procedures

EXAMPLE 1: Becoming a pro at writing an argument

After noticing that her students were having a hard time writing basic argument paragraphs, an elementary teacher decided to reteach and help students practice the procedure using the Procedural PRO tool. She began by explaining the value of being able to craft a solid argument. She then divided the writing procedure into three simple steps and **P**resented those steps to students.

> STEP 1: State your position or claim.
>
> STEP 2: Provide reasons and evidence to support your claim.
>
> STEP 3: Add a conclusion that summarizes your argument.

The teacher modeled the steps by using them to write a simple argument paragraph on the board. She made sure to explain potentially confusing terms like *claim*, *reasons*, and *evidence* as she went.

Once the model paragraph was complete, the teacher challenged students to use the steps to write their own paragraphs at their seats. She had them write about a simple and familiar issue, so that they could focus on the writing process rather than the content. And she walked around the room as students wrote, offering individualized guidance and feedback. (To ensure that students stayed on track, she had them stop and wait for feedback after completing each individual step.)

The teacher assigned several argument-writing tasks over the next several weeks, so that students could **R**ehearse the argument-writing procedure regularly. After each rehearsal, the teacher reviewed students' completed pieces and gave students feedback about their work. She focused her feedback on students' use of the individual steps. (Had students presented a clear claim? Had they provided reasons/evidence to support that claim? Had they wrapped up their argument?)

After weeks of practice, it became clear that students really **O**wned the procedure. They were able to execute the basic steps without help, and the quality of their writing had improved significantly.

EXAMPLE 2: Becoming a pro at balancing chemical equations

A chemistry teacher uses Procedural PRO to help students become "balancing equation pros." He begins by explaining the importance of balancing chemical equations. Next, he **P**resents and models the basic steps in the procedure—slowly, and one step at a time, using a concrete example. When he finishes, he asks for and answers students' questions. He then works through several more examples, explaining what he's doing and why. After each example, he checks how well students are following by surveying the class. ("Give me a thumbs-up if you've got it, a thumbs-down if you're lost, and a thumbs-to-the-side if you're getting it but need a bit more practice.")

Once students indicate that they're getting it, the teacher has them **R**ehearse as a class using an example he puts on the board. He instructs students to complete the first step at their seats, while he completes it on the board. When students finish, they look up to check and correct their work and ask for help if needed. The teacher then repeats the process for each successive step.

After completing several practice sessions over the course of the week using increasingly complex examples, students gain the confidence and skill they need to balance equations independently. In other words, they **O**wn the balancing equations procedure.

🌓 Teacher Talk

➔ It's true that this tool demands an investment of time up front, in the form of extensive teaching and modeling—but it's an investment that definitely pays off in the long run, in the form of improved student performance.

➔ Learn, and help students learn, where they are on the pathway to owning a procedure by having them periodically rate their comfort level using a simple scale. For example, 1 = I'm lost; 2 = I can do this with lots of help; 3 = I can do this with some guidance; 4 = I can do this on my own!

➔ Help students generate a permanent record of the procedures they learn in class by having them create "procedures binders" that include purpose, basic steps, and relevant examples. Encourage students to refer to their binders for guidance when completing specific tasks and to review their binders regularly, so that important procedures stay fresh in their minds.

➔ Explaining why a procedure is important (see Step 4) can be beneficial since students are more apt to try to master procedures whose purpose and value they understand.

➔ Dean et al. (2012) note that "if students practice a skill incorrectly, they will ultimately have difficulty learning the correct way to perform that skill" (p. 102). For this reason, it's important to give students regular feedback about their efforts and be sure that they really know what they're doing before having them practice without guidance (e.g., complete a problem set for homework). Ensure that students get the feedback they need by providing it directly or by giving them answer keys that they can use to assess their work, see where they're going wrong, and make corrections as needed.

➔ Adjust the amount of modeling and practice that you provide to fit the difficulty of the procedure and the needs of your students. Some procedures take days to learn; others might take months.

➔ Teach students to practice on their own the same way they do when using this tool—by rehearsing critical content multiple times rather than cramming all their studying into a single session. Distributing study time over several sessions can have a positive impact on performance (Donovan & Radosevich, 1999; Willingham, 2002).

How to Become a PRO at Procedures

I will … **P**resent the procedure.

- I will introduce the procedure and explain why it's important.

- I will model the steps in the procedure, explaining what I am doing and why.

- I will direct you through the basic steps.

- I will check that you understand how to execute the basic steps.

- I will ask for and answer any questions.

- I will continue teaching and modeling until you are clear about what to do.

WE will … **R**ehearse the procedure.

- We will practice the procedure until everyone feels comfortable with it.

- I will observe you as you practice and offer feedback to help you improve.

- I will point out potential pitfalls and suggest ways to avoid them.

- You may ask me questions or ask for help at any time.

YOU will … **O**wn the procedure.

- You will understand the procedure well enough to be able to use it independently.

Repetition, Variation, Depth of Thought (RVD)

What is it?

A tool that presents three powerful principles (**R**epetition, **V**ariation, and **D**epth of Thought) for designing effective and engaging practice sessions

What are the benefits of using this tool?

If you've ever watched a sports team practice, you've probably heard a coach say, "Take it again." Good coaches know that mastering a skill or play requires repetition. But they also know that too much repetition leads to boredom, which is why they use a variety of drills to develop each individual skill rather than using the same exact drill every time. Finally, good coaches help their players be the best they can be by teaching them to think deeply, analytically, and critically about what they do on the field. Like coaches, teachers can use the principles of repetition, variation, and depth of thought to make practice sessions both engaging and effective. This tool explains how.

What are the basic steps?

1. Identify a specific learning goal that you want students to achieve. (Think: What do I want my students to understand or be able to do?) Share that goal with students.

2. Develop a plan for helping students acquire the necessary knowledge or skills. (Think: How will I teach and/or model the relevant material?) Implement your plan in the classroom.

3. Help students review, practice, and deepen their understanding of what you taught them. Use the RVD principles as a guide.

    Repetition: Provide multiple opportunities for students to practice, reinforce, and expand their grasp of the targeted content. Practice can be teacher-directed, guided, or independent.

    Variation: Don't assign the same old worksheet every time. Prevent boredom by having students practice in different ways (as a class, in groups, alone), using different kinds of tasks.

    Depth of thought: Ensure that at least some of your tasks challenge students to think deeply, analytically, or originally about the content—not just recall memorized material.

    Tip: See Teacher Talk and the Task Creation Menu on page 178 for more on designing your tasks.

4. Explain the purpose of each practice activity and the way it relates to the overall learning goal. Remind students that learning new things takes time, that they'll have multiple opportunities to review and practice, and that you'll help them along the way.

5. Observe students as they work, or review their completed assignments. Help them achieve a higher level of understanding or performance by providing appropriate guidance and feedback.

6. Encourage students to take responsibility for their own improvement as well. Have them regularly assess their achievement or comfort level and set goals or make decisions accordingly (e.g., ask for help or do more practice problems if they're struggling).

How is this tool used in the classroom?

✔ To develop engaging and effective practice sessions

✔ To help students practice and deepen their understanding of critical content and skills

The examples that follow show how teachers address the repetition, variety, and depth-of-thought components of the RVD acronym. They also show how teachers assess (and have students assess) progress—and then use that information to guide subsequent teaching and learning decisions.

EXAMPLE 1: A math teacher introduced and modeled the order of operations procedure one step at a time. She then helped students work through increasingly challenging practice problems as a class.

The teacher further addressed the **R**epetition principle by providing multiple opportunities for students to review and practice what they had learned over the course of the week. To ensure that students didn't get bored during these follow-up practice sessions, she had them practice in a **V**ariety of ways—alone, with a partner, and by completing different kinds of tasks:

- First, students reviewed the basic steps in the order of operations procedure by completing a recipe card like the one at the right.

- The next day, students practiced applying the recipe to a series of simple problems with the help of a partner. One student attempted to solve the problem; the other student acted as a coach.

- Later in the week, students tackled comparable problems independently, using worksheets like the one at the right to show and explain their work. After checking their work using an answer key, students were asked to assess their level of proficiency on a scale of 1–5.

> **ORDER OF OPERATIONS**
>
> Ingredients: parentheses   multiplication   addition
>   exponents   division   subtraction
>
> Directions:
> 1. Start with expressions in parentheses.
> 2. Next, tackle exponents.
> 3. Then, do multiplication and division in order from left to right.
> 4. Finally, do addition and subtraction in order from left to right.

> **WORKSHEET**
>
> START WITH THIS: $10 - 2 \times 3 + 5^2$
>
> FIRST DO exponents   AND GET $10 - 2 \times 3 + 25$
> NEXT DO multiplication   AND GET $10 - 6 + 25$
> NEXT DO subtraction   AND GET $4 + 25$
> FINALLY DO addition   AND GET 29

- For homework, students were given a set of three increasingly difficult problem sets and encouraged to complete whichever one they felt was most appropriate based on their assessment. The teacher reviewed students' completed worksheets to see who was having trouble with what, and she worked with students to establish plans for improvement. ("What makes the next level harder? What will it take for you to go up a level?")

Finally, the teacher encouraged **D**epth of thought by challenging students to decide whether the order of operations really matters—and if so, why. She had students speculate about what would happen if operations were done in a different order, test their predictions, and draw conclusions.

EXAMPLE 2: A high school English teacher regularly incorporates the RVD principles into his vocabulary units. Instead of presenting terms once and moving on, he builds vocabulary knowledge over time by providing repeated exposures and practice opportunities (**R**epetition). He has students engage with the words in different ways every time (**V**ariety), using tasks like these that promote **D**epth of understanding rather than memorization:

- Define the concept/term in your own words.
- Create or find examples of the concept.
- Create a simile that shows your understanding of the concept.
- List the critical attributes of the concept.
- Compare/contrast the concept to another similar concept.
- Explain how the concept relates to at least two other concepts from this unit.
- Pretend that you are the concept and describe a day in your life.

The teacher enables students to see their vocabulary knowledge grow by having them rate their understanding of each term at the start of the unit, after each practice activity, and then again at the end. After each practice activity, he encourages students to think about what they can do to improve their understanding of the words they haven't yet mastered.

🌐 Teacher Talk

→ It's easy to fall into a rut and assign the same kind of practice task or worksheet over and over again. If you need some fresh ideas, the Task Creation Menu on page 178 can help. It identifies four distinct styles of tasks, and it provides concrete examples for each one. To achieve the **V**ariety that the RVD acronym calls for, simply use different styles of tasks from the menu. Use Understanding, Self-Expressive, and Interpersonal tasks to promote **D**epth of thought.

Note: The menu on page 178 isn't the only option. Designing tasks that engage different intelligences (Gardner, 1999) is another way to achieve the kind of variety that's called for by the RVD acronym. And engaging the thinking skills at the top levels of Bloom's Taxonomy or Webb's Depth of Knowledge model promotes depth of thought.

→ Clarify that practice sessions are formative, not summative—in other words, designed to promote improvement, not grade students on their performance. As a result, students should be taught not to worry about making mistakes while practicing. Explain that mistakes are natural and expected when learning something new and that they provide a valuable opportunity for you (and your students) to identify and target areas that need work.

→ Learning something new typically requires a lot more repetition than we think. For this reason, we suggest teaching, reinforcing, and having students practice new material more times, and over a longer period of time, than you think is necessary. Continue revisiting material even after a unit ends.

Tip: Help your students—and yourself!—appreciate the importance of repeated practice by having them think about a skill they're good at (e.g., making a layup, playing a video game, reciting number facts) and discuss what / how long it took for them to master that skill.

→ Because this tool is situated in a chapter about practice, it focuses on the use of RVD in a practice setting. But it's just as important to use RVD in an *instructional* context. To do this, present key content multiple times (**R**epetition) and in a **V**ariety of ways/modalities (e.g., via video, lecture, or reading). Promote **D**epth of thought by posing questions that require thinking deeply about the material (e.g., questions that ask students to analyze, evaluate, explain, synthesize, or apply).

Task Creation Menu: Four Different Styles of Tasks

INSTRUCTIONS: Use the menu below to help you design tasks that will engage students in deepening and demonstrating their grasp of the relevant content. To achieve the variety that the RVD acronym calls for, simply use different styles of tasks. Use Understanding, Self-Expressive, and Interpersonal tasks to promote depth of thought.

MASTERY TASKS require students to demonstrate factual knowledge or perform calculations/procedures with accuracy.

To create a Mastery task, you might ask students to

- Answer factual questions (who, what, where, when)
- List important facts, formulas, or steps in a procedure
- Define key terms or concepts
- Demonstrate, describe, or follow a set of procedures
- Put information in order (e.g., make a timeline)
- Make and label a visual display (e.g., a map or diagram)
- Perform calculations with accuracy

INTERPERSONAL TASKS invite students to connect personally with the content or with other people.

To create an Interpersonal task, you might ask students to

- Practice with a partner
- Teach or explain the material to someone else
- Coach or advise a classmate
- Consider the content from multiple people's perspectives
- Connect or apply the content to their personal lives/experiences
- Personify something (If you were ___, what would you feel/do?)
- Role-play

UNDERSTANDING TASKS ask students to analyze and/or explain; the goal is to promote or check for depth of understanding.

To create an Understanding task, you might ask students to

- Analyze similarities/differences
- Analyze causes and/or effects
- Analyze people's work or ideas, critiquing errors or logical flaws
- Analyze, interpret, or draw conclusions about data, texts, etc.
- Explain why or how
- Explain and/or justify their responses or thinking processes
- Find and explain connections (This is related to ___ because ___.)

SELF-EXPRESSIVE TASKS challenge students to express or apply their knowledge of the content in new and original ways.

To create a Self-Expressive task, you might ask students to

- Speculate or anticipate consequences (What if ___?)
- Represent key concepts visually
- Construct/formulate something original (e.g., solution, idea, rule)
- Use a simile to illustrate their understanding of a concept
- Apply their learning to a new and different context
- Express their learning in a creative or artistic way
- Synthesize multiple aspects of the content

Graduated Difficulty

What is it?

Inspired by the work of Muska Mosston (1972), this differentiating-by-readiness tool lets students choose which level to work at while practicing essential skills

What are the benefits of using this tool?

In order for students to practice critical skills in an efficient and effective way, they need to have a clear understanding of where they're going (What is the ultimate goal of the practice sessions?) and where they are now. The problem, of course, is that "figuring out where you are" isn't necessarily as easy as it sounds. In many cases, students don't realize how well—or poorly—they've mastered a specific skill until they're asked to apply it on an end-of-unit test. Graduated Difficulty addresses this problem by having students use three increasingly difficult practice tasks to assess and improve their proficiency *before* test time. By asking students to figure out what they can and can't do, this tool provides them with rich feedback about what to focus on and how to allocate practice and review time.

What are the basic steps?

1. Identify a skill you want students to practice. Develop three different tasks that will help them practice the selected skill, each at a different level of difficulty:

   • *Level 1 tasks* should be simple enough for all students to complete.

   • *Level 2 tasks* should be challenging for most students but doable by many.

   • *Level 3 tasks* should be challenging for all students. They should require the highest level of knowledge or proficiency that is demanded by your curriculum/standards.

2. Share the tasks—and the purpose of the tasks—with students. Instruct students to compare the different tasks, determine what makes one more difficult than another, and choose the task that feels right to them.

3. Prepare students to make good choices by discussing the consequences of selecting tasks that are too hard or too easy (too hard and they won't be successful, too easy and they won't improve).

   Tip: Use real-world examples to help students grasp the concept. ("What if you went skiing and stayed on the bunny hill the whole time? What if you tackled an expert slope before you were ready?")

4. Provide an answer key so that students can check their work and get feedback about their performance as they go.

5. Make it clear that students' work won't be graded and that students are free to change levels (up or down) at any time—the goal is to work at whichever level will help them improve.

6. Observe students as they work to see how they're getting along. Pose questions that will help them think about their decision-making process ("How did you select that level?"), but don't tell them what level to work at. Let them choose and learn from their choices.

7. Ask students to reflect on what they learned. See Teacher Talk for a list of questions you can use to help them analyze their choices and establish plans for improvement.

How is this tool used in the classroom?

✔ To have students practice, develop, and assess their grasp of key skills

✔ To make students responsible for monitoring and managing their own learning

EXAMPLE 1: A second-grade teacher used this tool to have his students practice and improve their ability to tell time. His Level 1 task involved telling time to the hour, his Level 2 task involved telling time to the half hour, and his Level 3 task involved telling time to the nearest five minutes.

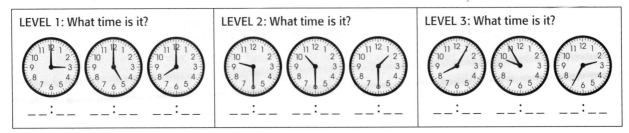

EXAMPLE 2: Portions of a French teacher's tasks are shown below. Notice that students will be practicing the same skill at all three levels (conjugating verbs), but that they'll be practicing it in different ways: by selecting the correct verb to complete a sentence (Level 1), by translating sentences from English to French (Level 2), or by writing a letter in French (Level 3).

LEVEL 1:

Circle the form of the verb that agrees with the subject pronoun at the beginning of the sentence.

1. Nous (voulez, veulent, voulons) visiter Normandie.

2. Ils (veulent, voulez, veut) aller à Nice.

3. Tu (veut, veux, veulent) regarder la télévision.

LEVEL 2:

Translate the following sentences into French. Pay close attention to the subject pronoun and the form of the verb that goes with that pronoun.

1. She wants to go to Paris.

2. They (f) want to visit Alsace.

3. You (pl) want to visit Champagne.

LEVEL 3:

Imagine that you're in France. Write a letter to a friend back home that describes the places you've already seen (cities, landmarks, etc.) and the places you hope to visit before your trip is over. Include at least three sentences that use the verb *aller*, three sentences that use the verb *vouloir*, and three sentences that use a regular *-er* verb. Word your letter so that you can use different subject pronouns—not *je* every time!

Note: Since there can't be an answer key for a task like this, bring me your finished letter and I will check it.

EXAMPLE 3: A music teacher presents students with pieces of music at three different levels of difficulty, tells them that the goal is to play one of the pieces without mistakes in a week's time, and lets them choose which piece to work on.

🌑 Teacher Talk

➜ Use questions like these to guide and focus the reflection process in Step 7:

- How did you go about deciding which level to work at? What criteria did you use?

- Do you feel like you made the right choice? Would you make the same choice again? Why?

- How did it feel to be able to choose your own task? Why?

- Did you learn anything about yourself and how you make decisions?

- How can this experience prepare you to study more effectively? To achieve at a higher level?

- What would it take to move up a level? How could you acquire the necessary knowledge/skills?

- Did you learn anything that could help you improve your performance in this or a future unit?

➜ There are many ways to establish different levels of difficulty. You can have students do the same exact type of task at every level (e.g., read the time on a clock), but make each level harder than the previous one as shown in Example 1. Another option is to have students complete a different type of task at every level as shown in Example 2.

➜ Graduated Difficulty works best with tasks that have right or wrong answers, but it can be used with other kinds of tasks as well. In these cases, students should be given a specific outcome to aim for or a list of criteria to satisfy at each level. For example, if students are practicing "pulling" a baseball, they might aim to pull the ball five times in a row off a batting tee (Level 1), in a batting cage (Level 2), against a pitcher throwing fastballs (Level 3), and against a pitcher throwing a mixture of pitches (Level 4).

➜ Find ways to challenge and engage students who complete Level 3 tasks successfully. One option: Invite them to create Level 4 tasks and the answer keys to go with them—and have them exchange their tasks with other Level 4 students. Another option: Have these students coach and assist a classmate.

➜ Some teachers choose *not* to indicate which level of task is which. Why? When tasks are labeled, some students pick based on the level alone ("I'm going to pick Level 3") rather than comparing the tasks and making an informed decision about which task is right for them. Leaving the tasks unlabeled forces students to examine the tasks more deeply (what makes one different from the next?), think about what they know, and decide which task is most appropriate.

➜ Teach students that effective studying/practicing involves deciding *how long* to practice as well as *what* to practice. In the context of Graduated Difficulty, this means deciding whether they need to complete an entire task before choosing to move up or down—or whether they can make that decision sooner. ("Since I got the first three questions wrong, I won't waste any more time at this level; I will move down.") Beyond the scope of this tool, this means making thoughtful decisions about how much time to practice or study specific things. ("Do I need to spend more time reviewing these vocabulary terms? Or do I know them well enough to move on to something else?")

➜ The fact that students learn at different speeds can pose challenges for classroom teachers. This tool acknowledges and addresses some of these challenges by providing options for students at different readiness levels. Letting students choose a practice task that's at the right level of difficulty for them enables everyone to work at a personally productive pace and experience confidence-building success. Encouraging students to make thoughtful decisions about their learning has the added benefit of fostering independence and self-regulation.

PART III

Tools for Helping Students Extend and Apply Knowledge

Identifying Similarities and Differences

One can state, without exaggeration, that the observation of and the search for similarities and differences are the basis of all human knowledge.

—Alfred Nobel

Simply put, identifying similarities and differences helps us make sense of the world. We ask, "Is this like that?" By answering the question, we enhance our existing mental representation or abstract schema for the information.

—Ceri B. Dean, Elizabeth Ross Hubbell, Howard Pitler, and Bj Stone, *Classroom Instruction That Works* (Second Edition)

Comparing and contrasting, or mentally placing items side by side to look for both similarities and differences, is fundamental to human learning. But just because the act of attending to similarities and differences is natural doesn't mean that students come to school knowing how to do it well. That's why the authors of *Classroom Instruction That Works* (Second Edition) highlight the benefits of providing "explicit instruction in the use of processes associated with identifying similarities and differences" (Dean et al., 2012, p. 121). These benefits include greater focus on essential information, increased ability to make inferences, and deeper insight. Not surprisingly, the benefits also include higher achievement: Dean et al. (2012) report that teaching students how to identify similarities and differences "produced an average effect size of 0.66, which is equivalent to a 25 percentile point gain" (p. 119).

The authors of *Classroom Instruction That Works* (Second Edition) make three recommendations designed to help teachers and their students realize the benefits associated with identifying similarities and differences. These recommendations are as follows:

- Teach students a variety of processes for identifying similarities and differences, including comparing, classifying, and exploring metaphors/similes/analogies.
- Guide students through the process of identifying similarities and differences.
- Provide supporting cues that draw students' attention to important features of the items being compared.

To help you put these important recommendations into practice and ensure that your classroom use of identifying similarities and differences leads to real gains in student achievement, we present the following four tools:

1. **Describe First, Compare Second** prepares students to make more thoughtful comparisons by providing clear criteria for them to focus on and by teaching them to describe items before comparing them.

2. **Comparative Controversy** develops comparison skills and content knowledge by having students take and defend positions on content-related controversies.

3. **Concept Attainment** helps students grasp the critical attributes of core concepts by having them compare examples and non-examples of those concepts.

4. **Metaphorical Thinking** helps students deepen their understanding of critical concepts by challenging them to make conceptual, rather than literal, comparisons in the form of metaphors, similes, and analogies.

Describe First, Compare Second

What is it?

A tool that prepares students to conduct thoughtful comparisons by teaching them to describe each item thoroughly before identifying similarities and differences

What are the benefits of using this tool?

If we expect students to master the skill of conducting a comparative analysis, then we need to provide "explicit instruction in the use of processes associated with identifying similarities and differences" (Dean et al., 2012, p. 121). This tool outlines a simple process for teaching comparison in the classroom.[*] The key to its success lies in its insistence on having students *describe* individual items before actually comparing them. Asking students to "describe first, compare second" is a simple instructional move, but it's one that we've seen pay off in countless numbers of classrooms with countless numbers of students.

What are the basic steps?

1. Select two items for students to compare (e.g., texts, objects, individuals, events, or concepts). Start with familiar items like plates and bowls or apples and oranges.

2. Ask students to describe each item individually using the Description Organizer on page 191. Guide the process by providing specific attributes, components, or criteria for students to focus on (e.g., Who are the main *characters* in each story? What is the basic *plot*?).

   Note: Very young students can work through Steps 2–5 as a class, and orally rather than on paper.

3. Have students use the information on their organizers to identify ways the items are similar and different. Encourage them to focus on the components they described in Step 2 when making these comparisons (e.g., How are the *characters* in the stories similar/different? The *plots*?).

4. Have students record the similarities/differences they identify on a Comparison Organizer (p. 192).

5. Assign a writing task that requires students to synthesize what they've learned from their analysis. Here are some options:
   - Explain how the items are similar and different.
   - Take a position on whether the items are more alike or different. Justify your position.
   - Compare how these two authors/texts addressed this theme, topic, or event.

6. Encourage students to use a "describe first, compare second" approach whenever they're faced with a comparison task (e.g., on a standardized exam).

7. Prepare students to handle comparison tasks independently by training them to scan task descriptions for hints about specific attributes/components to focus on, and by discussing the kinds of attributes they might want to focus on if attributes aren't provided. See Teacher Talk for details.

---

[*]This process is adapted from Silver Strong & Associates' Compare & Contrast strategy. For more on this strategy, see *The Core Six* (Silver, Dewing, & Perini, 2012) or *Compare & Contrast: Teaching Comparative Thinking to Strengthen Student Learning* (Silver, 2010).

How is this tool used in the classroom?

✔ To help students handle comparison questions more successfully

✔ To help students conduct more focused and organized comparisons

EXAMPLE 1: A second-grade teacher wants her students to compare two different Cinderella stories (the version popularized by Walt Disney and Rafe Martin's [1992] retelling of an Algonquin version). The Description and Comparison Organizers that they generated as a class are shown below. The comparison paragraph that one student used these organizers to write is shown on the next page.

Notice how the aspects of the stories that students described in the Description Organizer became the focus for both the Comparison Organizer *and* the final written piece. (In other words, students described, then compared, then wrote about the same five things: main characters, personalities, wants, ending, and lesson.) Teaching students to do this same thing—to use their organizers to guide the pieces that they write—will help them produce higher-quality comparison essays.

DESCRIPTION ORGANIZER

Story 1: Cinderella	Describe these things:	Story 2: The Rough-Face Girl
Cinderella two stepsisters prince fairy godmother	Main characters	Rough-Face Girl two sisters Invisible Being
Cinderella is good and sweet. Her stepsisters are mean.	What the three sisters are like	The Rough-Face Girl has a kind heart. Her sisters are mean.
They all want to marry the prince.	What the three sisters want	They all want to marry the Invisible Being.
The prince marries Cinderella instead of the mean sisters. They live happily ever after.	How the story ends	The Invisible Being marries the Rough-Face Girl instead of the mean sisters. They live happily ever after.
Good things happen to good people.	Lesson of the story	Good things happen to good people.

COMPARISON ORGANIZER ("TOP HAT" FORMAT)

Ways the stories are different

Cinderella:	The Rough-Face Girl:
Cinderella has a fairy godmother to help her.	The Rough-Face Girl doesn't have a fairy godmother.
Cinderella wants to marry a prince.	The Rough-Face Girl wants to marry the Invisible Being.

Ways the stories are alike:

In both stories, the main character is nice and her sisters are mean.

In both stories, the main character and her sisters want to marry the same person.

Both stories end the same way. The nice sister gets married and lives happily ever after. The mean sisters don't.

Both stories teach the same lesson that good things happen to good people.

COMPARISON PARAGRAPH

I am comparing two Cinderella storys. One is called Cinderella. The other is the rought face girl. One way both storys are alike is that the main character has two mean sisters. A second way they are alike is that in both storys all the sisters what to mary the same person but only the nice sisters gets to mary him at the end. Another way they are alike is that both storys teach you the same losson. Something that is differnt is Cinderella has a fairy god mother to help her and the rought face girl dosent but for the other resons I told you these two storys are a lot alike.

EXAMPLE 2: A high school math teacher wants his students to be able to explain in depth how quadratic equations are similar to and different from linear equations. Prior to making this comparison, students are asked to describe each type of equation separately by collecting information about the problem-solving processes, graph shapes, and solutions associated with both types of equations. The Description Organizer that one student created is shown below.

Description Organizer

Item or text #1: *Linear equations*	Describe these attributes, aspects, or components:	Item or text #2: *Quadratic equations*
$y = ax + b$	Standard Equation	$y = ax^2 + bx + c$
Select random values for x. Substitute and evaluate for y. Plot ordered pairs (x, y). Plot point b on the y axis to determine y intercept. Use slope (a) to determine additional points.	How to solve	Select random values for x. Substitute x and evaluate for y. Plot ordered pairs (x, y). A more complex process called completing the square is used to determine the vertex of the parabola and its general shape.
straight line – infinite number of ordered pairs that make the equation true	Shape of graph	Parabola
– given y, there is only one x value that makes the equation true.	Solution	– Infinite number of pairs that make the equation true. – Given y, there can be 0, 1, or 2 x values that make the equation true.

🌐 Teacher Talk

→ Prepare students to produce quality work by showing them examples of well-written comparison pieces, discussing the pieces' basic components and structures, and familiarizing students with linking/organizing words they can use to highlight similarities (e.g., *similarly, one similarity, both, likewise*) and differences (e.g., *in contrast, one difference, on the other hand, however*). You can also provide students with simple comparative frames that show how comparative writing is structured (see p. 114 for an example).

→ When students are comparing two texts, encourage them to include specific details and snippets from the texts on their organizers. Noting the page numbers where these items appear will help students incorporate these details into their final pieces.

→ Comparative writing tasks are common on standards-based tests. Here are some tips for helping students succeed on comparative writing tasks:

- Clarify that the word *comparing* typically implies comparing *and* contrasting. ("If a question or prompt asks you to *compare* two things, you should discuss the similarities *and* the differences.")

- Use sample tasks like the ones below to show students how test questions / task descriptions sometimes point to specific elements that they should focus on when conducting their comparisons.

  Task 1: Compare the kinds of adaptations that enable the animals you read about to survive in their various habitats. You may wish to address adaptations involved in finding food, regulating body temperature, or avoiding predators. (Here, the task suggests specific kinds of adaptations that students might want to compare.)

  Task 2: Compare George Washington's Farewell Address to the Monroe Doctrine. Analyze how both texts address similar themes and concepts regarding "entangling alliances."* (Here, the task asks students to focus on what the individual documents have to say about entangling alliances.)

- Talk to students about elements they might want to compare if none are suggested by the test question or task. ("If you're asked to compare characters, you might compare the characters' personalities, adventures, experiences, or interactions with other characters.")

- Use specific examples to teach students that comparative writing tasks won't always contain the words *compare* and *contrast*. Here is how a ninth-grade teacher did this using a task designed around Common Core Reading Standard RL.9–10.7:

  "This task is asking you to analyze representations of the fall of man in two different artistic mediums, including what is emphasized or absent in each one. The word *comparison* doesn't appear anywhere in the task description, but it's a comparison task nonetheless. How can we tell?"

*This task is adapted from Appendix B of the Common Core ELA/Literacy Standards, p. 129.

Description Organizer

Item or text #1:	Describe these attributes, aspects, or components:	Item or text #2:

Name: _____   Date: _____

"Top Hat" Comparison Organizer

Differences:

Item or text #1:

Item or text #2:

Similarities:

Comparative Controversy

What is it?

A tool that engages students in comparing and contrasting critical content as they take and defend positions on content-related "controversies"

What are the benefits of using this tool?

What if we could couple the research-based practice of identifying similarities and differences with controversy, a known motivator and achievement booster? By making this marriage, Comparative Controversy builds students' analytical skills and gets students engaged in exploring and debating critical content—even content they don't typically get excited about. At the heart of the tool are simple frames that force students to take and defend a position based on a comparative analysis of two or more items or topics. The debates that these frames spark tend to be animated and enthusiastic, as most students relish the opportunity to express and make a case for their ideas. Comparative Controversy also hones critical discussion skills, including listening carefully, disagreeing respectfully, and supporting ideas with evidence.

What are the basic steps?

1. Review the Comparative Controversy frames on pages 195–196. Pick one that fits your content.

2. Use the selected frame to develop a content-specific question that will provoke debate when presented to students. Confirm that your question is one that students can have legitimately different opinions about, not one that has a definitive right or wrong answer.

   Note: The goal is to develop questions or statements that require students to analyze similarities and differences between/among items and then use their analysis to take a position.

3. Present your question. Give students time to compare and contrast the items and develop a position. Clarify that there are no right or wrong answers, just different opinions—but that opinions must be based on a careful analysis of similarities and differences.

4. Prepare students to engage in a heated but respectful discussion by reviewing and modeling the following discussion guidelines (modify the list as needed):

   - State your positions clearly. Support them with relevant similarities, differences, or other details.
   - Treat your classmates as you'd want to be treated. If you're going to disagree, do it respectfully.
   - Question and critique each other's reasoning, not each other's intelligence.
   - Be passionate about your positions, but listen to other people's arguments as well.
   - Keep an open mind. Feel free to change positions in response to what you hear.

5. Invite students to share and justify their positions. Moderate the discussion by helping students recognize and strengthen poorly supported positions, identify similarities/differences they might've missed, transform personal attacks into thoughtful critiques, etc.

6. Help students reflect on what they learned, summarize critical similarities and differences, and assess how well they followed the discussion guidelines.

How is this tool used in the classroom?

✔ To develop students' comparative analysis skills

✔ To promote active conversations about (and a deeper understanding of) critical content

✔ To use controversy and debate as a means of stimulating student engagement

✔ To develop students' ability to support a position with solid reasons and evidence

✔ To promote essential speaking and listening skills

Teachers use the Comparative Controversy frames described on pages 195–196 to engage students in discussing key content and discussing it excitedly. Sample prompts show how the frames can work across grade levels and content areas.

🎯 Teacher Talk

➔ Remind students to support their positions with reasons and evidence by saying, "And you chose that position *because*?" (Students should respond with, "I think ____ because ____.")

➔ Be sure to leave time for reflection. Help students reflect on and analyze their decision-making process by calling attention to the criteria they use to make their choices. ("John argued that these paintings are more similar than different because their subject matter and color palette are almost identical. What criteria was Tameka using when she decided that the paintings were more different?") Help students solidify their understanding of the relevant content (and demonstrate they were listening) by challenging them to summarize their classmates' positions and reasoning. Prepare students to become more actively and appropriately engaged in future discussions by helping them assess—and think about how to improve—their performance. ("How well did you personally follow our discussion guidelines? How well did the class as a whole follow the guidelines? How can you/we do better next time?")

➔ Comparative Controversy provides an ideal opportunity to review and give students feedback about their use of behavioral guidelines that relate to sharing and discussing ideas—guidelines like listening carefully, disagreeing respectfully, and critiquing ideas rather than people. As always, remember to teach expected behaviors explicitly, provide reminders as needed, and offer specific and informative praise to students who exhibit the behaviors successfully. ("I appreciate that you questioned Santiago's logic rather than attacking Santiago personally.")

➔ As written, the tool develops oral argument skills, but you can target written argument skills instead by having students present and justify their positions in writing rather than orally.

Five Comparative Controversy Frames

More Alike or Different?

More Alike or Different? is useful when students are studying related pairs of items, events, concepts, or individuals. To use this frame, have students review what they know about each item, decide whether the items are more alike or different, and support their choices with relevant details. Asking students to decide whether two items are more alike or different and explain their reasoning forces them to examine the items more closely and attend to the most salient similarities and differences. Here are some sample prompts:

- Are spiders and insects more alike or more different?
- Are fractions and decimals more alike or more different?
- Are Ulysses S. Grant and Robert E. Lee more alike or more different?
- Are the heroines in these two stories more alike or more different?
- Are lithium and potassium more alike or more different?
- Are these two paintings more alike or more different?

Which Is More ... Better ... the Best ... the Most?

This frame asks students to make and defend judgments based on quality or degree. Prompts contain comparative or superlative words such as *more*, *better*, *best*, *most*, and *greatest*. Here are some examples:

- Which is the best season: spring, summer, winter, or fall?
- Which of these articles provides the most realistic advice for dealing with bullying?
- Which type of graph is best for presenting this kind of data?
- Which is the most powerful line in this text?
- Which of these scientific discoveries had the greatest impact on world history?

Which One Doesn't Belong?

This frame asks students to examine a set of three or four items, search for similarities and differences among the items, and identify one item that doesn't belong with the others. With the traditional use of this frame (see Silver, Brunsting, Walsh, & Thomas, 2012), the teacher deliberately selects one item in the set that is meant to be identified as the outlier (e.g., one non-right triangle among two or three right triangles). Here, however, the idea is to promote controversy by presenting students with a set of items that has no obvious outlier and allowing them to argue the case for any item they want ("This item doesn't belong with the others because ..."). Here are some sample prompts:

- Question mark, period, exclamation point: Which one doesn't belong?
- Butterfly, honeybee, mosquito, firefly: Which one doesn't belong?
- Square, rectangle, rhombus, trapezoid: Which one doesn't belong?
- Jazz, blues, soul, R & B: Which one doesn't belong?
- *A Raisin in the Sun*, *Death of a Salesman*, *The Glass Menagerie*: Which one doesn't belong?
- George Washington, Thomas Jefferson, Abraham Lincoln, Theodore Roosevelt: Which one doesn't belong?

Perfect Pairs and Odd Couples

With this frame, students are presented with a set of five or more related items that they've recently learned about (e.g., six organs in the human body, the ten amendments in the Bill of Rights, five classes of vertebrates, eight classic films). Students are then asked to decide which two items in the set they believe make a "perfect pair" (items they believe have a lot in common) and which two items are an "odd couple" (items that are very different from one another). Clarify that students can nominate any items they want for their pairings, as long as they can back up their choices with solid reasoning and details. Encourage students to support their choices with as many similarities or differences as they can think of. In response to the question "Which two planets in the solar system do you believe are an odd couple?," for example, a student might say something like this: "Mercury and Neptune are an odd couple, because almost everything about them is different! Mercury is closest to the sun, while Neptune is farthest away. Mercury is small and rocky, while Neptune is large and gaseous. Mercury is extremely hot during the day, whereas Neptune is always extremely cold."

Metaphorical Duels

Metaphorical Duels (Silver, Brunsting, Walsh, & Thomas, 2012) exploits the power of metaphorical thinking to promote depth of understanding. To use this frame, design two possible similes around a topic of interest, ask students which they feel is the most accurate, and have them justify their choices. Making the unusual connections that this frame requires forces students to think deeply and creatively about the critical attributes of the initial topic—a move that can have a powerful impact on comprehension and lead to deep insight. Here are some sample prompts:

- Is a good friend more like a teddy bear or a flower?
- Is prejudice more like an iceberg or a runaway train?
- Is the circulatory system more like a bicycle or a delivery truck?
- Is the scientific method more like a recipe or a map?
- Are graphing calculators more like microscopes or telescopes?
- Are hieroglyphics more like a comic strip or a short story?

Encouraging students to describe the attributes of the items they're comparing can help them make more thoughtful and well-supported choices. ("Before deciding whether prejudice is more like an iceberg or a runaway train, jot down everything you know about prejudice, everything you know about icebergs, and everything you know about runaway trains.")

Concept Attainment

What is it?

A tool that helps students build deep understanding of a core concept by presenting them with examples and non-examples of the concept and challenging them to identify its critical attributes

What are the benefits of using this tool?

Concept Attainment is a tool that harnesses the power of identifying similarities and differences and uses that power to help students build a deep understanding of important concepts. The tool presents students with both examples and non-examples of an essential concept and asks them to generate critical attributes that define the concept. Students then test and refine their list of attributes by analyzing and comparing additional examples and non-examples of the concept under investigation.

What are the basic steps?

1. Identify a concept that you want students to understand deeply. The concept should be one with clear critical attributes. The concept *mammal*, for example, includes these attributes: (1) vertebrates, (2) warm-blooded, (3) produce milk to feed young, and (4) have hair on bodies.

2. Tell students that they'll be working to develop a deep understanding of a mystery concept (the concept you identified in Step 1) by comparing *yes* and *no* examples of that concept. Then, present them with a series of *yes* and *no* examples.

   Note: Yes examples must have all the critical attributes of the concept. *No* examples can have none or some of the critical attributes.

3. Ask students to analyze the *yes* and *no* examples, identify what the *yes* examples have in common, and determine how the *yes* examples differ from the *no* examples. Ask students to use their analysis to develop an initial list of critical attributes of the concept.

4. Present additional *yes* and *no* examples. With each set of *yes* and *no* examples that you present, ask students to test and refine their list of attributes.

5. Work with the entire class to review the *yes* and *no* examples and develop a final list of attributes of the concept.

6. Identify/name the mystery concept that students have been working to understand. Explain why a deep understanding of this concept is important to future learning.

7. Ensure that students have internalized the attributes of the concept by assigning a task that asks them to demonstrate their understanding of those attributes. See Teacher Talk for task ideas.

How is this tool used in the classroom?

✔ To build students' understanding of important concepts

✔ To teach students how to use comparison to identify important attributes

✔ To develop students' ability to analyze and discriminate among items

EXAMPLE 1: A middle school science teacher is about to begin a lesson on predator-prey relationships. He uses Concept Attainment to help students build a deep understanding of what a predator is by discovering its critical attributes.

The teacher explains that he will present students with pictures of animals. Some of these animals will be *yes* examples, or examples that have all the critical attributes of a mystery concept they will be working to understand. Others will be *no* examples, which may have some of—but not all—the critical attributes of that concept. Students will have to analyze the attributes of the animals carefully to answer three questions: What do all the *yes* examples have in common? How are the *yes* examples different from the *no* examples? How can you use the *yes* and *no* examples to identify the critical attributes of the mystery concept?

The teacher begins by presenting three pictures: cat (yes), dog (yes), and kangaroo (no). Based on these three animals, some of the initial *yes* attributes that students generate include *meat eaters*, *runners* (as opposed to hoppers), and *common pets*. The teacher presents more pictures: tiger (yes), brontosaurus (no), killer whale (yes), horse (no). With this round of examples, students recognize that some of their initial attributes like *runners* and *common pets* are wrong. They also notice that all the *yes* examples have sharp teeth. Other students point out that the brontosaurus is slow, but that all the *yes* examples are fast. The teacher records all the attributes that students generate, then presents more pictures, including an eagle (yes), a praying mantis (yes), and a rabbit (no) to allow students to continue to test and refine their list of attributes.

At this point, the class tentatively agrees on this set of attributes: (1) eats meat, (2) has teeth or other body parts to help it tear into meat, and (3) can move or strike quickly. With this, the teacher holds up one more picture, a vulture, and surprises many students when he tells them that it is a *no* example. He challenges students to figure out why the vulture, which eats meat, has a sharp beak and claws, and can fly and swoop is a *no* example. As students re-examine the examples, they realize that all the *yes* examples kill and eat live animals, while the vulture eats dead animals. Together with the teacher, the class develops a final set of attributes:

- Hunts live animals and kills them
- Has body parts (e.g., sharp teeth, claws, beaks) to help kill and eat other animals
- Is fast or uses stealth to hunt live animals

The teacher then tells students that they have just figured out all the critical attributes of predators. To test their understanding of the predator concept, he presents them with pictures of various birds, insects, fish, and other animals and challenges them to determine which are predators based on the critical attributes they have discovered.

EXAMPLE 2: An elementary math teacher uses Concept Attainment to help students build their understanding of symmetry by presenting pairs of *yes* and *no* examples like these:

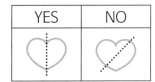 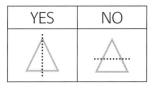 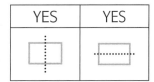 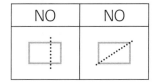

To test students' understanding of the symmetry concept, the teacher asks students to draw two *yes* examples and two *no* examples and to explain why each is / is not symmetrical.

EXAMPLE 3: A first-grade teacher uses Concept Attainment to help students discover important phonics rules and concepts. In this example, her goal is to help students recognize that when the letter *C* is followed by an *E, I,* or *Y,* it usually makes a soft-C sound. She begins by saying lots of C-words aloud and writing them in one of two columns (*yes* or *no*) as shown at the right. She then challenges students to figure out how the *yes* words are alike and how they differ from the *no* words. Once students recognize that the *yes* words all start with a soft-C sound and the *no* words don't, the teacher asks if students notice anything else that the soft-C words have in common. After she focuses their attention

YES	NO
celery	cat
cement	cloak
city	coat
circle	can
cymbals	crayon
cycle	cut

on the spellings of the words, students recognize that the letter *C* is followed by an *E, I,* or *Y* in the soft-C words, but not in the hard-C words. The teacher talks to students about how this knowledge can help them. ("If you encounter an unfamiliar C-word while reading—and the *C* is followed by an *E, I,* or *Y*—what kind of sound is the *C* likely to make?") She then tests their ability to apply this knowledge by going around the room, displaying words containing *C*s, and having students say whether each *C* is likely to make an "s" sound (soft *C*) or a "k" sound (hard *C*). She concludes the lesson by letting students know that the *E, I, Y* rule isn't perfect, but that it works often enough to be useful while reading.

Variation: Attribute Sort

Classification is one of the ways that the authors of *Classroom Instruction That Works* (Second Edition) encourage teachers to engage students in identifying similarities and differences. Attribute Sort is a variation on Concept Attainment that requires students to classify items according to their attributes or characteristics. You can ensure that an Attribute Sort is more than a simple memory task by asking students to analyze and sort items that you haven't already discussed in class. You should also ask students to justify their categorization based on the characteristics of the items within each category.

A high school art teacher used Attribute Sort to develop and test students' understanding of important stylistic elements associated with major artistic movements. She provided students with pictures of twenty-five paintings from the twentieth century and challenged them to sort the paintings into the various movements they had studied (Cubism, Abstract Impressionism, Dadaism, Social Realism, Surrealism, Pop Art). Recognizing that some movements share characteristics and that some painters belong to multiple movements, the teacher made sure students understood that the task was less about getting all the answers right and more about explaining their choices based on the characteristics of each painting. Each time students assigned a painting to a particular movement, they had to explain their choice ("I think that *Crying Girl* is representative of Pop Art because …").

🌐 Teacher Talk

➔ Think carefully about the *yes* examples and *no* examples that you use and the order in which you present them. In most cases, it is wise to begin by presenting simple examples that will help students generate an initial set of attributes. Then, as the lesson progresses, try to fold in examples that will challenge students' initial assumptions, add new perspective to their thinking, and help them see what they may have missed. For example, if you want students to discover the critical attributes of a desert by comparing *yes* and *no* descriptions of different places on Earth, your initial *yes* examples should probably include hot deserts only. Because cold deserts are counterintuitive for many students, presenting cold deserts later in the lesson will likely promote deeper thinking—and rethinking—about the critical attributes of deserts.

➔ Use guiding questions like these to help students keep their thinking focused on the critical attributes of the items under examination:

- Can you describe the attributes of the *yes* examples?

- How do the *yes* examples differ from the *no* examples?

- Based on what attributes would you group the *yes* examples?

- Are there any attributes on your list that you're more or less sure of? Why?

➔ A simple task idea to ensure that students have internalized the attributes of the concept (Step 7) is to have them generate additional *yes* and *no* examples of the concept, as illustrated in Example 2. Another way is to present students with additional items and challenge them to explain why each item is either a *yes* or *no* example of the concept, as shown in Example 1.

➔ Although we have chosen to place this tool in Chapter 8 (Identifying Similarities and Differences), it is also a good fit for Chapter 9 (Generating and Testing Hypotheses) because it requires students to generate hypotheses and then test and refine those hypotheses in light of new information.

Metaphorical Thinking

What is it?

A tool that uses metaphors and similes to help students build a deep understanding of key concepts

What are the benefits of using this tool?

Metaphors and similes help students understand abstract ideas through the lens of familiarity. (How is a chemical reaction like a recipe? How is a revolution like a volcano?) Yet, too often, teachers think of metaphorical thinking activities as "fluff"—exercises to be used only after "real learning" has already taken place. Metaphorical Thinking (adapted from Silver, Strong, & Perini, 2007) does more than give students a creative way to compare ideas; it uses the clarifying power of metaphors and similes to engage students in serious, analytical thinking about important concepts and their critical attributes. Its use in the classroom can lead to breakthroughs of insight on the part of students.

What are the basic steps?

1. Explain that metaphors and similes help build deep understanding by challenging us to make connections between items that are not literally alike—and that students will be using metaphorical thinking to deepen their understanding of important and abstract concepts.

2. Pick a concept you want students to understand deeply. Pair it with a concrete item that shares critical attributes or conceptual similarities with the original concept, not literal similarities. See Teacher Talk for more on selecting your items.

   Example: You might pair *democracy* (concept) with *diamond* (concrete item) because both can have flaws, both are desired by many people, and both can take a long time to create.

3. Present the pair of items to students. Explain that their immediate task is to identify ways the items are similar—and that the ultimate goal is for them to use those similarities to help them get a better, deeper understanding of the original concept.

4. Have students begin by listing everything they know about each item, starting with the concrete one. Provide readings or other source material that they can use to supplement their existing knowledge about the two items, and have them update their lists accordingly.

5. Ask students to think about ways the two items are similar. Challenge them to identify as many similarities/connections as they can, using the information on their lists to help them. Encourage them to strive for unusual and original connections; see Teacher Talk for more on how to do this.

6. Invite students to share and explain the similarities they found / connections they made. Record their ideas. Ask them which similarities/connections they think are the most informative and why.

7. Conclude by helping students define or summarize what they learned about the original concept and reflect on the value of the metaphorical thinking process. ("How did this exercise help you deepen your understanding of the original concept and its key attributes?")

How is this tool used in the classroom?

✔ To make abstract concepts easier for students to grasp through metaphorical comparison

✔ To enhance students' understanding of critical concepts and their attributes

✔ To encourage divergent thinking and facilitate breakthroughs of insight

Teachers from all grade levels and content areas use this tool to help students develop a deep understanding of important concepts. A list of sample questions that reflects this diversity is provided below, along with three fleshed-out classroom examples.

Note: The sample questions on the list are written as similes rather than metaphors, but they could just as easily be expressed as metaphors (e.g., "How is the Earth's atmosphere a blanket?" instead of "How is the Earth's atmosphere like a blanket?").

- How is the Earth's atmosphere like a blanket?
- How is democracy like a diamond?
- How is friendship like a raft?
- How is a habitat like a classroom?
- How is prejudice like an iceberg?
- How is the nervous system like a computer?
- How is a function like a person?
- How is the solar system like a musical composition?
- How is a community like an orchestra?
- How is a revolution like a volcano?
- How is factoring like panning for gold?
- How is courage like a suit of armor?
- How is a writer's revision process like dentistry?

EXAMPLE 1: Before beginning a unit on the American colonies, a fifth-grade teacher wants students to build their understanding of the relatively unfamiliar concept of a colony by comparing it to a concept they know well—a child. To prepare students to make rich comparisons, the teacher asks them to jot down everything they know about children. She also provides them with a short reading on colonies and asks them to jot down important facts and details as they read. The teacher then challenges students to find as many connections as they can between colonies and children. As students share their ideas, the teacher captures them on the board. Some of the connections students make include the following:

- A colony is like a child because both a colony and a child need support and protection from their parent country / parents.
- The younger the children and colonies are, the more support and protection they need.
- Colonies and children are not independent. They are under the control of their parent country / parents.
- Children don't always agree with their parents. Colonies don't always agree with their parent country.
- Sometimes colonies and children rebel as they get older.
- Parents and parent countries are always responsible for their children/colonies no matter where they are.

EXAMPLE 2: A middle school teacher used Metaphorical Thinking to help his students review and solidify their understanding of basic principles about the periodic table. He challenged them to review their notes about the periodic table, think through everything they knew about jigsaw puzzles, and then generate ways the periodic table is like a jigsaw puzzle. The responses that one student generated are shown below. Notice how this student's responses reflect some of the core understandings about the periodic table that the teacher had designed this activity to reinforce.

The periodic table of the elements	A jigsaw puzzle
Each element in the periodic table is unique.	Each piece in a traditional jigsaw puzzle is unique.
Elements are organized into groups based on their properties.	Puzzle pieces can be organized into groups based on their properties.
Organizing elements into groups is useful because it can help you predict how those elements will react.	Organizing puzzle pieces into groups (blue pieces, edge pieces, corner pieces, etc.) is useful because it can help you predict where the pieces will go.
You can predict the properties of a missing element based on where it falls in the table.	You can predict the properties of a missing piece based on where it is in the puzzle. (You could tell if it was an end piece, what colors it would have in it, etc.)
The periodic table is easier to use and understand the more you work with it.	Jigsaw puzzles are easier to put together the more you play with them.

EXAMPLE 3: A fourth-grade teacher doesn't just use metaphors to deepen her students' understanding of abstract concepts; she uses them to deepen students' understanding of characters from literature. Here, she attempted to help students get a better understanding of Fudge, a key character in Judy Blume's *Tales of a Fourth Grade Nothing*, by having them compare Fudge to a thunderstorm. The responses that one group of students developed, along with the students' reflections about what they learned by making this comparison, are shown below.

Thunderstorms	Fudge
Thunderstorms can ruin your plans.	Fudge ruins people's plans. For example, he ruins the Hatcher family's plans to have normal dinners.
Thunderstorms do damage. They can cause floods and knock down trees.	Fudge does damage. For example, he ruins Peter's school project, and he even eats Peter's pet turtle, Dribble.
No one can control a thunderstorm.	No one can control Fudge. He throws tantrums to get his way. For example, he throws a tantrum in the shoe store to try and get the shoes he wants.
We have to deal with thunderstorms. They are part of life.	Peter has to deal with Fudge because he has no choice. Fudge is part of the family.
We need thunderstorms. They bring water and help things grow.	The novel needs Fudge because he makes it funny and interesting.

Reflection: Comparing Fudge to a thunderstorm helped change our opinion of Fudge. Before, most of us saw Fudge as bad and annoying. But thunderstorms are not all bad because we need them. Now, we can see that Fudge is also needed because he is family and because he makes the book more interesting.

🔵 Teacher Talk

➡️ When picking an item for comparison (Step 2), list attributes or elements you want students to understand about the initial concept—and then identify a concrete item that possesses some or all of those same characteristics. If you want students to understand that the circulatory system follows a specific route and transports "things" from one place to another, for example, you might have students compare it to a subway system, since a subway system shares those same exact attributes. Don't pair items that share literal similarities (e.g., fables and folktales), since that kind of pairing won't require thinking metaphorically.

➡️ Encourage students to move beyond the obvious when making their comparisons (Step 5). Don't let them stop after their initial responses; instead, pose questions that help them expand their thinking. If students noted that "democracy is like a diamond because both are precious," for example, you could push them to think further with questions like these: Can there be flaws in both? What happens when there are flaws? How about how they're made? Can you find any similarities there? Are there any risks or downsides associated with either democracy or diamonds?

Another way to encourage students to move beyond the obvious is to turn the generation of similarities/connections into a game. Challenge students to come up with as many similarities and connections as they can, and award points to students who make connections that no one else did.

➡️ Don't overlook the importance of modeling. Many students will be new to this way of thinking. And many will stop at one or two obvious connections and think they're done. To help students become more comfortable and fluent with metaphorical thinking, show them how you make a metaphorical comparison. Choose a basic metaphorical comparison whose items students will be familiar with (e.g., How is a story like a vacation?) and think out loud as you walk through the process of listing important attributes, looking for similarities and connections based on those attributes, and stretching your mind to make unusual connections. Clarify that metaphorical comparisons don't have to be perfect—in other words, that it's not necessary for all attributes to match up, just some.

Variation: Analogies

Analogies are another form of comparison highlighted in *Classroom Instruction That Works* (Second Edition). Like metaphors and similes, analogies engage students in making conceptual, rather than literal, comparisons. The difference is that an analogy compares two pairs of items and focuses students' attention on the relationship between the items in each pair. Some of the most common analogical relationships include *tool and its use* (microscope is to cells as telescope is to stars), *part to whole* (coda is to blues song as conclusion is to essay), *role/function within a system* (immune system is to body as police force is to community), and *cause or contributing factor/effect* (the Boston Massacre is to the American Revolution as the assassination of Archduke Ferdinand is to World War I).

To use this technique, develop a relevant analogy that will enhance student learning. For example, students who are learning about Gutenberg and the printing press might be challenged to complete this analogy: Gutenberg is to the print revolution as _____ is to _____. Students may complete the analogy with any pair they choose but must be able to explain their reasoning.

Generating and Testing Hypotheses

What is required of a working hypothesis is a fine capacity for discrimination.

—Jean-Francois Lyotard

Although we often think of generating and testing hypotheses as a task for science class, students can engage in this process in all content areas. When students create thesis statements, make predictions based on evidence, or ask "If I do this, what might happen?" they are using the process of generating and testing hypotheses.

—Ceri B. Dean, Elizabeth Ross Hubbell, Howard Pitler, and Bj Stone,
Classroom Instruction That Works (Second Edition)

The final category of instruction highlighted in *Classroom Instruction That Works* (Second Edition) is generating and testing hypotheses. It is important to note that this category includes a variety of processes that involve generating and testing ideas—not just the kind of formal hypothesizing that we associate with science class, but similar processes that go "by different names in other content areas—predicting, inferring, deducing, or theorizing" (Dean et al., 2012, p. 135).

Whatever we call these processes, they have great value in the classroom. They promote deeper understanding of content, they enhance student motivation by tapping into the "natural inclination to solve problems," and they develop "critical thinking skills such as analysis and evaluation" (Dean et al., 2012, p. 137). They also give teachers a powerful way to help students extend and apply what they know—one of three key goals the authors of *Classroom Instruction That Works* (Second Edition) recommend that teachers keep in mind during instructional planning.

Given these varied benefits, it should come as little surprise that research on generating and testing hypotheses shows significant gains in student achievement. The most rigorous studies analyzed by Beesley and Apthorp (2010) produced an average effect size of 0.58, which is the equivalent of a 22-point percentile gain.

The question then becomes not *whether* we should build the practice of generating and testing hypotheses into our classroom but *how*. The authors of *Classroom Instruction That Works* (Second Edition) recommend engaging students in a variety of structured tasks for generating and testing hypotheses. They also recommend asking students to explain their hypotheses and conclusions. The three tools in this chapter were designed with these recommendations in mind.

1. **From Challenges to Controversies** presents eight easy-to-use frameworks for engaging students in generating and evaluating ideas across content areas.

2. **Mystery** involves students in generating and testing hypotheses as they work to solve content-related mysteries (e.g., the mystery of why the dinosaurs disappeared).

3. **Because** gets students in the habit of explaining the thinking behind hypotheses, conclusions, and other ideas by prompting them to "give a because" when sharing their ideas. ("Why do you think that? Can you give me a *because*?")

From Challenges to Controversies

What is it?

A collection of eight easy-to-use task frameworks that require students to extend and apply critical content knowledge as they generate and test ideas; the frameworks are adapted from Boutz et al. (2012) and Dean et al. (2012)

What are the benefits of using this tool?

We tend to think of generating and testing hypotheses as something that only happens in science class, but the basic process of generating and testing ideas is one that can and should be encouraged across content areas. This tool makes that easy to do by presenting eight types of tasks that involve generating and testing ideas—not just formal hypotheses, but predictions, solutions, designs, and more. Collectively, these task types help students develop a variety of valuable thinking skills, including hypothesizing, analyzing, evaluating, and justifying. When tasks are framed around critical content, they deepen and reinforce students' understanding of that content as well.

What are the basic steps?

1. Familiarize yourself with the eight different task frameworks described on pages 208–209.

2. Select a framework. Use it to develop a question/task that will engage students in extending and/or applying what they've learned about a specific topic, issue, or skill. Use the classroom examples on pages 208–209 as models; see page 211 for additional guidance and question stems.

3. Introduce the question and the framework you selected to students. Explain how students will work through the various steps in the framework (alone, in groups, or as a class) and how they will communicate their ideas (orally, graphically, in writing, or using some other format).

4. Instruct students to apply their existing knowledge and skills—or acquire and apply new knowledge/skills—to the question at hand. ("Use what you know about what the sun does to predict what would happen if it stopped shining" or "Research this issue and then generate …")

5. Guide and give students feedback about their work. Pose questions that will help them expand and evaluate their thinking (e.g., "Are there other possibilities?" or "Why do you think that?").

6. Use students' performance to assess students' understanding of and ability to apply the relevant content knowledge and thinking skills/capacities (e.g., Were students able to apply what they had learned about crafting an argument to present and defend their choice for best class pet?).

How is this tool used in the classroom?

✔ To have students generate and test ideas in response to authentic types of questions

✔ To engage students in extending and applying critical content knowledge and thinking skills

From Challenges to Controversies: Eight Task Frameworks to Choose From

FRAMEWORK	STEPS	CLASSROOM EXAMPLES
Design Challenges ask students to generate the best possible design for achieving a specific goal.	1. Pose a question that challenges students to develop the best possible design for achieving a goal. ("How might you ___?") Clarify the criteria for success as well as any relevant constraints. 2. Instruct students to use what they know to predict the kinds of designs that are likely to work. Have them generate, test, and refine possible designs—and submit their best one. 3. Test (or otherwise evaluate) students' designs as a class. 4. Discuss why the most successful designs were so successful and what can be learned from those designs (e.g., what materials keep liquids hot, what design features prevent toppling).	How might you • Design the tallest block tower that doesn't topple over? • Design an egg carton that offers optimal protection from dropping-related damage? • Design a cup that will keep a drink warm for an extended period of time? • Design the most efficient computer program for executing this task? • Design the most convincing anti-smoking public service announcement? • Redesign the zoo's gorilla enclosure so as to promote the health and happiness of the gorillas while providing maximum visibility and entertainment for visitors?
Informed Prediction Tasks present students with a "what if" scenario and ask them to generate possible outcomes.	1. Present students with a "what if" question or scenario. 2. Instruct students to use what they know to predict possible outcomes (or causes). 3. Invite students to explain what they predicted and why. 4. Discuss and/or evaluate the merit of students' predictions.	• What if the sun stopped shining? • What if we had a base-60 number system like the ancient Babylonians instead of base-10? • What if there wasn't any oil in the Middle East? • What if Rasputin had never lived? • What if we increase the steepness of the ramp? How might that affect our results? • What if you traveled into the future and found that the United States was no longer the superpower it is today. What might have caused this change in status?
Problem-Solving Tasks ask students to analyze problems, generate possible solutions, and evaluate those solutions.	1. Identify a goal that's worth achieving (real or hypothetical). 2. Identify barriers/constraints (problems) that are getting in the way. 3. Challenge students to generate solutions/strategies that would overcome these problems. ("How might we …") 4. Ask students which strategies/solutions seem most likely to work. If possible, let students test their ideas.	• How might we get our classmates to sleep longer at nap-time given that the classroom is bright, noisy, and full of distractions? • How might we give a great concert despite the fact that our bass drum was damaged? • How might we reduce the spread of communicable diseases at our school despite the fact that we only have $100/month in the budget to allocate toward solutions?
Systems Analysis Tasks help students appreciate the importance of a specific part in a system by having them predict the effect(s) of changing that part in some way.	1. Ask students to identify the parts of a system, describe how each part functions, and explain the purpose of the system as whole. 2. Have students explain how the parts affect one another. 3. Pick–or have students pick–a part of the system. 4. Ask students to predict what might happen if the part were changed in some way (e.g., reduced in size or capacity). 5. Let students test their ideas if possible (e.g., via simulation).	What might be the effect of • Removing (or changing the levels of) a component of an ecosystem? • Changing the function or efficiency of an organ within an organ system? • Reducing capacity within a system of transportation (e.g., fewer runways at an airport)? • Eliminating, changing the role of, or increasing/decreasing the power of a particular entity within a system of government (e.g., a branch, department, or political party)?

Decision-Making Tasks require students to analyze different options, pick one, and defend their choice.	1. Pose a question that requires students to consider alternatives and make an informed decision. 2. Tell students what criteria they should use to analyze the various alternatives, or let them choose their own criteria. 3. Ask students to explain and defend their decisions. (What did I decide? How did the criteria guide my decision-making process?) *Variation:* Have students use specific criteria to evaluate someone else's decision (e.g., a politician's or literary character's).	• Which of these animals would make the best class pet? • Which of these emperors would make the best US president? • Which of these snack menus would have the most positive impact on student health? • Which of these plans for bringing back American jobs is most likely to work? • If you were the coach, what play would you call in this situation? • Do you agree that bombing Hiroshima and Nagasaki was President Truman's best option for ending the war in the Pacific? Use the criteria on the board to compare the options that were available to Truman and decide what you would've done if you were president.
Experimental Inquiries challenge students to generate hypotheses and develop ways to test them.	1. Ask students to generate possible and plausible explanations ("hypotheses") for something that they or others have observed. If needed, present relevant background information first. 2. Invite students to share their hypotheses as a class. 3. Help students develop one or more ways to test their hypotheses. Clarify that hypotheses can be tested in different ways (e.g., by making observations or performing experiments or calculations). 4. Ask students to predict how their tests will likely turn out if their hypotheses are correct (i.e., what results they expect). 5. Have students conduct their proposed tests if possible and determine whether the results support or contradict their hypotheses.	• Why might the lamp in our book nook not be turning on? • Why might the grass on this side of the playground be brown rather than green? • Why might the teeth in this beaker have decayed faster than the teeth in that one? • Why might some foods need to be refrigerated, but not others? • What might explain the drop in new lung cancer cases? • Look at the picture and evidence file. What might have caused the accident? • How might birds know when it's time to fly south for the winter? • Why might the number of flu cases be higher in winter months? • Why might different parts of the Earth experience summer at different times of year?
Historical Investigations have students explore debatable or unresolved issues of historical significance (e.g., cause of an event, motive for an action, impact of a policy).	1. Identify a debatable or unresolved issue surrounding a historically significant event, individual, or institution. 2. Present a question or hypothetical scenario that will get students thinking about that issue. 3. Instruct students to explore the issue, develop a position/thesis, and support it with evidence. 4. Evaluate the strength and clarity of students' arguments.	• What factor do you believe was most responsible for the fall of the Roman Empire? • What might explain Adolph Hitler's rise to power? • What was President Lincoln's primary motive in signing the Emancipation Proclamation? • Would the Cuban people be better off if the Cuban Revolution hadn't happened? • If the stock market hadn't crashed, would the Great Depression have happened anyway? • Could a flu outbreak as widespread and deadly as the one in 1918 happen again?
Controversy Tasks are similar to Historical Investigations, but ask students to focus on current "hot topic" issues.	1. Identify an issue that people have different theories/positions on. 2. Pose a question that will get students thinking about that issue. 3. Challenge students to research the issue, evaluate the various positions/options, and decide which they think is the strongest. 4. Have students make the case for the position they selected (i.e., present the position and support it with evidence).	• Will school vouchers be good for education? • Would a minimum wage hike help or hurt workers? • If the goal is raising achievement, will our school's new homework policy be likely to help? • What would be the best strategy for reducing teen pregnancy rates? • What's the best way to stimulate the economy during a recession? • How should we define *civilization*?

🌐 Teacher Talk

➔ What kinds of questions do scientists ask themselves? What about historians? Engineers? Anthropologists? This tool engages students in thinking about the kinds of questions that professionals in the real world explore, and its eight task frameworks help students generate and evaluate possible responses. Developing their responses requires students to apply and elaborate on what they know about the relevant content. It also gives them an opportunity to apply and refine their ability to use critical thinking and problem-solving skills. The kinds of skills that the frameworks engage (e.g., analytical thinking skills, problem-solving skills, communication skills, argument skills) are particularly valuable ones because they're both authentic and transferrable—the kinds of skills that can help students thrive not just in the classroom but also in the real world.

➔ Your instructional goals should determine *when* you present the question you develop in Step 2 (during a lesson/unit or at the end) and *in what context* (classwork assignment, homework assignment, test item, or end-of-unit project).

The task menu below shows how a teacher used three of the tool's frameworks to develop end-of-unit assessment tasks around a unit on climate change. Her goal was to test students' grasp of the relevant content using authentic tasks rather than a traditional paper-and-pencil test.

Climate change task sampler: Choose ONE task to complete.		
CONTROVERSY TASK Are recent, unprecedented warming trends due to natural or human causes? Present your position in an editorial. Be sure to define climate change, explain the controversy, and defend your position (rebut the alternative one as well) using relevant evidence.	SYSTEMS ANALYSIS TASK Sea ice is the foundation of the Arctic marine ecosystem. Investigate the degree to which the extent and age of sea ice has changed over the last several decades. Describe what, if any, impact these changes in sea ice will have on the health of the ecosystem.	INFORMED PREDICTION TASK Prepare a presentation in which you use tables, charts, computer simulations, and/or other data to predict ways the tourism industry will be affected if temperatures continue to rise at the same rate they have been over the past hundred years.

➔ Giving students choices about their learning can enhance their motivation and success. Here's how one teacher built the element of choice into a Decision-Making Task: "FDR made a lot of important decisions in his first hundred days as president. Pick one that you want to evaluate, describe the criteria you'll use to do it, and present the results of your analysis in writing."

Another way to incorporate choice is to create a sampler of tasks around a specific topic and let students choose which task(s) to complete. See the climate change sampler above for an example.

➔ In this tool, teachers generate the questions (Step 2), but the ultimate goal is to have students generate and explore their own questions. You can help students develop this capacity by familiarizing them with the question stems on page 211 and asking them to use the stems to develop questions of their own that interest them. ("Read this article. Then, use the question stems we discussed to generate three questions that interest you.")

➔ Can this tool be used with very young students? Yes! Primary-grade examples have been provided for most of the frameworks, and the frameworks can be simplified and scaffolded as needed.

Question-Generating Guidance

The frameworks in this tool are designed to help students work their way through questions that involve thinking hypothetically and exploring possibilities. Hypothetical-thinking questions often include the words *if, might, would,* and *could*.

If questions often take the following forms:

- What if ___?
- What might happen if ___?
- If ___ hadn't happened (or had happened differently) . . .

Might questions often take the following forms:

- How might ___?
- Why might ___?
- What might explain ___?
- What might have caused/motivated ___?
- What might be the outcome/effect of ___?

Would/could questions often take the following forms:

- Would ___ be good/bad for ___?
- Would ___ have been a better decision/option/strategy?
- Which of these options would be the most/least likely to work?
- Which of these options would be the best/worst ___?
- Could ___ happen (or happen again)?

Use the question stems above and the classroom examples on pages 208–209 to help you generate appropriate kinds of questions for the tool's eight task frameworks.

Mystery

What is it?

A tool that sparks interest and engagement by presenting students with a content-related "mystery" that needs to be solved; students use teacher-provided clues to develop and test possible solutions

What are the benefits of using this tool?

Students often view the process of generating and testing hypotheses as something they're forced to do in science class, not something they like to do. But when we present students with puzzling phenomena and challenge them to generate possible explanations (hypotheses), the process of generating those explanations is one they actually enjoy. This tool makes generating and testing hypotheses exciting by presenting students with content-related mysteries and asking them to generate and test possible solutions. The element of mystery serves to pique student interest, while the generating/testing process develops both content knowledge and critical thinking skills, including analyzing data, synthesizing information, and supporting ideas with evidence.

What are the basic steps?

1. Identify an event, phenomenon, or concept that you want students to understand and explain. Frame it as a mystery that students will need to investigate/solve (e.g., "How is it possible that a giant metal boat can stay afloat when this tiny piece of metal sinks in a glass of water?").

2. Develop a clear idea of the solution/explanation you want your students to generate. List the big ideas students will need to understand in order to arrive at the solution you have in mind.

3. Create a set of clues that will enable students to discover the solution and the big ideas that underpin that solution. Clues can take any form you want—data tables, images, maps, sound clips, factual information in sentence form, etc. See Teacher Talk for more on generating clues.

4. Divide students into teams. Present the mystery, give each team a set of clues, and tell students to
   - Examine the clues carefully. Group related clues together, and give each group a descriptive label. (Clarify that students may place the same clue in more than one group.)
   - Summarize the key ideas from each group. (Think: What are the clues telling you?)
   - Identify connections between or among clue groups. (Do you see common threads or themes?)
   - Think about how the clues/groups are connected to the mystery as a whole.
   - Generate a tentative solution that's supported by the clues. Be ready to share and defend it.

5. Invite students to share their ideas and solutions—and the clue evidence that supports those ideas/solutions—both as they work and at the end of the lesson. Use probing questions to help students evaluate and refine their ideas. See Teacher Talk for specific suggestions.

6. Assess and reinforce students' grasp of the relevant content at the end of the lesson by asking students what they learned and by reviewing the critical concepts/ideas as a class.

How is this tool used in the classroom?

✔ To provide an authentic and engaging context for students to generate and test hypotheses

✔ To help students acquire critical content knowledge in a fun and active way

✔ To develop students' ability to analyze and interpret data—and support ideas with evidence

Teachers across content areas use this tool to help students generate possible explanations of mysterious phenomena or observations. Mysteries are usually presented as *why* or *how* questions. Multiple sample questions are shown below, along with two fleshed-out classroom examples.

- Why is it better to sneeze into your elbow than into your hand?
- How did an untrained colonial militia defeat the mighty British army?
- Why does the sun rise and set every single day?
- In 2010, a fossil of a giant whale was discovered in a desert in Peru. How did it get there?
- How is it possible that airplanes don't fall out of the sky even though they're so heavy?
- How did people tell time before there were clocks?
- Why is George Washington considered a great war hero when he lost more battles than he won?
- How is it possible that burning a forest can be good for its health?
- Why was there an explosion of mystery novels and detective stories in the Victorian era?
- What painters painted and how they painted it changed dramatically between the Middle Ages and the Renaissance. Why? What explains the change?
- The illustrations in this box are from a story that someone was planning to write but never did. What story do you think the author might have intended to write? Why do you think so?
- There's only one correct order in which to perform mathematical operations. Can you discover what it is just by examining these clues?

EXAMPLE 1: A middle school social studies teacher wants her students to understand the various factors that gave rise to the Age of Exploration. Instead of having students read about the topic in their textbooks, she uses the Mystery tool to help them discover the key factors for themselves. To get them interested, she frames the content as a mystery: "For much of European history, no real efforts were made to explore the world by sea. Why, all of a sudden, was there an 'exploration explosion' in the fifteenth century?"

She then organizes students into teams and challenges them to solve the mystery using clues that she provides (slips of paper with relevant information drawn from a textbook). Students are instructed to organize related clues into groups and use the groups they create to develop some possible hypotheses for why the time was right for exploration in the fifteenth century. One such clue group is shown below, along with the hypothesis that students generated after examining it.

Clue 4: The science of mapmaking had become sophisticated and increasingly accurate by Columbus's time.

Clue 9: Inventions like the astrolabe and mariner's compass made longer and more difficult trips possible.

Clue 20: New ships called caravels were faster and easier to navigate than any ship before.

We hypothesize that the time was right for exploration in the fifteenth century because advances in technology and mapmaking made farther, safer trips possible.

Additional clue groups (not shown) lead students to hypothesize that other factors were also responsible for triggering the Age of Exploration, including the desire to spread Christianity, find new routes for the silk and spice trades, and gain control of new territories and wealth.

After a round of discussion in which students share their hypotheses and the "clue evidence" that supports them, students use the textbook passage from which the teacher generated her clues to check and refine their ideas. ("How do the ideas you generated compare with those in the text?")

EXAMPLE 2: Instead of telling students why scientists think dinosaurs became extinct, a high school teacher challenges them to generate plausible explanations (hypotheses) on their own. To spark their interest, he frames the dinosaur disappearance as an intriguing mystery for them to solve: "We've just learned that the dinosaurs dominated the earth for over 150 million years. So how is it possible that they became extinct? Today, you'll get a chance to investigate and solve that mystery using a set of clues that I will give you."

The teacher divides students into teams of four and presents each team with an identical set of thirty-five clues. (To create the clues, he pulled bits of information from an article that presented a commonly accepted explanation for the dinosaurs' demise.) As students begin working to analyze and group the clues, the teacher walks around to listen in on, probe, and guide their thinking.

Students in one of the teams notice that there are multiple clues about tropical plants—and they group those clues accordingly. They create a plankton group as well, as shown below.

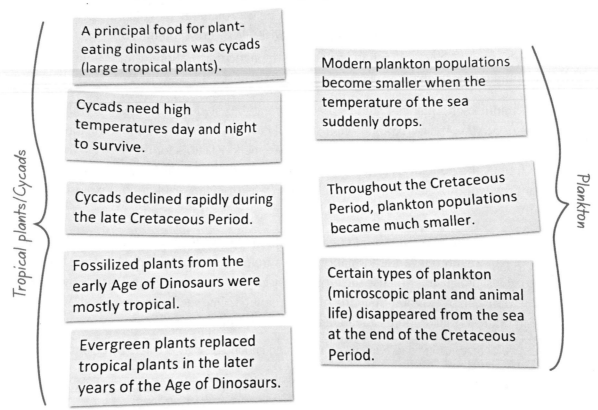

When they examine their groups more closely, the students notice some common themes. They notice, for example, that clues in both groups highlight changes in population that occurred during the Cretaceous Period. (Populations of tropical plants and plankton both declined rapidly.)

They also find multiple temperature-related clues—clues that lead them to hypothesize that a drop in temperature was what caused the cycad and plankton populations to decline.

When their teacher asks how the clues they've examined so far might relate to the mystery of why the dinosaurs died out, these students hypothesize that a shortage of food, triggered by a drop in temperature, might have caused the dinosaurs' demise. ("We learned that cycads declined, and cycads were a major source of food for the dinosaurs.")

But what might have caused such a drop in temperature? After grouping and labeling additional clues (not shown), team members hypothesize that the drop in temperature was caused by a giant meteor that hit the earth and created a large cloud of dust that blocked out sunlight.

At the end of class, after teams have shared and critiqued each other's hypotheses (and supporting clues), the teacher challenges students to develop a brief, written explanation—backed by clue evidence—that synthesizes the class's ideas about the factors that led to the demise of the dinosaurs. One student's explanation can be viewed at www.ThoughtfulClassroom.com/Tools.

Variation: Yes/No Inquiry

This variation on Mystery is adapted from the work of J. R. Suchman (1966). Like Mystery, Yes/No Inquiry begins with an intriguing phenomenon or mystery concept. Also similar to a Mystery lesson, Yes/No Inquiry withholds the solution and challenges students to discover it for themselves. Students collect data by asking yes/no questions.

In its simplest form, Yes/No Inquiry can be used to challenge students to identify a particular concept or object. Rather than simply guessing at the concept, students—guided by their teacher—learn how to formulate questions that focus on critical attributes. For example, an elementary teacher might select a shape and challenge students to ask yes/no questions that help them zero in on critical attributes of the shape in question (e.g., Does the shape have sides? Does the shape have more than three sides? Does it have parallel sides? Does it have angles of equal size?).

The same process of asking yes/no questions can be used by students to generate and test hypotheses about phenomena they observe. A science teacher, for example, might challenge students to use yes/no questions to generate a plausible explanation for something they observe during a demonstration (e.g., why, when ice cubes are placed in two identical-looking beakers filled with clear liquid, do the ice cubes float in one of the beakers but sink in the other?). At the end of the demonstration, students would be instructed to

- Record everything they know about the situation
- Generate one or more hypotheses to explain what they observed (e.g., why the ice cubes floated in one beaker but sank in the other)
- Pose yes/no questions to the teacher to help them test their hypotheses
- Develop what they believe is the best explanation for the phenomenon

🎯 Teacher Talk

➜ Here are some things to keep in mind when generating your clues:

- Clues should contain information that will help students generate their own ideas and solutions; they shouldn't *tell* students the solution. Check that the clues you generate give students enough information to develop the generalizations and conclusions you expect them to make.

- Clues can be derived from primary or secondary sources—and they can be copied directly or rewritten/summarized for length or age-appropriateness. You might, for example, reprint an entry from a captain's log or summarize information from an article on the whaling industry.

- Build different types of clues into your lessons (e.g., maps, tables, or images in addition to written-out factual information) so that students get practice interpreting different forms of data.

➜ Use probing questions to help students articulate, evaluate, and expand their thinking, both as they work (Step 4) and when they're sharing their ideas as a class (Step 5). For example: How did you group the clues and why? What did you learn from each group? Do you see any connections between groups? How might the information from these groups relate to the mystery as a whole? What solution did you develop? What clue evidence supports this solution? Are there any clues you've failed to account for or that contradict your proposed solution? Is your logic sound?

➜ Help students evaluate the explanations that they and their classmates generate (Step 5) by having them review each team's ideas, identify potential issues (e.g., flaws in logic, failure to account for critical information, information that doesn't fit), and decide which explanation is best supported by the evidence. Alternatively, you can have students compare their solutions with the actual solution. ("Read this article. How does the author's explanation compare with yours?")

➜ Clarify that it's not a problem if students generate a different solution/response than you had in mind at the start of the activity as long as their response is supported by solid evidence. In fact, you can use students' differing solutions as a way to introduce the idea that there are many instances in "real science" where multiple hypotheses are plausible and supported by evidence.

➜ At first, some teachers wonder if the time it takes to plan a Mystery lesson is worth it. In our experience, once teachers see the curiosity and engagement that the tool generates—and its ability to promote active, authentic learning—they don't tend to ask the "is it worth it" question anymore. To reduce the workload, collaborate with teachers at your school to develop and share Mystery lessons. And remember that once you've created a Mystery lesson, you can reuse it every year.

➜ If you're having trouble developing a Mystery lesson, find a passage or article that explains how or why something happens, identify the question the passage is answering (e.g., How can fish breathe underwater?), and extract a set of short clues. (If you can't frame the question in a way that makes the topic sound intriguing, pick a different how/why topic.) Mystery lessons can also be built off of "Yes, but why?" questions that challenge students to look into the causes behind phenomena. ("We all know that the ocean has high and low tides. The question is *why*? What's causing them?")

➜ Instead of *giving* students clues, you can have students discover the relevant information (clues) for themselves. To do this, set up "discovery stations" where students complete a task (e.g., watch a video, make observations, perform an experiment) and jot down what they learn.

Because

What is it?

A tool that teaches students to explain the thinking behind their ideas by training them to support their hypotheses, predictions, conclusions, and inferences with "becauses" ("I predict that the piece of wood will float in the water *because* …")*

What are the benefits of using this tool?

The authors of *Classroom Instruction That Works* (Second Edition) point out that asking students to explain their thinking as they generate and test hypotheses promotes deeper understanding (Dean et al., 2012). Therefore, we need to get students in the "explaining habit" when they use the various thinking practices that the authors of *Classroom Instruction That Works* (Second Edition) associate with generating and testing hypotheses. These thinking practices include hypothesizing, making predictions, drawing conclusions, making inferences, and formulating theses. The Because tool gives teachers a simple way to build and reinforce the explaining habit whenever students engage in these practices. Best of all, regular use of this tool helps create a classroom culture in which student behaviors such as elaborating on ideas, justifying conclusions, and clarifying one's thinking become the norm.

What are the basic steps?

1. Tell students that you want them to get in the habit of supporting their ideas with "becauses." ("Whenever you make a hypothesis, conclusion, inference, or prediction, I want you to give me a *because* that explains your reasoning.")

2. Help students build this habit by writing the word *because* in an easily visible location (e.g., on the board or a piece of poster paper). If students forget to give you a "because," prompt them to do so by pointing at the word. For example:

   Teacher: So what do you predict will happen if we take two fractions that are less than one and multiply them together?

   Student: I think the product will get smaller. [Teacher points at the word *because* to remind the student to keep talking.]

   Student: Because you'd be taking a fraction of a fraction that's already less than one.

3. Use students' responses to gauge their understanding of the content and their ability to support their ideas with evidence, reasons, and/or examples. Respond accordingly.

---

*This tool is adapted from the work of Cathy Mitchell, a teacher at Robert Kerr Elementary School in Durand, MI.

How is this tool used in the classroom?

✔ To get students in the habit of supporting their ideas with reasons and evidence

✔ To help students extend and elaborate on their thinking

✔ To develop and assess students' understanding of key content

The examples that follow illustrate some of the many ways this tool can be used in the classroom—specifically, to help students support the thinking behind hypotheses, predictions, inferences, conclusions, and theses. Note that while the steps on page 217 focus on the tool's use in classroom lessons and discussions, the tool works just as well with written assignments (see Examples 5 and 6).

EXAMPLE 1: Asking students to explain predictions

A kindergarten teacher uses this tool to have students explain the thinking behind their predictions during an art lesson.

Teacher:	What do you think will happen when we add this white paint to the blue paint?
Student:	I think we will get a lighter blue.
Teacher:	*Because?*
Student:	*Because* when we added white to the green paint, we got a lighter green. And when we added white to the purple paint, we got a lighter purple.

EXAMPLE 2: Probing the logic behind students' hypotheses and conclusions

A third-grade teacher regularly engages students in generating and testing hypotheses—and he uses the Because tool to probe their thinking at multiple points in the process. For example, he asks them to give *becauses* when they're explaining the thinking behind their hypotheses:

Teacher:	Why might some of our classmates' basil plants be growing better than the others?
Student:	I think it's *because* they're getting more light.
Teacher:	And you generated that hypothesis *because*?
Student:	*Because* the plants that are growing best are the ones near the window.
Teacher:	Great. So, how could you go about testing your hypothesis? Let's design an experiment…

He also asks students to give *becauses* when they're explaining why their experimental results do/don't support their hypotheses:

Teacher:	That's great that you completed your experiment! Do the results support your hypothesis?
Student:	Yes.
Teacher:	*Because*?
Student:	*Because* the plants I put near the window grew the best, the plants I put farthest away from the window didn't grow as well, and the plants I put in the closet where it's totally dark died. That's exactly what you'd predict to happen if my hypothesis was correct.

EXAMPLE 3: Encouraging students to explain inferences

A high school English teacher uses Because to have students explain and justify the inferences and interpretations they develop while reading literature.

Teacher:	So, now that we've all read Emily Dickinson's famous poem, "Because I Could Not Stop for Death," let's think: What might the poet be trying to tell us about death?
Student 1:	I think she is telling us that we should accept death.
Teacher:	And you think that *because*?
Student 1:	*Because* she's not afraid of death in the poem.
Teacher:	Do the rest of you agree with that interpretation?
Student 2:	I agree that Dickinson wants us to accept death *because* the description of the carriage ride sounds so nice. She sees children playing at recess and fields of grain.
Student 3:	I disagree that it's about accepting death. I think it's about not being ready for death.
Teacher:	*Because*?
Student 3:	*Because* the tone of the fourth stanza is totally different from the first three stanzas. The fourth stanza talks about how the dew "drew quivering and chill."
Teacher:	And that's significant *because*?
Student 3:	*Because* it shows a change in her attitude toward death. In the beginning, she seems happy and the carriage ride seems nice. But in the fourth stanza, it suddenly gets cold, and she's not dressed for the cold.
Teacher:	Interesting. And what about the last two stanzas? How do they fit in with your interpretation?

EXAMPLE 4: Probing the thinking behind students' conclusions

A high school history teacher regularly uses Because to probe student thinking and get students in the habit of supporting their conclusions with reasons and evidence.

Teacher:	How did you come to the conclusion that the Stamp Act helped lead to the American Revolution?
Student:	*Because* the Stamp Act really angered a lot of colonists.
Teacher:	*Because*?
Student:	*Because* the Stamp Act was a tax, and they didn't think it was a fair one.
Teacher:	*Because*?
Student:	*Because* they felt it was unfair to be taxed without representation in Parliament.
Teacher:	True, but is it really fair to say that the Stamp Act actually contributed to the revolution?
Student:	Yes, *because* the taxation issue it raised didn't go away. With each new unfair tax, more colonists wanted to rebel.

EXAMPLE 5: Challenging students to explain conclusions

A second-grade teacher designed the activity below to help students draw conclusions based on the attributes of shapes—and explain the thinking behind their conclusions.

Examine the three shapes below. Then, draw a new shape that belongs with these three shapes. Explain why your new shape belongs with the others. See if you can give at least two *becauses*.

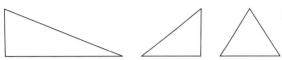

Draw your shape here:

EXAMPLE 6: Helping students develop a well-supported thesis

A high school history teacher prepares students to write strong thesis essays by having them write out their thesis statements and three "becauses" before they begin working on their essays.

My thesis is that the rise of print culture was the primary factor behind the spread of the Enlightenment.

I believe this is a valid thesis BECAUSE...

1. Books, newspapers, and pamphlets allowed information to spread to many more people than ever before.

2. Important ideas about politics and scientific discoveries couldn't be hidden by governments or by the Church once they were in print.

3. Access to new ways of thinking about freedom and democracy caused many people to question authority.

 Teacher Talk

→ Because of this tool's placement in Chapter 9, we've focused on uses that support the thinking practices associated with generating and testing hypotheses. But the tool can be used for many other purposes as well. For example, you might use it to help students identify flaws in logic or procedures ("This solution is incorrect *because*..."), to check for understanding during a lecture ("And you think that DNA and RNA are more similar than different *because*?"), or to invite students to share and justify their opinions ("I enjoyed the poem *because*...").

→ If you consistently prompt students to include *becauses* in their responses, they'll get to the point where they feel a response is missing something if it doesn't include a *because*. When visiting classrooms that use this tool on a regular basis, we've seen many students ask each other for a *because*. ("Hey, where's your *because*?")

→ This tool gets students in the habit of supporting their ideas with reasons and evidence—a skill that's highlighted in all college and career readiness standards.

PART IV

From Tools to Design

Conclusion:
Putting It All Together

There are three responses to a piece of design—yes, no, and WOW! Wow is the one to aim for.

—Renowned graphic designer Milton Glaser

To be skilled conductors of instruction, teachers must intentionally select the best mix of instructional strategies to meet the diverse needs of students in their classrooms.

—Ceri B. Dean, Elizabeth Ross Hubbell, Howard Pitler, and Bj Stone,
Classroom Instruction That Works (Second Edition)

In the first nine chapters of this book, we presented a diverse collection of research-based tools for raising student achievement. We also prepared you to use these tools in your classroom by providing clear implementation steps and concrete examples to use as models. The goal of this chapter is to show you how you can combine individual tools from the book, along with principles of effective instructional design and knowledge about how students learn, to design more focused, learning-driven, and effective instructional plans. To guide you through this process, we present four tips that can help you put it all together like an expert.

Tip 1: Think Backward

Expert teachers know what they want for their students. They operate with a well-defined vision of what their students will learn—and what the results of that learning will look like. One way to achieve this kind of expert vision is to use a process that Jay McTighe and Grant Wiggins (2014) call "backward design." Designing backward means planning with the end results of learning in mind and building assessment and instruction to achieve these results.

When designing backward, it's important to identify and articulate the knowledge, understandings, and skills that students will develop and apply over the course of a learning sequence. An ideal tool for achieving this level of clarity is Learning Window (pp. 13–16). You can use a Learning Window to help you transform your standards into four distinct types of learning goals: knowledge goals, understanding goals, skill-acquisition goals, and dispositional goals / habits of mind.

But a vision of student learning requires more than clear goals. Expert teachers also know that the goals we establish need to be worth the instructional time it will take to achieve them—and that the ultimate aim is *transfer:* "The point of school is not to simply excel in each class, but to be able to use one's learning in other settings" (McTighe & Wiggins, 2014, p. 2). Thus, as you think through your learning goals and commit them to your Learning Window, ask yourself this: Do the goals I am focusing on have meaning and applicability beyond this particular unit?

The sample Learning Windows on pages 14 and 15 show how two teachers used the Learning Window tool to unpack their standards and convert them into clear, classroom-level learning goals. Notice that many of the goals in their Learning Windows focus on transferrable understandings, skills, and habits of mind, so that the unit on fables, for example, is not just about reading fables but also about deriving universal understandings, mastering real-world skills, and developing habits of mind associated with lifelong success.

Tip 2: Assess Beyond the Test

When it comes to developing culminating assessments, expert teachers ensure that the assessments they design are aligned with classroom learning goals. Expert teachers also strive to assess beyond the test by moving beyond traditional paper-and-pencil tests that assess recall of factual information. Instead, they develop tests and tasks that require complex and authentic types of thinking—and that challenge students to apply/transfer what they've learned to new and different contexts.

A tool that can help you develop culminating assessment tasks that challenge students to apply their learning in new and different ways is From Challenges to Controversies (pp. 207–211). This tool presents eight different frameworks that engage students in responding to authentic types of questions; thus, it can be of great help in designing tasks that require transfer. A social studies teacher used the tool's Historical Investigations framework to help her design this culminating assessment task for her unit on early exploration of the Americas:

Explorers or Exploiters?

As you know from our unit, the Age of Exploration was a time of unprecedented accomplishment. It was also a time that saw terrible cruelty inflicted upon native populations. So, how should historians remember this period? For your final task, you will conduct a historical investigation by researching conflicting accounts of the interactions between explorers and native populations. Based on your research and what you have learned about the accomplishments of the explorers we have studied, you will take a position on how we should remember this period. In your position paper, you must use specific details from the sources to support your position.

Tip 3: Design Instructional Sequences That Support How Students Learn

Expert teachers are also expert instructional designers, and they design their lessons and units to ensure that students can achieve the established learning goals and successfully complete the relevant assessment tasks. Built into their designs is the understanding that learning is not something that gets poured into students' minds; rather, learning is a process—a journey during which students' memories become stronger and their understanding becomes deeper over time. A simple model of this journey, derived from the findings of cognitive science, involves three distinct learning phases: attention, concentration, and consolidation (Goodwin, Gibson, Lewis, & Rouleau, 2018).

Over the years, we have found that the best way to help teachers increase their expertise as designers—to help them craft instructional sequences that capture students' attention, build students' concentration, and help students consolidate and extend their learning—is to invite them to think of instruction as a series of five episodes. These episodes, which are highlighted in the figure below, reflect universal elements of good instruction as identified in some of the most highly regarded instructional frameworks (Hunter, 1984; Wiggins & McTighe, 2005; Marzano, 2007; Dean et al., 2012). Notice that each of the five episodes is guided by a clear instructional purpose—and that the purpose of each episode is driven by what cognitive science teaches us about the learning process.

EPISODE 1:
Preparing students
for new learning

Learning begins with *attention*.

Therefore, during this episode, teachers capture students' attention and help students activate prior knowledge. Teachers also direct students' attention to the learning to come by establishing clear learning targets.

EPISODE 3:
Deepening and
reinforcing learning

Learners need opportunities to *consolidate* learning.

Therefore, during this episode, teachers engage students in strategic practice to help them solidify their understanding of key content and increase their mastery of new skills.

EPISODE 2:
Presenting new learning

Learning requires *concentration*.

Therefore, during this episode, teachers do more than present content; they help students actively process the content and assemble information into big ideas and important details.

EPISODE 5:
Reflecting on and
celebrating learning

This entire process is enhanced through active *reflection*.

Therefore, during this episode, teachers help students look back on, learn from, and celebrate their learning—and their learning process.

EPISODE 4:
Applying and
demonstrating learning

Learners further *consolidate* and extend learning by applying it.

Therefore, during this episode, teachers challenge students to demonstrate, synthesize, and transfer their learning.

This framework makes it easy to design instructional sequences that support how students learn. To use the framework as a lesson or unit design tool, select tools from this book (or from other resources) that will help you achieve the purpose of each episode. We've provided three sample instructional sequences (see pp. 226–228) to help you see what the outcome of this design process looks like.

The figure below shows how a primary-grade teacher used the five-episode framework and tools from this book to build an instructional sequence for his fables unit. The Learning Window that drove the development of this sequence and that maps out the goals this teacher was trying to target can be found on page 14.

Fables: A Study in Overcoming Challenges (Sample Unit)

EPISODE	INSTRUCTIONAL SEQUENCE
Preparing students for new learning	**Start with a Story (pp. 109–111):** Invite students to share personal stories about overcoming challenges. Look for patterns in students' responses. Connect students' responses to the theme of the unit by explaining that students will be reading two fables from different cultures and exploring lessons those fables teach about overcoming challenges. **Vocabulary Knowledge Rating (pp. 90–93):** Introduce and have students rate their initial understanding of key vocabulary terms (e.g., *fable, moral, challenge, overcome*), including select adjectives that describe characters from the fables (e.g., *resourceful, persistent, cautious*).
Presenting new learning	**S-O-S Graphic Organizers (pp. 112–118):** Review the critical attributes of a fable using a custom-made "fist list" organizer. (Students record one attribute in each finger.) **Describe First, Compare Second (pp. 187–192):** Ask students to read similar fables from two different cultures: "The Tortoise and the Hare" by Aesop and "The Tortoise and the Antelope" from the Ngoni people. Have them describe the following components of each fable: characters, reason for race, challenge, how the winner overcomes the challenge, lesson.
Deepening and reinforcing learning	**Describe First, Compare Second (continued):** Challenge students to identify critical similarities and differences between the two fables, using the descriptions they generated above to guide their comparisons. Use students' descriptions and comparisons to assess their understanding of the fables. **Because (pp. 217–220):** Have students examine pairs of adjectives that could be used to describe particular characters, decide which adjective is a better descriptor, and provide a "because" to support their position (e.g., "*Overconfident* is a better adjective to describe the hare than *lazy* because . . .").
Applying and demonstrating learning	**Comparative Controversy (pp. 193–196):** Have students demonstrate their learning by writing an opinion essay that responds to the following "more alike or different" question: Are the two fables more alike or more different? Encourage students to use details from the fables to support their ideas. **Student-Generated Assessment Criteria:** Prior to having students write their essays, prepare them for success by helping them examine top-notch examples from a previous year's class and use those examples to identify the characteristics of high-quality work. **PEERS (pp. 33–34):** Organize students into pairs to have them review and refine their opinion essays. Listen in as students work to assess their ability to give and receive feedback.
Reflecting on and celebrating learning	**Vocabulary Knowledge Rating (revisited):** Have students reflect on and assess how their understanding of key terms has grown. **Reflection:** Ask students to think back on their learning and respond to these questions: What have the fables taught you about overcoming challenges? Why might different cultures have different ways of teaching the same lesson?

Below is a middle school teacher's design for a unit on the early exploration of the Americas. To understand the standards and learning goals that this teacher was trying to address, see her Learning Window on page 15.

Early Exploration of the Americas: A Study in Perspective (Sample Unit)

EPISODE	INSTRUCTIONAL SEQUENCE
Preparing students for new learning	**Hooks & Bridges (pp. 87–89):** Show a video of President Kennedy's speech about putting a man on the moon. Discuss why the time was right in the 1960s for such rapid advancement. Connect the discussion to the Age of Exploration: Why was the time right in 1492 (and why not 1392 or 1292)? Bridge students' brainstorms to the unit to come.
Presenting new learning	**Mystery (pp. 212–216):** Help students discover why the time was right by having them examine clues and develop/test hypotheses about key factors that stimulated this new Age of Exploration. Challenge students to demonstrate their learning by creating a flag that contains symbols/icons that reflect key factors they identified.
	4-2-1 Summarize (pp. 148–150): Use this tool to develop and assess students' understanding of the reading "Christopher Columbus: A Very Complicated Man."
	Jigsaw (pp. 80–82): Organize students into four-member teams so they can learn about and report back on key conquistadors: de Soto, Cortez, de Leon, Pizarro. Assess and refine student understanding by listening in as students work and by reviewing key ideas at the end.
Deepening and reinforcing learning	**Argument Essay:** Have students reinforce their learning and practice their argument-writing skills using the following prompt: Did the times make Columbus, or did Columbus make the times? Students should take a position and justify it with evidence from the Columbus reading above or from other appropriate sources.
Applying and demonstrating learning	**From Challenges to Controversies (Historical Investigations framework, p. 209):** Ask students to research conflicting accounts of interactions between explorers and native populations, using at least one primary source. Challenge students to use details from their research—and what they learned during the unit—to take and defend a position on how historians should remember this period (explorers versus exploiters).
	Guiding & Grading Rubrics (pp. 35–40): Present and discuss the rubric for the Historical Investigations task above. Ensure that students understand the "success criteria" for their research, their understanding of the content, and their written products before they begin.
	Stop, Read, Revise (pp. 49–50): Have students read and revise their Historical Investigations essays before submitting them, using the Seven Cs to guide their work.
Reflecting on and celebrating learning	**"Then and Now" Reflection:** Ask students to review the unit learning goals and respond to the following questions: What were your thoughts and feelings before the unit started? What do you think and feel now? How have your thoughts and feelings changed?

Note that the five-episode approach to instructional design is not reserved for designing units. It can also be used to think through the design of almost any lesson, starting with how you will prepare students for the lesson, all the way to how you will have students reflect on what they learned. The figure below shows how a math teacher used the five episodes to design a lesson aimed at helping students master the order of operations.

Order of Operations: A Study in Procedure (Sample Lesson)

EPISODE	INSTRUCTIONAL SEQUENCE
Preparing students for new learning	**Hooks & Bridges (pp. 87–89):** Pique students' interest with this hook: "List as many things as you can think of that follow a specified order (the seasons, a recipe, etc.). Why is order so important? What might happen if we do things out of order?" **Do, Look, Learn (pp. 127–129):** Present the following equation: $2 \times 12 + 3 \times 4 = $ ___ . Have students DO the operations in different orders and see what happens. Help them LOOK back on the activity and discuss what they LEARNED about the importance of order.
Presenting new learning	**Procedural PRO (pp. 171–174):** Present the basic steps in the order of operations procedure using a two-column graphic organizer—steps on the left and steps applied to sample problems on the right. Provide multiple opportunities for students to **R**ehearse the procedure. Have students continue practicing until they **O**wn the procedure. Use the principles from the Repetition, Variation, Depth of Thought tool below to guide the practice.
Deepening and reinforcing learning	**Repetition, Variation, Depth of Thought (pp. 175–178):** Have students practice the order of operations procedure **R**epeatedly, using a **V**ariety of activities (e.g., list steps, work through problems as a class, check and correct a partner's work). Encourage **D**epth of thought by having students convert word problems into equations that specify the proper order of operations.
Applying and demonstrating learning	**From Homework to HOME Learning (pp. 167–170) / Graduated Difficulty (pp. 179–181):** For home learning, have students compare three increasingly difficult problem sets and complete whichever one feels "challenging but right" for them. Encourage students to determine what makes each set harder and what it will take to move up a level.
Reflecting on and celebrating learning	**Reflection:** Review students' home learning assignments as a class. Help students reflect on and celebrate areas of strength and develop plans for addressing any challenges.

Tip 4: Diagnose and Adjust in Real Time

In the classroom, the ability to diagnose and adjust is the difference between simply teaching content and making sure students actually learn it. That's why expert teachers don't just deliver instruction; they also continually assess the effectiveness of that instruction where it matters most: in terms of student learning. To enable this kind of continual monitoring, we need to make formative assessment an integral part of our instructional designs. Formative assessment is assessment that's used for the purpose of gauging and advancing—rather than evaluating—student learning.

The good news is that many tools from this book can serve not only as instructional techniques but also as formative assessment techniques. How so? By making learning visible (e.g., by having students create products or share ideas), these tools provide evidence of student learning that we can then use to improve future instruction. A tool like 4-2-1 Summarize (pp. 148–150), for example, is primarily an instructional tool for developing students' summarizing skills. But the summaries that students generate provide valuable assessment data regarding their grasp of the relevant content and the sophistication of their summarizing skills.

Many other tools in the book have formative assessment built into their structures as well, with steps that show you how to make learning visible and use what you learn to promote student achievement. Therefore, when you select tools to create an instructional sequence, you can often use the same tools to collect evidence of student learning and progress. Armed with this information, you can make more expert decisions about how to help your students improve.

. . .

Throughout this book, we have encouraged you to select tools that address particular needs or challenges in your classroom. But we also encourage you to see tools as elements in a larger design. By incorporating tools into your classroom thoughtfully and intentionally—by tying them to clear goals and rich culminating tasks, by employing them at the most opportune times in a learning sequence, and by using them to open windows into students' thinking and learning processes—you can turn your classroom into a place where high levels of engagement and deep learning occur every day. We are certain that you and your students will appreciate the results.

Epilogue: Looking Back to Go Forward

At this point in the book, we've done what we set out to do. We've provided a variety of tools aligned to the *Classroom Instruction That Works* framework, and we've shown you how teachers use these tools in their classrooms. Now it's up to you to try the tools in your classroom, reflect on how well they work, and think about steps you can take to get them working even better.

The reflection form on the next page was designed to help you look back on your practice and use what you learn to establish concrete plans for improvement. We encourage you to use the form regularly and save your responses, along with copies of relevant artifacts (e.g., lesson plans, handouts, classroom posters, samples of student work). Creating this kind of "reflection journal" will enable you to look back on and learn from your experiences, document growth over time (yours and your students'), and share what you've been doing with colleagues and/or supervisors. A sample journal entry is shown below.

REFLECTING ON MY PRACTICE

1) What tool did I use? On what date? With what group of students or class?

   I used the Power Previewing tool with the entire class on October 12th.

2) Have I used this tool before? *No.*

3) How did I build the tool into my lesson plans? And for what purpose?

   I used the organizer to have students preview an article about why honeybees are disappearing. My goal was to help them really engage with the text and get more out of it than they usually do when I assign these kinds of articles.

4) Did I use the tool as written or modify it in any way? (Explain any modifications.) *Used as is.*

5) What worked well? What (if any) issues or challenges did I face?

   Students were definitely examining the text more closely than usual, but many of them seemed overwhelmed by the text and the organizer. In particular, they didn't seem confident about where to look for important information or what to write down.

6) What might I do differently the next time I use this tool to make it work even better?

   I should've used a shorter and simpler article the first time. I will make sure to do that next time. I will also spend some additional time reviewing the text features that are described in the "P" of the organizer so students are clearer about where to look for important information. And I will do some more modeling and practicing as a class.

7) How did the tool affect me, my students, and/or our classroom environment?

   (Did it affect factors like engagement, effort, or collaboration? Did it promote better behavior, thinking, or learning? Did it enhance my teaching, my relationships with students, or the classroom environment?)

   My better readers were really focused and deeply interacting with the text while working on their organizers. Even the students who were struggling were examining the text more closely than I expected.

8) Would I use this tool again and/or recommend it to a colleague? Why or why not?

   Yes, because I think it has real potential to promote more focused and active reading—and a better understanding of assigned texts. It's also a good tool for reviewing critical text features. I think the issues I encountered resulted from picking an overly difficult text and not doing enough reviewing and modeling. I thought our previous lessons on text features would've carried over, but I should've reviewed to be sure.

Reflecting On My Practice

1) What tool did I use? On what date? With what group of students or class?

2) Have I used this tool before?

3) How did I build the tool into my lesson plans? And for what purpose?

4) Did I use the tool as written or modify it in any way? (Explain any modifications.)

5) What worked well? What (if any) issues or challenges did I face?

6) What might I do differently the next time I use this tool to make it work even better?

7) How did the tool affect me, my students, and/or our classroom environment?

(Did it affect factors like engagement, effort, or collaboration? Did it promote better behavior, thinking, or learning? Did it enhance my teaching, my relationships with students, or the classroom environment?)

8) Would I use this tool again and/or recommend it to a colleague? Why or why not?

References

Alderman, M. K. (2008). *Motivation for achievement: Possibilities for teaching and learning* (3rd ed.). New York: Routledge.

Antil, L. R., Jenkins, J. R., Wayne, S. K., & Vadasy, P. F. (1998). Cooperative Learning: Prevalence, conceptualizations, and the relation between research and practice. *American Educational Research Journal, 35*, 419–454.

Aristotle. (n.d). *Aristotle > quotes > quotable quote.* Retrieved from https://www.goodreads.com/quotes/4184-for-the-things-we-have-to-learn-before-we-can

Aristotle. (n.d). *Aristotle > quotes > quotable quote.* Retrieved from https://www.goodreads.com/quotes/1146512-the-beginning-seems-to-be-more-than-half-of-the

Aronson, E., Blaney, N., Stephin, C., Sikes, J., & Snapp, M. (1978). *The jigsaw classroom.* Beverly Hills, CA: Sage Publishing Company.

Beesley, A. D., & Apthorp, H. S. (Eds.). (2010). *Classroom instruction that works, second edition: Research report.* Denver, CO: Mid-continent Research for Education and Learning.

Blachowicz, C. L. Z. (1986). Making connections: Alternatives to the vocabulary notebook. *Journal of Reading, 29*(7), 643–649.

Bloom, B. S. (Ed.). (1985). *Developing talent in young people.* New York: Ballantine Books.

Boutz, A. L., Silver, H. F., Jackson, J. W., & Perini, M. J. (2012). *Tools for thoughtful assessment: Classroom-ready techniques for improving teaching and learning.* Ho-Ho-Kus, NJ: Thoughtful Education Press.

Brookhart, S. M. (2008). *How to give effective feedback to your students.* Alexandria, VA: ASCD.

Brownlie, F., & Silver, H. F. (1995). *Mind's eye.* Paper presented at the seminar Responding Thoughtfully to the Challenge of Diversity, Delta, BC.

Carroll, L. (1865). *Alice in Wonderland.* Retrieved from https://www.goodreads.com/quotes/449586-alice-would-you-tell-me-please-which-way-i-ought

Chappuis, J. (2009). *Seven strategies of assessment for learning.* Portland, OR: Educational Testing Service.

Churchill, W. L. (n.d.). *Winston Churchill quotes.* Retrieved from https://www.brainyquote.com/quotes/quotes/w/winstonchu385862.html

Clark, J., & Paivio, A. (1991). Dual coding theory and education. *Educational Psychology Review, 3,* 149–210.

Costa, A. L. (2008). *The school as a home for the mind: Creating mindful curriculum, instruction, and dialogue* (2nd ed.). Thousand Oaks, CA: Corwin Press.

Dean, C. B., Hubbell, E. R., Pitler, H., & Stone, B. (2012). *Classroom instruction that works: Research-based strategies for increasing student achievement* (2nd ed.). Alexandria, VA: ASCD.

Donovan, J., & Radosevich, D. (1999). A meta-analytic review of the distribution of practice effect: Now you see it, now you don't. *Journal of Applied Psychology, 84*(5), 795–805.

Dweck, C. S. (1975). The role of expectations and attributions in the alleviation of learned helplessness. *Journal of Personality and Social Psychology, 31*(4), 674–685.

Dweck, C. S. (2007). The perils and promises of praise. *Educational Leadership, 65*(2), 34–39.

Dweck, C. S. (2016). *Mindset: The new psychology of success* (updated ed.). New York: Ballantine Books.

Ericsson, K. A., Prietula, M. J., & Cokely, E. T. (2007). The making of an expert. *Harvard Business Review, 85*(7/8), 114–121.

Franzke, M., Kintsch, E., Caccamise, D., Johnson, N., & Dooley, S. (2005). Summary Street: Computer support for comprehension and writing. *Journal of Educational Computing Research, 33*(1), 53–80.

Gambrell, L. B. (n.d.). *Comprehension strategy instruction that works.* Marlborough, MA: Sundance. Retrieved from http://www.sundancepub.com/articles/31246_CSK_GambrellMono.pdf

Gardner, H. (1999). *Intelligence reframed: Multiple intelligences for the 21st century.* New York: Basic Books.

Glaser, M. (n.d.). *88 essential quotes about design.* Retrieved from http://www.printmag.com/imprint/89-essential-quotes-about-design/

Goodwin, B., Gibson, T., Lewis, D., & Rouleau, K. (2018). *Unstuck: How curiosity, bright spots, and peer coaching can unleash your school.* Manuscript submitted for publication.

Hattie, J. (2012). *Visible learning for teachers: Maximizing impact on learning.* New York: Routledge.

Hattie, J., & Timperley, H. (2007). The power of feedback. *Review of Educational Research, 77*(1), 81–112.

Herber, H. (1970). *Teaching reading in the content areas.* Englewood Cliffs, NJ: Prentice Hall.

Hill, J. D., & Miller, K. B. (2013). *Classroom instruction that works with English language learners* (2nd ed.). Alexandria, VA: ASCD.

Holgate, S. A. (2012, July 20). *How to collaborate.* Retrieved from http://www.sciencemag.org/careers/2012/07/how-collaborate

Hunter, M. (1984). Knowing, teaching, and supervising. In P. Hosford (Ed.), *Using what we know about teaching* (pp. 169–192). Alexandria, VA: ASCD.

Johnson, D. W., & Johnson, R. T. (1999). *Learning together and alone* (5th ed.). Boston: Allyn & Bacon.

Kagan, S., & Kagan, M. (2015). *Kagan cooperative learning.* San Clemente, CA: Kagan Publishing.

Koutselini, M. (2009). Teacher misconceptions and understanding of cooperative learning: An intervention study. *Journal of Classroom Interaction, 43*(2), 34–44.

Lyman, F. (1981). The responsive classroom discussion: The inclusion of all students. In A. Anderson (Ed.), *Mainstreaming digest* (pp. 109–113). College Park: University of Maryland.

Lyotard, J. (n.d.). *Jean-Francois Lyotard quotes.* Retrieved from https://www.brainyquote.com/quotes/quotes/j/jeanfranc370937.html

MacGregor, J. (2015, December). Meet Lin-Manuel Miranda, the genius behind "Hamilton," Broadway's newest hit. *Smithsonian Magazine.* Retrieved from https://www.smithsonianmag.com/arts-culture/lin-manuel-miranda-ingenuity-awards-180957234/

Martin, R. (1992). *The rough-face girl.* New York: Putnam and Grosset.

Marzano, R. J. (2007). *The art and science of teaching: A comprehensive framework for effective instruction.* Alexandria, VA: ASCD.

Marzano, R. J., Pickering, D. J., & Pollock, J. E. (2001). *Classroom instruction that works: Research-based strategies for increasing student achievement.* Alexandria, VA: ASCD.

Mathan, S. A., & Koedinger, K. R. (2002). An empirical assessment of comprehension fostering features in an intelligent tutoring system. In S. A. Cerri, G. Gouarderes, & F. Paraguacu (Eds.), *Intelligent Tutoring Systems, 6th International Conference, ITS2002* (Vol. 2363, pp. 330–343). New York: Springer Verlag.

McTighe, J., & Wiggins, G. (2014). *Improve curriculum, assessment, and instruction using the Understanding by Design framework.* Retrieved from http://www.ascd.org/ASCD/pdf/siteASCD/publications/ASCD_UBD_whitepaper.pdf

Medina, J. (2008). *Brain rules.* Seattle, WA: Pear Press.

Moss, C. M., & Brookhart, S. M. (2009). *Advancing formative assessment in every classroom: A guide for instructional leaders.* Alexandria, VA: ASCD.

Mosston, M. (1972). *Teaching: From command to discovery.* Belmont, CA: Wadsworth Publishing.

National Governors Association Center for Best Practices, Council of Chief State School Officers. (2010a). *Common Core State Standards for English language arts & literacy in history/social studies, science, and technical subjects.* Washington, DC: Author.

National Governors Association Center for Best Practices, Council of Chief State School Officers. (2010b). *Common Core State Standards for mathematics.* Washington, DC: Author.

Nietzsche, F. W. (n.d.). *Friedrich Nietzsche quotes.* Retrieved from https://www.brainyquote.com/quotes/quotes/f/friedrichn134602.html

Nobel, A. B. (n.d.). *Alfred Nobel quotes.* Retrieved from https://www.brainyquote.com/quotes/quotes/a/alfrednobe556200.html

Paivio, A. (2006). *Dual coding theory and education.* Draft chapter for the conference on "Pathways to Literacy Achievement for High Poverty Children," The University of Michigan School of Education, September 29–October 1, 2006. Retrieved from http://readytolearnresearch.org/pathwaysconference/presentations/paivio.pdf

Palincsar, A. S., & Brown, A. L. (1985). Reciprocal teaching: Activities to promote reading with your mind. In T. L. Harris & E. J. Cooper (Eds.), *Reading, thinking and concept development: Strategies for the classroom.* New York: The College Board.

Pashler, H., Bain, P., Bottge, B., Graesser, A., Koedinger, K., McDaniel, M., & Metcalfe, J. (2007). *Organizing instruction and study to improve student learning* (NCER 2007-2004). Washington, DC: National Center for Education Research, Institute of Education Sciences, US Department of Education. Retrieved from http://ncer.ed.gov

Paul, A. M. (2012, March 17). Your brain on fiction. *The New York Times.* Retrieved from http://www.nytimes.com/2012/03/18/opinion/sunday/the-neuroscience-of-your-brain-on-fiction.html

Pfeiffer, J. W., & Jones, J. E. (Eds.). (1974). *A handbook of structured experiences for human relations training* (Vol. 1, 2nd ed.). La Jolla, CA: University Associates Publishers and Consultants.

Potter, H. B. (n.d.). *Beatrix Potter quotes.* Retrieved from https://www.goodreads.com/quotes/327250-thank-god-i-have-the-seeing-eye-that-is-to

Pressley, M. (1979). *The mind's eye.* Escondido, CA: Escondido Union School District.

Pressley, M. (2006). *Reading instruction that works: The case for balanced teaching* (3rd ed.). New York: The Guilford Press.

Raphael, T. E. (1986). Teaching question-answer relationships, revisited. *The Reading Teacher, 39,* 516–522.

Rowe, M. B. (1972, April). *Wait-time and rewards as instructional variables: Their influence on language, logic, and fate control.* Paper presented at the National Association for Research in Science Teaching, Chicago, IL.

Schooling, P., Toth, M., & Marzano, R. J. (2013). *Creating an aligned system to develop great teachers within the federal Race to the Top initiative.* Bloomington, IN: Marzano Research Laboratory. Retrieved from http://www.marzanocenter.com/files/Marzano-Race-to-the-Top-White-Paper.pdf

Shakespeare, W. (1959). *The Tragedy of Macbeth.* New York: Washington Square Press.

Shakespeare, W. (1965). *The Tragedy of Hamlet, Prince of Denmark.* New York: Washington Square Press.

Shute, V. J. (2008). Focus on formative feedback. *Review of Educational Research, 78*(1), 153–189.

Silver, H. (2010). *Compare & contrast: Teaching comparative thinking to strengthen student learning.* Alexandria, VA: ASCD.

Silver, H. F., & Boutz, A. L. (2015). *Tools for conquering the Common Core: Classroom-ready techniques for targeting the ELA/literacy standards.* Franklin Lakes, NJ: Thoughtful Education Press.

Silver, H. F., Brunsting, J. R., Walsh, T., & Thomas, E. J. (2012). *Math tools, grades 3–12: 60+ ways to build mathematical practices, differentiate instruction, and increase student engagement* (2nd ed.). Thousand Oaks, CA: Corwin.

Silver, H. F., Dewing, R. T., & Perini, M. J. (2012). *The core six: Essential strategies for achieving excellence with the Common Core.* Alexandria, VA: ASCD.

Silver, H. F., & Perini, M. J. (2010). The eight Cs of engagement: How learning styles and instructional design increase student commitment to learning. In R. J. Marzano (Ed.), *On excellence in teaching* (pp. 319–342). Bloomington, IN: Solution Tree Press.

Silver, H. F., Perini, M. J., & Boutz, A. L. (2016). *Tools for a successful school year (starting on day one): Classroom-ready techniques for building the four cornerstones of an effective classroom.* Franklin Lakes, NJ: Thoughtful Education Press.

Silver Strong & Associates (2007). *Word works: Cracking vocabulary's CODE* (2nd ed.). Ho-Ho-Kus, NJ: Thoughtful Education Press.

Silver, H. F., Strong, R. W., & Perini, M. J. (2001). *Tools for promoting active, in-depth learning* (2nd ed.). Ho-Ho-Kus, NJ: Thoughtful Education Press.

Silver, H. F., Strong, R. W., & Perini, M. J. (2007). *The strategic teacher: Selecting the right research-based strategy for every lesson.* Alexandria, VA: ASCD.

Stafford, T. (2014, April 21). Five secrets to revising that can improve your grades. *The Guardian.* Retrieved from https://www.theguardian.com/education/2014/jan/08/five-secrets-of-successful-revising

Stiggins, R., Arter, J., Chappuis, J., & Chappuis, S. (2006). *Classroom assessment for student learning: Doing it right—using it well.* Portland, OR: Educational Testing Service.

Suchman, J. R. (1966). *Developing inquiry.* Chicago: Science Research Associates.

Suskind, R. (1998). *A hope in the unseen: An American odyssey from the inner city to the Ivy League.* New York: Broadway Books.

Tobin, K. (1987). The role of wait time in higher cognitive level learning. *Review of Educational Research, 57*(1), 69–95.

Tomlinson, C. A. (2001). *How to differentiate instruction in mixed-ability classrooms* (2nd ed.). Alexandria, VA: ASCD.

Wiggins, G., & McTighe, J. (2005). *Understanding by design* (2nd ed.). Upper Saddle River, NJ: Prentice Hall.

Wilhelm, J. D. (2012). *Enriching comprehension with visualization strategies: Text elements and ideas to build comprehension, encourage reflective reading, and represent understanding* (Rev. ed.). New York: Scholastic.

Willingham, D. T. (2002). Allocating student study time: "Massed" versus "distributed" practice. *American Educator, 26*(2), 37–39. Retrieved from https://www.aft.org/periodical/american-educator/summer-2002/ask-cognitive-scientist

Wormeli, R. (2005). *Summarization in any subject: 50 techniques to improve student learning.* Alexandria, VA: ASCD.

Index of Tools

About the Authors

Harvey F. Silver, EdD, cofounder and president of Silver Strong & Associates, has more than forty years of experience as a teacher, administrator, and consultant. He is a regular speaker at national and regional education conferences, addressing a wide range of topics, including differentiated instruction, thoughtful assessment, school leadership, tools and strategies for meeting today's standards, and lesson/unit design. Dr. Silver also conducts workshops for schools, districts, and educational organizations around the world. He is the co-author of several education bestsellers, including *Tools for Thoughtful Assessment*, *Tools for a Successful School Year*, and *The Core Six*. He has also collaborated with Matthew Perini to develop the Thoughtful Classroom Teacher Effectiveness Framework, a comprehensive teacher evaluation system that is being implemented in school districts across the country.

Cheryl Abla, MA, believes deeply in all students' capacity to achieve at high levels and is passionate about helping educators use their full potential to make a positive impact on students. At McREL International, Cheryl trains and coaches K–12 teachers and school leaders on effective instructional strategies, classroom technology, teacher coaching, English-language-learner supports, and creating engaging school cultures and climates. Prior to joining McREL, she taught grades 1–12 for over twenty years; served as a national facilitator for the FACES, Inc. character education program; and was the director of both a Parents as Teachers district program and a Migrant Education Even Start district program. Drawing on her extensive and diverse classroom experience, she has presented at educational conferences around the United States and the Pacific and has authored several articles for McREL's *Changing Schools* magazine.

Abigail L. Boutz, PhD, has taught, tutored, and mentored students at the elementary through college levels, most recently at the University of California, Los Angeles, where she served as a lecturer for the Life Sciences Department, a university field supervisor for the Teacher Education Program, and an academic coordinator for the Undergraduate Research Center/Center for Academic and Research Excellence. During her tenure with Silver Strong & Associates, she has designed training modules and workshop materials on classroom tools and strategies, learning styles, and instructional leadership. She has also co-authored three award-winning titles in the Tools for Today's Educators series: *Tools for Thoughtful Assessment*, *Tools for Conquering the Common Core*, and *Tools for a Successful School Year*.

Matthew J. Perini, MA, senior director of content development for Silver Strong & Associates, has authored numerous books, curriculum guides, and articles on a wide range of topics, including reading instruction, formative assessment, and effective teaching practices. Most recently, he collaborated with Harvey Silver and Abigail Boutz on *Tools for a Successful School Year*, winner of both a Teachers' Choice Award and an Independent Publisher Book Award (IPPY). Matthew has been a driving force in the development of Thoughtful Education Press, the publishing division of Silver Strong & Associates. He serves as both a contributing author and series editor for Thoughtful Education Press's award-winning Tools for Today's Educators line of books.